Frontiers of Management

This edited collection, first published in 1989, stems from the second annual meeting of the British Academy of Management, held at Cardiff Business School in 1988. With the focus on important areas of change affecting management practice and theory – in markets, technology and organizational structure - this volume contains a selection of material presented at the conference by leading scholars in the field. Their contributions provide multi-disciplinary views of organizational strategy, across a wide spectrum of business and industry, which will be of significant interest to any students of business structure and management.

Frontiers of Management

Research and Practice

Edited by
Roger Mansfield

First published in 1989
by Routledge

This edition first published in 2013 by Routledge
2 Park Square, Milton Park, Abingdon, Oxon, OX14 4RN

Simultaneously published in the USA and Canada
by Routledge
711 Third Avenue, New York, NY 10017

Routledge is an imprint of the Taylor & Francis Group, an informa business

Publisher's Note
The publisher has gone to great lengths to ensure the quality of this reprint but
points out that some imperfections in the original copies may be apparent.

Disclaimer
The publisher has made every effort to trace copyright holders and welcomes
correspondence from those they have been unable to contact.

A Library of Congress record exists under LC control number: 89032950

ISBN 13: 978-0-415-72098-4 (hbk)
ISBN 13: 978-1-315-86663-5 (ebk)

Frontiers of Management

Edited by Roger Mansfield

R
Routledge
London and New York

First published 1989
by Routledge
11 New Fetter Lane, London EC4P 4EE

Simultaneously published in the USA and Canada
by Routledge
a division of Routledge, Chapman and Hall, Inc.
29 West 35th Street, New York, NY 10001

Phototypeset in 10pt Times by
Mews Photosetting, Beckenham, Kent
Printed and bound in Great Britain by
Mackays of Chatham PLC, Chatham, Kent

British Library Cataloguing in Publication Data

Mansfield, Roger, *1942–*
    Frontiers of management.
    1. Business firms. Management
    I. Title
    658
    ISBN 0-415-04471-5

Library of Congress Cataloging-in-Publication Data

Frontiers of management: research and practice / [edited by] Roger
Mansfield.
        p. cm.
    ISBN 0-415-04471-5
    1. Industrial management – Congresses. I. Mansfield, Roger, M.A.
HD29.F77   1989
658.4–dc20   89-32950
                                                 CIP

Contents

Contents

Tables

Figures

Preface

This book stems from the second annual meeting of the British Academy of Management which was held at Cardiff Business School in September 1988. The British Academy of Management is a recent foundation which was established to encourage research and scholarship in the field of management and to provide a forum for those involved in this to exchange ideas. It was established partly as a way of focusing attention to the research activities of business schools and management departments at a time when increasing pressures were being placed on them to meet immediate teaching and training objectives. It was also established to try and provide a forum and a focus for those who wanted to develop management as a subject as opposed to the variety of disciplines on which the study of management draws. In its short history, the academy has achieved some of its initial objectives. It is to be hoped that in the publication of this book and the variety of future publications of the academy, that a growing number of those interested in understanding management will be reinvigorated in order to make a greater contribution to its practice.

Section One

Understanding Management

Chapter one

Management research and the development of management practice

Roger Mansfield

Introduction

The practice of management has changed and arguably developed significantly in recent years. If we think back to the early years of the present century, most of the changes or advances in management practice at that time were largely as a consequence of managers learning from experience. In some cases, this was a question of learning from their own experience, in other cases, learning from the experience of others who made available their thinking by means of consultancy or through books and articles.

As the century has progressed, more and more time, money and resources has gone into systematic research into the theory and practice of management. Now, many of the developments in the practice of management stem from the output of academics largely located in the world's business schools. At the same time, managers continue to learn and develop their ideas based upon their own experience and the experience of others.

Various papers in this book describe ways in which the research process can be better carried out in order to give outputs of use to managers or suggest findings from management research which may be of use to the practising manager.

The nature of the problem

The difficulty involved in managing and doing research to understand better the processes involved in management largely stem from the inherent complexity of the management task. The practising manager, at any level, from the supervisor up to the chief executive has to deal with a range of problems which occur synchronically. In real life, these problems are multi-faceted and do not come with the convenient labels used in business schools such as organizational behaviour or financial management or marketing. Most real-life problems have aspects of all

3

these involved in them and the manager has to comprehend the inter-action between the different issues involved in any single real-life problem. Systems approaches to the understanding of organizations and management within them have made clear the very large number of interconnections between different aspects of the systems which the manager has to cope with on a day to day as well as a long-term basis. A further difficulty of major dimensions stems from the time-scale involved in management action. In general, management is not about the here and now even though the pressures felt by managers are often most acute when dealing with immediate problems requiring immediate solutions. Good management, at any level, and particularly at the highest levels in an organization, is about managing not just for the present but also for the future. This immediately creates difficulties for the practising manager to learn from his experience and the management researcher to conduct studies which give answers which have a long-term meaning-fulness. It may well be, particularly in strategic areas, that one can only learn whether one has done it rightly or wrongly, if at all, many years after the event. However, during that span of years, many other deci-sions will have had to be taken and actions initiated even before the results of the earlier actions are fully understood. An inevitable consequence of this is that, in general, management research, even when well conducted, can only be indicative in terms of best practice. It is rarely possible to validate fully the conclusions of a study even for the situa-tion in which the research has been carried out, let alone for its generalizability to other situations.

However, the complexity of management problems and the long time-scale involved in seeing their implications, should not be used as an excuse for taking little or no notice of the fruits of experience or the findings of research studies. Rather, they should be indicators suggesting that such results should be treated with care and interpreted in the on-going context in which the manager must operate.

One of the difficulties involved in management research and its interpretation is that most of the models employed tend to have been derived in the physical sciences, where research typically follows the experimental method. Experiments in management are rarely possible and quasi experiments or natural experiments are generally a poor substitute. There is a further difficulty in the social sciences generally that the research, whether carried out by academics or by managers, is interactive with the subject of that research. It is not possible to carry out management research which has no effect upon the situation being researched. Neither is it possible to stop managers learning from the on-going experience which is being studied and adapting their behaviour accordingly ahead of the final evaluation of the study of that process.

Method of research

In the articles which form the chapters of the present work, a variety of different research methods are examined explicitly or implicitly through the presentation of results stemming from the application of such methods. Each of these methods and many others not described in this volume have certain virtues and certain problems associated with them. Some methods such as case studies have the virtue of giving us an in-depth picture of a particular set of circumstances. Others provide us with systematically comparable data through a wide variety of different situations. Others fall somewhere between these two categories. The strengths of each of the methods is closely linked to its weaknesses. Thus, a case study in providing us with a depth of knowledge of a situation, fails to provide us with data from other situations to allow comparison, whereas, on the other hand, methods which give us systematically comparable data across a range of situations typically are relatively superficial by comparison with the case approach. Some methods are at their strongest in exploring relatively unknown areas and issues, others are better when moving towards a hypothesis-testing approach to research. However, it must be recognized that the benefits of research depend not only on the research itself but the ability to gain insights and knowledge as a consequence of that research. In this respect, no method can claim to have a monopoly or can it be suggested that any method leaves us no better informed than we were before. It is, therefore, essential that a variety of methods are employed either within a single study or across a range of studies in order that a variety of different sorts of information, data and findings are made available for people to think about and reflect upon.

Of course, research can be seen as merely the systematization of learning from experience. In this respect, it must be reckoned that for any amount of data gathered by researchers, substantially more is gathered in a non-systematic way by practising managers. All of this information and the conclusions drawn from it is relevant to the search for improved practice in management.

The development of management practice

In reality, the practitioner of management learns from his own experience as well as from reading the research findings of academics and others involved in systematic study. He is very close to the academic researcher in that both are trying to make sense of a wide variety of ideas and information coming from a range of different sources in order to understand better the processes and problems of management. Through the ever-increasing literature reporting on experience and research in the management area as well as through business school courses and a host of seminars and meetings conducted for a range of purposes, all these actors are involved in an on-going large-scale social process, part of the objectives of which are the better management of human affairs. Only by understanding the way the practice of management has developed, the findings of research studies and the ideas of creative thinkers can we hope to develop, in a positive sense, the practice of management.

It is probably true in this area as in so many others that the vast majority of researchers and managers are involved in making very small increments to an existing body of knowledge, and opinion. A very small number of managers or researchers will have radically new ideas which may bring forward significant developments in and of themselves in the practice of management. When those new ideas occur there is a problem both of their recognition and of their evaluation. Many new ideas may be accepted and practised because of their inherent plausibility or because of the advocacy of their creators rather than because of their intrinsic value. To make progress in the development of the practice of management, both managers and researchers must be involved in a large-scale experimental process where there is a preparedness to consider and try out new ideas, and a determination to evaluate as critically as possible the consequences of the implementation of those ideas and a willingness to learn from that evaluation.

The practice of management remains, in large part, an art rather than a science. What we mean by that is that our knowledge is so significantly limited that logic and evidence will only achieve a certain amount without the addition of judgement and intuition or even guess work. It is probably true that research in management is also more of an art than a science although there may be great utility in applying widely understood scientific principles. The reason for this is that in most areas if we designed the best study we are able to in order to investigate a particular issue, it would almost certainly involve massively larger resources than those available and take far too long to be practical. Research then is usually about finding the most useful and valuable short cut which allows it to move into the world of practical possibilities whilst not losing some of its merits in providing systematic information and conclusions to guide future researchers and practitioners.

As was suggested at the beginning of this chapter, writing on management has moved from a situation where it was predominantly based on experience to one where it is predominantly based on research. However, the optimism that appeared to be extant in the 1950s and 1960s that scientific research could provide the answers to management problems would seem to have been either misplaced or wildly optimistic in terms of timescale. It is now, I believe, widely accepted that research has probably shown us more things we do not know than things we do. It is in this light that we must judge its utility and make the best of the findings available allied to our own experience in making progress in the development of the practice of management.

If there is a conclusion that comes from our knowledge of management and management research at the present time, it is almost certainly along the lines that, if in doubt, simplify, rather than the natural reaction of many managers and even more researchers to, if in doubt, complicate. Both in the acquisition of knowledge and in the practice of management, simple solutions are often the most practical, given our present state of knowledge.

Chapter two

The discipline of management and academic defensive routines

Chris Argyris

Schools of business and management are being viewed increasingly by other faculties as places where new and exciting research and teaching are to be found. With this increased status, the faculty of these schools are feeling a decreasing sense of being beholden to the faculties of the disciplines from which many of them came. With this increased sense of confidence and autonomy, there is also an increased interest in developing the identity and integrity of management as a profession. In this connection a recent review of the status of business education reports that one of the most important concerns of faculty and deans is the problem of integration among the disciplines toward a coherent theory and practice of management (Porter and McKibbin, 1988).

In order for management to become a discipline, it must find ways to integrate knowledge from the functional discipline (e.g. marketing, finance, production, accounting, as well as disciplines such as psychology, sociology, economics, and political science). Many academics espouse the belief: indeed it is seen as a truism. But their attempts to implement it, leave something to be desired. Indeed, I do not believe it is grossly unfair to suggest that we may espouse this belief strongly as a way to resist making it come true in practice.

Forces that facilitate integration

All professions are concerned about their respective worlds of practice. Practice, in turn, is carried out by human beings under the pressures and constraints of everyday life. It is important, therefore, that the substance of practice, in this case management, includes the knowledge that is relevant to its effective implementation. But the knowledge that is relevant is vast. It must be packaged in a way that it can be stored in the human mind and retrieved under real-time conditions and pressures. This requires the development of models and theories that organizes and integrates the knowledge that is relevant for practice.

The second force toward implementation is created by the fact that fundamental to management is taking action. Action, in turn, must be effective and effectiveness means producing consequences that are intended and not those that are unintended. Managerial actions, therefore, should be subjected to the most stringent tests that are possible in the world of practice. This, in turn, means that actions should be crafted in ways that are falsifiable. Falsifiability requires an *a priori* hunch or hypothesis which, in turn, comes from a theory of management.

Forces that inhibit integration

Each discipline that contributes to a theory of management is represented by a community of scholars with norms about appropriate behaviour. Kuhn (1970) has shown that many of these norms are inherently conservative. They do not encourage co-operation with and the integration of several different disciplines; indeed they discourage these activities. Hence a force against integration.

Dilemma of academics as practitioners

As scholars, we espouse the importance of comprehensive and falsifiable theories. Yet, as I hope to show, our actions are not likely to facilitate this objective. Thus we have two important inconsistencies. First, there is the inconsistency between our espoused theories and beliefs about the pursuit of knowledge and our actions. Second, our theories-in-use are also inconsistent with our espoused theories.

Scholarship and science supposedly abhor inconsistency. As researchers, whenever we see inconsistency we go after it with due deliberate speed. Yet our predisposition to deal with the inconsistencies embedded in the practice of scholarship is not very strong. We appear to live with this inconsistency. Why?

Many scholars reply that one answer is obvious from Kuhn's (1970) research. Scholars behave as they do because they conform to the community norms. That may be an explanation of what has occurred, but the moment it is used to predict our future behaviour, the descriptive generalization takes on the status of a prescriptive generalization. If we act consistently with Kuhn's generalization, it is because we choose to do so. We are personally causally responsible for choosing to adhere to actions that are consistent with Kuhn's description generalization. These choices cannot be explained without implying some sort of rules that tell us to act in accordance with the norms. The theories-in-use represent prescriptive stances.

As scholars, we turn a descriptive generalization into a prescriptive one without much empirical research on how this occurs. Imagine if any of us did that in an article or book. We would be taken to task for not realizing that moving from description to prescription cannot be done by a simple flip in framing.

By what processes do we appear to flip from descriptive propositions to prescriptive ones in milliseconds? We do so, I will argue, by using the same processes most human beings use. We either act as if we are not acting inconsistently or admit that we are and assert that we are helpless to act otherwise.

Organizational defensive routines

Such actions are consistent with organizational defensive routines. An organizational defensive routine is any action or policy that prevents organizations or communities or individuals from experiencing embarrassment or threat and, at the same time, prevents them from discovering and reducing the causes of the embarrassment or threat (Argyris, 1985).

In order to produce defensive routines individuals hold, at least, four rules in their heads.

1. Produce behaviours or messages that are inconsistent.
2. Act as if they are not inconsistent.
3. Make the inconsistency undiscussable.
4. Make the undiscussability undiscussable.

Permit me a few examples.

I respect the norms and rules of your discipline, you respect mine

The first routine begins with acknowledging that there are differences of views and methods. This is usually followed with, 'Of course I respect your right to think and act as you do. I expect you to show me the same respect.' The strategy is to appeal to mutual respect, and to tie it to the adherence of the norms and rules in each one's respective discipline. In the name of respect and implied civility, the individual is asked not to confront the very factors that would have to be confronted if the new ideas are to be respected. Examples of conversations that are consistent with this strategy are:

1. My theory is incomplete but it predicts; we arrive at the correct conclusion. In my field, prediction is more important than explanation.
2. Sure, our models are distant from reality. They are idealized. Physics is built this way.
3. Yes, I can see how those variables are important in your field. They are not in mind. (After some pressing) we don't use these because they are too soft and difficult to measure.

4. That's not true. So-and-so has done some research, and he is (let us say) an economist. (Yet the individual is seen as a deviant.)
5. That's an interesting point. But surely it is self-evident, is it not, that people act (in the way that is consistent with our discipline)?

I respect your right to say what you are saying, but disagree with you. I will examine rigorously and empirically the basis of the difference but if we are seen by colleagues as misunderstanding each other, I will not examine the dynamics of the misunderstanding

This second defensive routine often occurs in debates in the journals and less so face-to-face. First, each scholar asserts that the other is doing important work in his or her discipline. The argument continues that the points being made by the other are either not relevant, or they show a misunderstanding of the field, or they are being worked on and it will take a while for the results to appear. The bottom line message is that the other is wrong, and each one should get on with their work, which can feed back to reinforce the first defensive routine.

I would like to nominate my debate with Professor Herbert Simon (Argyris, 1973 a, b; Simon, 1973) as an excellent example of this defensive routine. We both informed the other of gaps and inconsistencies, we told each other how the other was wrong and, looking back, I believe, passed each other like ships in the night (Argyris, 1973; Simon, 1973).

By the way, the editor at that time asked how we wished to deal with the differences. Professor Simon suggested a mathematical solution which would guarantee that the number of pages in each reply would decrease dramatically so that we would not go on forever. I rejected that solution because it would not get at the defensive behaviour on both our parts. I recommended that we meet to examine the reasoning behind the way we were dealing with the differences in views, not simply the substantive differences. Professor Simon rejected this proposal as too time consuming, and probably not likely to be profitable.

I agree that such activities might take time. I do not agree that they are not profitable if we are to confront the defensive reasoning each of us uses to defend our disciplines and, of course, ourselves.

Alderfer (1972) conducted such a study of Professor Dunnette and myself which, at least, the graduate students present and several readers who wrote to each of us felt that more such studies should be conducted.

We need more research on how we pass each other by design while we are conversing with each other, and act as if the passing is not by design. I had an opportunity to observe and participate in a set of conversations between psychologists and sociologists on the one hand, and economists on the other hand. In order to tell my story, I will call the first group the 'social scientist' and the second group the 'economist'.

11

The story is written from observing their conversations, having access to their written memoranda, and the opportunity to interview them.

The social scientist began by advocating his views that he believed the economist rejected. For example, organizations require (1) an authority system for the purpose of control, (2) a sense of solidarity in order to facilitate co-operation, and (3) shared values to legitimize long-term direction and sustain loyalty.

The economist reported that economists have been writing about stable authority systems as long as the social scientists. But in the interest of being co-operative, he withheld this view because to state it would be tantamount to asserting the social scientist did not know the economic literature.

Second, the economist was aware of the sociological literature on solidarity and group pressure, which raised questions about the pre-eminence of economic motives. But most of the research, he believed, was case studies such as those on 'rate busting' and 'banana time'. The economist felt that he needed more comprehensive data to reject his theory. He also believed that the social scientist should know that. He concluded that he should not say any of this because that, too, may be seen as a personal attack by the economist upon the social scientist.

Third, the economist was aware that the social scientist wanted to teach him that 'individual rewards may undermine solidarity, enhance envy, and make co-operation difficult'. The social scientist seemed to believe that undermining solidarity by individuals who show a sense of performance responsibility is a bad thing. But, argued the economist, that is a normative position. Again, he did not discuss this because, after all, attacking the foundations of another discipline is not good manners.

The social scientist was trying, in as co-operative and thoughtful manner as he could muster, to alert the economist to possible gaps in his perspective. The more he talked, the more he sensed an antipathy. But in the interest of being co-operative and sticking to substance, he bypassed this issue and covered-up that he was bypassing.

The economist was also trying to be co-operative and thoughtful. He believed that he knew valid responses to the comments made by the social scientist. The trouble was that the responses could be seen as a personal attack. He did not wish to create any antipathy, so he too bypassed and covered-up. The result was that important substantive issues were never discussed because each side doubted the credibility of the other side, and hence bypassed talking about the issues. All this was done in the name of not upsetting the other. Yet both sides attributed a sense of antipathy to the other and, of course, did not say so.

I like what you are saying because it reminds us of the gaps in our discipline but, come to think of it, so-and-so (an acknowledged leader in our field) said the same thing decades ago

Recently I listened to a thoughtful analysis of some of the limits of economic theory by Amitai Etzioni based on his forthcoming book (1988). As soon as he finished, one distinguished economist responded in effect:

> This was a thought provoking and excellent presentation by Amitai, a colleague who I have known for years, and respect very highly. Some economists may get a bit defensive hearing his ideas, but I think he does all of us a service by pointing out gaps and inconsistencies in our discipline. (Then he smilingly added) This talk reminds me of my undergraduate days (in the 1940s) in economics where Professor Schumpeter used to say that a lot of important problems are covered-up in the phrase, 'All other things equal . . . ' So some of us are aware of what Amitai is saying. He serves to remind us that it is important to think about these issues.

I made an informal one-on-one survey of three present graduate students and two recently minted doctoral faculty from the department. They could not ever recall any student conducting research in the area that Etzioni was describing. Moreover, they could give examples of subtle and not-so-subtle cues that to conduct such research during the early part of their career could be disastrous in terms of appointments and promotions. Bowman (forthcoming) gives the same advice to younger faculty in the field of strategy.

The indiscussability of mixed messages

Embedded in these defensive routines are mixed messages, messages with inconsistent meanings. For example:

This is an excellent and exciting paper	yet	It describes problems known by us for decades
It is important to conduct research like this	yet	You may harm your career if you conduct such research, especially early in your career
I respect your rules and expect you to respect mine	yet	If you follow my request then we do not have to deal with the problem that you wish to deal with

You should conduct more systematic descriptions of the territory	yet	Others have been describing the same territory; why don't you use it to fill in your gaps.

As I said before, in order for mixed messages to work, the crafter of the message must deliver it as if it is not inconsistent. Moreover, the inconsistency is made undiscussable, and, its undiscussability is undiscussable. Anyone violating these rules is likely to get into trouble.

I recently participated in a faculty seminar to focus on the relationships between economic, on the one hand, and social science disciplines such as organizational behaviour, social psychology and sociology on the other. During one session several non-economists described economists as 'not being concerned about people', 'trying to subsume other disciplines into their own', etc. I felt that these attributions were true of some economists, and similar ones could be made about the scholars in the disciplines represented by those making the negative evaluations. One participant, a non-economist, said that he was getting a bit tired of economist-bashing. Much of what was being said was only half true. He added that he was beginning to resent what was going on, and wondered why it was happening. He added by asking if anyone felt the same way. 'Maybe I'm all wrong. Maybe I'm becoming unfairly defensive', he said. Before anyone could answer, the chairman ruled such a discussion out of order. He assured the speaker that everyone's intentions were clean, that the characteristic of sound academic discussion was freedom to speak your mind.

I remember agreeing with the comment that there should be freedom to speak one's mind. I also remember feeling that the speaker was doing just that. I also believed that a discussion of his question might get a faulty reasoning embedded in several of the accusations made by the non-economists.

After the seminar I asked the chairman why he disallowed the discussion. He replied that he realized that disallowing the discussion was a violation of his own rule of freedom to speak one's mind. He would not have disallowed the discussion if, at the outset of the seminar, it had been made clear that such discussions would be permissible. The players would have then known the rules, and crafted their conversations accordingly. He did not want to legitimize unilaterally a 'somewhat psychiatric' discussion.

I could understand the bind that he experienced because he was the kind of individual that would not mind participating in a discussion of the kind that he disallowed. Yet he suppressed his own values to those of the community. In addition, all of this was not discussed. He did not say in the group what he said to me. And he must have felt that the undiscussability of that subject was undiscussable once the seminar began.

This story points up how descriptive statements such as those made by Kuhn about the conservatism of the norms of the community of scholars become translated into prescriptive statements. The tacit strategy is as follows:

1. Interpret the acceptance of the norms as signs of maturity and co-operativeness.
2. Interpret changing the norms as signs of being a troublemaker or even a traitor.
3. Keep the interpretation covered-up and cover-up the cover-up.
4. Publically deny all this but make it clear through threats to progress in one's career of the dangers of violating Kuhn's description of reality.

Strategies for enhancing integration

Conduct research that makes it possible for 'other' disciplines to achieve their objectives more effectively

Recently economists such as Leibenstein (1987), Nelson and Winter (1982), and Simon (1978) have argued that greater attention be paid by economists to procedural rationality, the study of procedures that have to be carried out to achieve the ends embedded in substantive rationality. For example, Leibenstein suggests at least thirteen kinds of data needed to carry out a maximizing decision. Most of the ones listed could not be crafted without attention to variables from social psychology, sociology, and political science (Leibenstein, 1987, pp. 15–16). His book provides insights into how behavioural scientists could assist economists in better understanding procedural rationality.

One strategy that I have found rewarding is to ask how can my discipline help some other discipline carry out its present research programmes. For example, there are three stages in economic analyses; property rights, information and allocation (Kay, 1984, pp. 13–14). Stage 2, is concerned with collecting all relevant information; the less noise the better. I have been concerned with studying the barriers that people create to inhibit the production of valid information in the world of practice. Defensive routines are a prime example. Recently, I tried to show how organizational defensive routines inhibited the production of valid economic information that was needed to formulate long-range economic strategies in business firms. I also tried to create the conditions where the noise was reduced and the amount of valid economic information was increased. As I saw the contribution to economists, it was the creating of conditions that made it more likely that they could get the economic information that they needed to test and implement features of their theories of the firm (Argyris, 1987).

Conduct research that makes it possible for 'other' disciplines to achieve their objectives more effectively, and to question important features of their theory

The second strategy is an extension of the first. In the first, the research facilitates a discipline, in the second, it does the same but it also questions a basic concept.

For example, let us take agency theory as formulated by Jensen *et al.* (1987). Their theory is based upon the assumption that human beings are basically *R*ational, *R*esourceful, *E*valuative, and *M*aximizing (RREM). RREM, they argue is a descriptive and not a normative concept. If human beings do not always behave this way, it is because some forces are blocking them. For example, recall the sociological research on group pressures to restrict production. Succumbing to these pressures is consistent with sociological man. That is a view of human nature brought on by sociologists; not by human beings if they were free to act according to their true nature. Recently Baker *et al.* (1988) published a paper that illustrates the way that RREM features are suppressed. They cite an array of research that suggests few employees are paid for performance. Most are overpaid because they are given scores much higher than their performance merits. They get these inflated grades because their managers do not want to get into hassles. The managers smooth over the conflict.

Our own research supports the findings of smoothing over and other organizational defensive routines. We conducted several interventions to help some managers to reduce the defensive routines they own, and those of the organization. The inflation of scores began to be reduced and the variance in performance ratings began to increase. The employees soon began to act more consistently with the RREM assumption.

There is nothing in agency theory, that I am aware of, that helps individuals unfreeze their 'sociological' or 'psychological' man theories in order to bloom into RREMs. The intervention required a theory that had a different assumption about human nature. Briefly, human beings are capable of acting consistently with all three theories (if not more).

Impose an additional stewardship, teaching for practice

The third strategy is for faculty to take seriously our responsibility for educating line managers. I do not include the teaching of technicians in our respective fields, we do take that task seriously. Anyone who asserts that they are a psychological tester, a market researcher, or an accountant can easily be tested by whether or not they know their discipline. Grant me, for the sake of argument, that a key feature of managing others is to control, co-ordinate, and influence their actions in ways that produce consequences intended by a manager. Grant also that whatever knowledge we teach, it must be enactable by practitioners under the constraints of everyday life.

If it is true that most disciplinary propositions are descriptive, and intendedly so, then we have a responsibility to transform them into enactable propositions. This means that descriptive propositions must be translated into a prescriptive form. For certain generalizations such as how to prepare a balance sheet, the translation from description to prescription is not too difficult. But for the myriad of generalizations that have to do with leading people especially to perform difficult and complex tasks that may have non-trivial consequences the translation problem is itself non-trivial. For example, a favourite form of generalization in my discipline is usually stated as X (f) Y. Usually some relationship is plotted, let us say, a curvilinear relationship. For example, research suggests that under low frustration creativity may increase. As the frustration goes above a threshold, regression sets in, and creativity is reduced.

If a manager were in a meeting, and he wished to create and manage frustration to keep it below the threshold point, how would he do it? How would he 'measure' where the subordinates were along the curve, and still get the task done? Would he tell the subordinates that he was doing this?

The leadership literature states that authoritarian leadership tends to produce dependence, and the dependence, in turn, produces frustration. In the form that I just presented the proposition it is, I believe, enactable. It is close to the form that can be found in the original Lewin, Lippitt, and White studies of leadership climates. Yet Lewin's own colleagues conducted years of follow up research in order to produce more rigorous generalizations. As they became more rigorous, the knowledge became less enactable (Argyris, 1980).

Knowledge for leading people in everyday life must usually deal with more than a few variables as well as many relationships among those variables. Scientists typically deal with that by developing analytical techniques such as multivariate analysis. The diagnoses that are usually produced are not enactable. They are simply more sophisticated versions of the X as a function of the Y.

Enactable knowledge may be configured as action maps. These maps describe a multitude of variables, on different levels of analysis, that can be stored in the human mind, retrieved under everyday conditions, and used to design and implement actual solutions in specific situations.

17

The maps have the feature of presenting generalized knowledge without losing the capacity to deal with the individual case (Argyris and Schon, 1988).

I realize that there are some scholars in professional schools who are not concerned about the implementation of the ideas that they teach. One such scholar said to me, 'I really don't worry about implementation'. Another said, 'I think if I were honest I would say I am proud that the ideas are not applicable'. As they spoke, I wondered how they would feel if medical doctors, lawyers, accountants, and other professionals whose services they needed were educated by faculty with their values. By the way, the second speaker told me that he would not say in his MBA clases what he just told me. The first speaker said that he never discussed his values around the enactability of the knowledge that he teaches, but the issues often arise because the students sense his views and question him. Faculty who think that they hide these views, I believe, are kidding themselves. I have just finished observing twenty classes, covering a range of disciplines. I found that students are quite sensitive to how far they can press a faculty member and jeopardize their grades. Defensive routines in class!

Both scholars, when pressed, admitted that applicability of knowledge is important, especially in professional schools. Both also believed that knowledge becomes more applicable as it cumulates and matures. In a recent study that I conducted of subjects reviewed in the *Annals of Psychology and Sociology*, about fields such as leadership, motivation, organizational behaviour, and organizational design, additivity hardly existed (Argyris, 1980). Additivity is a sound idea, but if it is not pursued vigorously by researchers, it is likely to take on the role of a defensive routine to permit us to continue whatever we wish to pursue.

I feel strongly that scholars should be free to pursue their interests. I feel equally strongly that we should be confrontable and influenceable on our defensive behaviour that can be shown to retard the production of valid information. If it works, don't mess with it. In discussing these ideas with several colleagues, they pointed out that some may argue that the present system works, so why try to change it? First, I am not saying that the present system does not have some advantages. I am pleading for research to make it even more effective.

Second, the criterion 'it works' has never been defined, to my knowledge, in ways that it can be publicly tested and subjected to being disconfirmed. In order for the test to be falsifiable, the proposition must be put to a test that is independent of the reasoning of those who have formulated it. If all we do is ask the players, all we can conclude is that the people who say it works are correct because they say it. Clearly that is not acceptable by even the most rudimentary standards of science.

Third, there is, in my opinion, an even more fundamental issue.

The present situation violates the basic value of freedom for social scientists to explore issues wherever they arise. What are the ethics of espousing an opposition to the tyranny of ideas and, at the same time, inhibiting the study and change of our own barriers to freedom of inquiry. What I am suggesting, therefore, is that we reduce the domain of what is undiscussable and hence difficult to influence.

Nor am I making a plea for an immediate focus on the development of one central paradigm. I agree with Bowman (forthcoming) that such activity may be unwise, given the state of our field. Indeed, the result of what I am recommending might be a greater differentiation for the time being, rather than integration. Successful integration does not only mean the speedier development of a genuine discipline of management, it means that our self-limiting barriers will be reduced.

References

Alderfer, P. (1972) 'Conflict resolution among behavioral scientists', *Professional Psychology* Winter: 41–7.

Argyris, C. (1973a) 'Some limits to rational man organizational theory', *Public Administration Review* 33; 253–67.

Argyris, C. (1973b) *Public Administration Review* 33: 354–7.

Argyris, C. (1980) *Inner Contradictions of Rigorous Research*, New York: Academic Press.

Argyris, C. (1985) *Strategy, Change and Defensive Routines*, Cambridge, MA: Ballinger.

Argyris, C. (1987) 'Bridging economics and psychology', *American Psychologist* 42; 456–63.

Argyris, C., Putnam, R., and Smith, D. (1985) *Action Science*, San Francisco: CA Jossey-Bass.

Argyris, C. and Schon, D. (1988) 'Rigor or relevance: Normal science and action science compared' (manuscript).

Baker, G., Jensen, M., and Murphy, K.J. (1988) 'Compensation and incentives: Practice vs. theory', Harvard Business School Division of Research, Working Paper, pp. 88–36.

Bowman, E.H. in *Perspectives on Strategic Management*, James W. Fredrickson (ed.), Cambridge, Mass.: Ballinger, forthcoming.

Etzioni, A. (1988) *The Moral Dimension: Toward a New Economics*, New York: The Free Press.

Jensen, M.C., Meckling, W.H., and Baker, G.P. (1987) 'Models of man', Harvard Business School Teaching Notes, 7 September.

Kay, N.M. (1984) *The Emergent Firm*, New York: St Martins Press.

Kuhn, T.S. (1970) *The Structure of Scientific Revolutions*, 2nd edn, Chicago: University of Chicago Press.

Leibenstein, L. (1987) *Inside the Firm: The Inefficiencies of Hierarchy*, Cambridge, Mass.: Harvard University Press.

Nelson, R.R. and Winter, S.G. (1982) *An Evolutionary Theory of Economic Change*, Cambridge, Mass.: Harvard University Press.

Porter, L.W. and McKibbin, L.E. (1988) *Management Education and Development*, New York: McGraw Hill.

Simon, H.A. (1973) 'Organizational man: rational or self-actualizing', *Public Administration Review* 33: 346–53.

Simon, H.A. (1978) 'Rationality as process and as product of thought', *American Economic Review* 68: 1–16.

Chapter three

Longitudinal methods to study change: theory and practice

Andrew M. Pettigrew

Introduction

Longitudinal studies in the social sciences have always been a minority taste. Academic careers cannot wait for time-series data.

Of course, there has been some charting of longitudinal research strategies in the social sciences. Encouraged by the then (British) Social Science Research Council, Wall and Williams (1970) offered a useful review of the literature up to the late 1960s. More recently Goldstein (1979) and then Tuma and Hannan (1984) have set out some of the theoretical and practical problems of conducting long-itudinal studies of development and change. In the narrower fields of organizational analysis and business strategy the reviews by Kimberly (1976) and Miller and Friesen (1982) have also proved useful, as has the work by Boruch and Pearson (1988) on longitudinal surveys.

Empirically the 1980s has brought us time-series studies of processes of strategic change (Pettigrew, 1985a; Edstrom, 1986; Johnson, 1987; Child and Smith, 1987). Whipp and Clark (1986) produced longitudinal studies of the design innovation process. Topics such as ideologies (Engwall, 1985, decision-making (Lucas, 1987), political processes (Feldman, 1987), and organizational structure and strategy (Mintzberg and Walters, 1982) have all attracted longitudinal research. Although the above-reported studies have tended to use single or comparative case studies, often using historical or historical and real-time data, other studies have used repeated surveys (Brousseau, 1978) and quasi experiments (Wall *et al.*, 1986). Published longitudinal research in organizations is still unusual, but appears to be increasing, and there is variety in what is being studied and how it is being carried out and reported.

Enough is now known about the reality of research activities in the natural and social sciences to recognize research as a craft process and not merely the application of a formal set of techniques and rules. All research involves the application of skills, knowledge,

21

and the person in a variety of different problems in varying contexts, and in that sense it is a craft activity involving skills of individual judgement within a system of collective rules and communication. All researchers make choices. In making those choices no-one starts with their mind a blank and waits for it to be filled with evidence. Our training, experience, and predilections influence our preferred research strategies. In that sense this chapter about longitudinal processual research in organizations has to be autobiographical in tone and content.

My first experience of social science research was working with social anthropologists on a study of cultural change among the Basibolo Sect of the Sebeii people in Uganda. My task was to plot the distribution of the remaining flat-roofed houses of the Basibolo so that another researcher could return a few years later and check my snap shot observations against the later pattern. Thus introduced to field-observational methods it was not an enormous jump to direct my research effort into organizational settings and conduct a series of longitudinal studies of decision-making processes (Pettigrew, 1973a; Mumford and Pettigrew, 1975), occupational specialization as an emergent process (Pettigrew, (1973b, 1975), the creation of organizational cultures (Pettigrew, 1979), and long-term processes of strategic decision-making and change (Pettigrew, 1985a, b, 1987).

Much of the learning from that experience was distilled after the fact and presented as inarticulate reflection from practice in Pettigrew (1985b). This paper is an attempt to build on the 1985 statement of theory of method about contextualist research by incorporating some of the learning from the programme of research now underway at the Centre for Corporate Strategy and Change, University of Warwick.

Since 1985 the building of a programme of research at the Centre for Corporate Stratregy and Change (CCSC) has allowed the broadening and deepening of the mid-1980s statement of contextualist longitudinal research on change. Pulling together an interdisciplinary team of full-time and experienced researchers has not only developed our starting meta level analytical approach to change (the context–content–process formulation), it has also reinforced the crucial need for such a broadly based and theoretically non-restrictive set of analytical principles. In a research centre where:

1. the content areas of change vary from business strategy and structure to human resource management, to strategic service change in health care organizations;
2. where comparative and longitudinal research is underway in around 50 organizations in 8 industries in the private sector, and also in the National Health Service (NHS), and,

3. where the interdisciplinary project teams include individuals with doctorates in modern history, sociology, social policy, psychology, organizational theory and organizational development;

there is clearly a requirement for a meta level analytical approach to provide the identity and coherence within which creative choices can be made. A key purpose of this paper is to make explicit the epistemological and methodological stance of the Centre. In doing this I shall highlight progress and problems. In attempting to reveal our theory of method I recognize the difficulties of trying to make explicit much that is still uncodified and tacit. As Donald Schon (1983) has reminded us even the willing reflective practitioner probably knows more than can be said.

This paper is divided into three sections; the first provides a brief outline of the meta level analytical approach guiding the Centre's research on change together with a statement of some of the central research questions in our empirical work. Section two reveals key areas of practice in conducting comparative and longitudinal field studies. Here some of the craft skills in doing longitudinal research are discussed and suggested routes to simplification of the complex data sets generated in contextualist research are highlighted. The final section points to the strengths and weaknesses of the Centre's approach and identifies some of the major areas of learning from carrying out our first generation projects.

Strategic change processes in context

The Centre's research agenda is the study of strategic change processes in context. Thus far the study of corporate strategy and change has been carried out in three streams of work, which are:

1. The management of strategic and operational change and competitiveness;
2. Studies of the human resource transformation of organizations;
3. Research on the management of strategic service change in the National Health Service (NHS).

Within the above three streams of research a number of detailed research questions arise. These include the following:

1. What are the factors which affect the maintenance and improvement of competitive performance? What role do managerial processes of strategic assessment, choice, and change play in sustaining and developing competitive performance. Are firms which are effective in managing strategic and operational changes those which continue to remain competitive?

23

2. What are the factors and processes which affect the survival and regeneration of firms in mature industries? Many firms do not make major strategic changes until they experience a business crisis. How can change processes be managed on a more continuous basis to avoid the necessity of enforced and painful eras of change?

3. What is the relationship between changes in a firm's business environment, business strategy and technology and its human resource policies and practices? How should employment policies, methods of recruiting, training and developing, and reviewing employees change, as businesses and their technologies change? What new skills, knowledge, capabilities and beliefs are appropriate as their strategies change? How will the role and style of personnel and training specialists need to change to design and implement new policies and practices in the human resource management area?

4. In the NHS, and indeed in many organizations in the public sector, the jugular management problem is how to close the gap between strategic intent and operational implementation. At the District level in the NHS, what are the factors associated with the context of the District and the management culture, structure, and process in the District which lead to strategic intentions for change being operationally implemented?

The overall research challenge in our work is to connect up the content, contexts, and processes of change over time to explain the differential achievement of change objectives. Theoretically the Centre's approach challenges rational, linear theories of planning and change where actions are seen as ordered and sequenced in order to achieve rationally declared ends and where actors behave mechanistically and altruistically in the pursuit of organizational goals. Instead, the task is to explore the complex, haphazard, and often contradictory ways that change emerges and to construct a model that allows for an appreciation of conflicting rationalities, objectives and behaviours. There is an explicit recognition that change is multifaceted; involving political, cultural, incremental, environmental, and structural, as well as rational dimensions. Power, chance, opportunism, accident are as influential in shaping outcomes as are design, negotiated agreements and masterplans (Pettigrew, 1985a). The conventional split between policy formulation and implementation is also questioned and these processes are not viewed as discrete or chronological but as interactive and muddled (Quinn, 1980).

Building on the above conceptual approach, the primary research questions can be summarized as follows:

- what are the main motors/pressures for change? (direction from which the change springs, the role of context and action)
- what are the antecedent conditions for the strategic changes and how influential are they?
- what are the principal impediments/facilitators in the change process?
- how can the pace and extent of change be explained?
- what contexts are change-receptive or change-inhibiting and why?
- how does the total organization change agenda and the interrelationship between change objectives affect outcomes ('change load')?
- how are organizational change priorities ranked and balanced and emergent issues anticipated?
- what are the varying effects of organizational culture, leadership, managerial competence and performance on implementation and change?
- who are the powerful change constituents and how do they legitimate their actions?
- what combinations of features external to the organization (outer context) and internal to the organization (inner context) help explain the rate, pace, and timing of strategic changes?

Contextualism as a mode of analysis

The recent success of books such as Burrell and Morgan (1979) and Morgan (1986) is testimony to the lack of theoretical explicitness of much work in organizational analysis. However, if we as social scientists are not always as explicit as we might be about what theoretical assumptions we are taking into or leaving out of our work, we are equally guilty of not being clear about the theory of method which guides our empirical inquiries. Challenged in 1983 to articulate the theory of method guiding my research on change I chose to present my approach to contextualism using and developing the 1940s writing of the philosopher Stephen Pepper (1942). My 1983 response was eventually published in Pettigrew (1985b, 1985d).

Greiner (1985) offered some initial reflection on Pettigrew (1985b). He considered the treatment of ontology and epistemology abstract and asked for yet more concrete detail on what contextualism meant in the practical day to day conduct of research. Before I try again to explain what contextualism means both as a mode of analysis and a source of the Centre's meta level perspective on change, I should perhaps comment on why context and process-sensitive research is so necessary.

An answer to the 'why' question is provided in a broad review of the literature on change made elsewhere (Pettigrew, 1985a). In that review the point is made that with a few limited noteworthy exceptions (Berg, 1979; Kervasdoue and Kimberly, 1979), much research on organization change is ahistorical, aprocessual, and acontextual in character. In this respect, the area of organization change merely reflects the biases inherent in the social sciences generally and in the study of organizations in particular. There are remarkably few studies of change that actually allow the change process to reveal itself in any kind of substantially temporal or contextual manner. Where the change project is treated as the unit of analysis the focus is on a single event or a set of discrete episodes somehow separate from the immediate and more distant antecedents that give those events form, meaning, and substance. Such episodic views of change not only treat innovations as if they had a clear beginning and a clear end but also, where they limit themselves to snapshot time-series data, fail to provide data on the mechanisms and processes through which changes are created. Studies of transformation are, therefore, often preoccupied with the intricacies of narrow changes rather than the holistic and dynamic analysis of changing.

The suggestion made here is that one way to respond to the above weaknesses in the literature on change is to encourage a form of research which is contextualist and processual in character (Pettigrew, 1985b). A contextualist analysis of a process such as change draws on phenomena at vertical and horizontal levels of analysis and the interconnections between those levels through time. The vertical level refers to the interdependencies between higher or lower levels of analysis upon phenomena to be explained at some further level; for example, the impact of a changing socioeconomic context on features of intra-organizational context and interest-group behaviour. The horizontal level refers to the sequential interconnectedness among phenomena in historical, present, and future time. An approach that offers both multilevel or vertical analysis and processual, or horizontal, analysis is said to be contextualist in character.

In summary the key points to emphasize in analysing change in a contextualist mode are:

1. The importance of interconnected levels of analysis.
   (a) Target changes should be studied in the context of changes at other levels of analysis.
   (b) The search is for patterns of reciprocal connectivity between levels.
   (c) A source of change is the asymmetries between levels of context.
   (d) Processes at different levels have their own momentum, rates, pace and trajectory.
   (e) Some levels of context may impact more visibly and rapidly than others and thus in the short term sources of change may appear undirectional rather than multidirectional.

2. The interconnectedness of the past, present and future.
   (a) Antecedent conditions shape the present and the emerging future. History is not an event in the past but is alive in the present.
   (b) History is about events and structures, acts and underlying logics.
   (c) There are no predetermined timetables; trajectories of change are probabilistic and uncertain because of changing contexts.
3. The importance of context and action.
   (a) It is not a question of nature *or* nurture, or context or action, but context *and* action.
   (b) Context is not just a stimulus environment but a nested arrangement of structures and processes where the subjective interpretation of actors perceiving, comprehending, learning and remembering helps shape process.
4. The nature of causation about change.
   (a) Causation is neither linear nor singular. Changes have multiple causes and are to be explained more by loops than lines. 'The shifting interconnectedness of fused strands', as Mancuso and Ceely (1980) put it.
   (b) The directions of change follow multiple paths; there is no necessary path to development, the trajectory could involve growth, decline, decay, death, or regeneration.

Thus contextualism offers an analytical mode to study change not tied to a particular theory of change. It provides an approach capable of drawing on concepts from a variety of disciplines and several levels of analysis. Featherman and Lerner (1985) conclude their review of what they call developmental contextualism by drawing attention to its intellectual pluralism. 'Different modes of analysis and causal explanation do not need reduction or integration into one over-arching theoretical paradigm: evidence from distinct paradigmatic approaches can accrue or co-exist to account for a complex phenomenon' such as change (Featherman and Lerner, 1985: 672). Furthermore, contextualism offers a meta level approach capable of exploring several content areas of change in multifarious contexts through time. Thus reality can be caught in flight whilst at the same time there is a commitment to embeddedness as a principle of analysis.

If the first section of this chapter describes and explains our theory of method, what of the practical problems of implementing our chosen approach? The task of the next section is to describe and discuss some of the practical issues we encountered in conducting longitudinal research in organizational settings.

Practising longitudinal research in organizational settings

It should be clear from the outline of our research in the first section of this paper that our research strategy is to pursue longitudinal research by means of the comparative case-study method. Our case studies involve comparisons across firms in the same sector, between firms in different sectors, and sometimes as in our human resource work we make direct sector to sector comparisons. Time is captured in our work through a combination of retrospective and real-time analysis. Thus far, the retrospective element can provide us with up to a 20-year time series while for reasons of funding we have been restricted to a real-time analysis of up to 3 years. In earlier work on strategic change in ICI (Pettigrew, 1985a) a real-time analysis of 10 years was achieved which was complemented by 20-plus-years of retrospective data, but this is an ideal rarely accomplished in organizational analysis. The kind of intensive comparative analysis practised in the Centre means that a practical load for two senior and experienced full-time staff is 10 case studies over a 3-year period. Our research strategy is resource intensive, intellectually challenging, and highly demanding of the social and political skills of the Centre staff.

Given all the variants of longitudinal research sketched by Kimberly (1976), Miller and Friesen (1982) and others, why have we adopted the comparative case study method? The simple answer is because the longitudinal comparative case method best suits the research topic being pursued, the contextualist mode of analysis adopted, and the broad research objectives we have in mind.

Let us examine some of the broad research goals pursued by social scientists. They may include:

1. precision of measurement
2. generality over actors and situations
3. realism of context
4. theoretical and conceptual development
5. contribution to particular and general questions of policy and practice

Given the limited character of our knowledge of change in organizational settings, and in particular how so much change research is acontextual, ahistorical, and aprocessual (Pettigrew, 1985a, 1987a, b) the time is ripe for intensive and contextually sensitive studies of changing. We thus give primacy to realism of context and theoretical and conceptual development as research goals, and by the very nature of the research process engaged in and the kinds of data collected, thereby create some of the circumstances to ask and answer questions of policy and practice. Given that the contextualist explicitly works towards goals three, four and five does not, of course, preclude the use of measurement. Indeed the generation of apposite measures, that is measures invented and sensitively linked to the subtleties and nuances of a particular context or contexts, is an important consideration for the style of research described here. Equally well the exploration of processes in context does not have to imply single case study analyses, although such case studies can be valuable as part of the task of raising new empirical areas for study and articulating novel frames of reference. Where comparisons are being built into the research design these can involve multiple cases in different settings, or multiple incidents in the same physical setting but at different points in chronological time, or different states or phases in a group or any other system's pattern of development. Where comparisons are being attempted a prime analytical requirement should be to demonstrate how variability in context influences the shape, pace, and direction of the change processes under investigation.

The longitudinal comparative case method provides the opportunity to examine continuous processes in context, to draw in the significance of various levels of analysis and thereby to reveal the multiple sources and loops of causation and connectivity so crucial in identifying and explaining patterns in the process of change.

Having clarified our research strategy and objectives it remains for me to discuss some of the practical problems in implementing our favoured approach. I have collected together a range of implementation issues under the following headings:

1. truth is the daughter of time
2. site selection
3. data collection and degree of involvement
4. research outputs, audience and presentation
5. routes to simplification

Truth is the daughter of time

For the practitioner of longitudinal research issues of time are critical and pervasive. How does the choice of the time series influence the perspective of the researcher? When does the process begin and end? When is the appropriate moment to make assessments about outcome evaluation? Is time just events and chronology or is time a socially constructed phenomenon which influences behaviour? Are there varying time cycles at levels of analysis beyond the focal level of investigation? Does the appreciative system of the researcher change over time and therefore is what the researcher is capable of thinking and saying conditional on when pen is put to paper?

First there is the crucial issue of time and perspective. Time sets a frame of reference for what changes are seen and how those changes are explained. In the micro-events which surround our particular lives and in the daily trumpetings of the media change has an ever-present illusion of reality. The more we look at present-day events the easier it is to identify change; the longer we stay with an emergent process and the further back we go to disentangle its origins, the more we can identify continuities. Empirically and theoretically, change and continuity need one another. Process and context, change and continuity are inextricably linked. Any adequate theory or theories of change has to deal with continuity and change. Any adequate empirical inquiry into change has to be capable of revealing the patterns, causes, and movements from continuity to change and vice versa. There is, therefore, no option for the analyst of change but to collect time-series data which allows the present to be explored in relation to the past and the emerging future.

But when does a change process begin and end especially where the unit of analysis is the continuous process in context and not the change episode or project? When does the field researcher start and stop collecting data? Does one stop peeling the layers from the onion only when the vapours inhibit all further sight? There are, of course, no absolute answers to such questions. Pragmatically, judgements will be made in the light of the themes and research questions being pursued, the empirical setting of the research, the nature and quality of researcher-subject relationship in any site, and funding or other resource constraints. An example is perhaps in order. In Hardy's (1985) research on factory closures a judgement had to be made as to when the process of closure began. One choice point was when the senior management announced the closure. Another was when the senior management agreed to stop investing in the factory in question. The latter choice point preceded the closure announcement by around 5 years in one of Hardy's cases. With the management pursuing a conscious long-term strategy of allowing the factory to wither on the vine it was not a difficult choice to begin the data collection at the earlier of the two options. However, not all choice points are as empirically evident as that.

The issue of when to conclude the data collection and analysis is closely linked to the problem of when to make judgements about outcome evaluations in a change process. The time-series data on the birth, evolution, impact and fate of internal consultancy groups reported in Pettigrew (1975, 1985a) illustrates how judgements of impact and fate are sensitive to time and the vagaries of shifting internal and external contexts. But judgements about impact are not only conditioned by the time point of observation but also by the subjective interpretations of actors involved in and around the change process. Often contradictory accounts are obtained from different respondents. Where this has occurred, the Centre's approach is to expose the alternative accounts, rather than accord one privileged status. We are essentially presenting a pluralist analysis, where different versions of reality are revealed by the range of actors who operate with a variety of interests and perceptions.

Questions of evaluation are also linked to core problems such as the meaning of 'change' in the research. In our health service research, Ferlie and Pettigrew (1988) argue that this apparently simple concept can be defined in a variety of ways. There is the speed of health service change question. How quickly has the health authority changed its pattern of service? There is the quantity of service change question. What have been the changes in inputs such as hospitals, beds, staff and number of new facilities? There is the quality of service change question. To what extent has there been developments of new roles, new working practices and attitudes? Finally there is the process of service change question, as experienced by the members of the organization. Has the change been driven through, but at the cost of wrecked relationships, leaving the health authority unable to contemplate further change?

Aside from the core question of what change means in longitudinal research there is also the equally important issue of the meaning of time in temporal analysis. As Elchardus (1988) has recently argued 'time is increasingly recognised as an issue in its own right and not just a secondary factor that becomes relevant when the question of social change is raised' (1988: 36). For a citizen such as myself whose grand passion is antiquarian horology it is easy to assume a single means of time reckoning: clock time. But as Whipp (1988) reminds us 'time is more diverse and necessarily social and subjective' (1988: 211). Time is not just 'out there' as neutral chronology it is 'in here' as a social construction. In certain kinds of organization there are socially constructed time frames build around, for example, the design and development cycle of a car or the long process of taking an idea for a new drug from the laboratory to the marketplace.

Time is a socially meaningful phenomenon, something to which value is attached and which we conceive to try and understand continuity and change. In trying to make sense of order and movement, time is clearly more than just events and chronology. We follow Ladurie (1979) in seeking to tame the event 'the long sequence of simple and uncomplicated events'. Instead events are stepping stones in the search for the study of structures, 'the persistent patterns of the long term' Ladurie (1979: 111). Or as Morgan (1986: 267) puts it 'we need to try and understand how the discrete events that make up our experience of change . . . are generated by a logic unfolded in the process of change itself.' What is critical is not just events but the underlying logic that gives events meaning and significance. Understanding patterns in the process is the goal.

Lerner and Kauffman (1985) remind us that there is the added complication that there may be different patterns in the process occurring at different levels in a contextualist analysis. What they call the non-equivalent temporal metric across levels of analysis. The firm may be changing more quickly or more slowly than the sector or sectors of which it is a part. Furthermore, Lerner and Kauffman (1985) use an example from developmental psychology to illustrate the general point that time may not have an identical meaning at all the pertinent levels of analysis. Thus infant neuromuscular change can be detected in weeks but social-institutional change may take years to reveal itself. Thus it may be difficult to detect the influence of changes on one level on another – a perennial problem for the longitudinal researcher using a contextualist mode of analysis.

Finally there is the issue of time and the appreciative system of the researcher. Collecting and analysing comparative and longitudinal data on change processes is a highly complex social and intellectual task. There are times when one feels overwhelmed by detail. Later in the process one may feel a temporary often illusory sense that order is prevailing. There are indeed patterns, not only in this case but across these cases in quite different contexts. At some point in time the painful process of writing must begin and end. When one puts pen to paper will influence what one can see and say. The meta level appreciation of a complex data set takes time. Truth is indeed the daughter of time.

Site selection

There is an intentional or design component in the process of choosing and gaining access to research sites but the process is best characterized by the phrase 'planned opportunism'.

From the perspective of the CCSC one can identify a longer-term planning activity where the issue of the research strategy of the Centre is linked to matters of academic and practitioner relevance, funding strategies and explicit network building to open up site options. At the level of short-term planning for individual research projects there are clear decision rules that can be invoked to inform the choice of research sites. The short-term decision rules bound up with research design are dependent on the success of the longer-term planning activity, and vice versa.

The selection of research sites is shaped by the choice of research topics and questions being posed, together with the language with which the research domain is expressed. In this sense any longer-term planning is only possible in so far as a research area is fundable. Like it or not funding decisions are very much a product of a jointly intellectual, social, and political process. Topic areas rise and fall in their academic and practitioner salience and relevance. In saying this I make no simple dichotomy between academic salience and practical relevance. The most jugular practical problems contain within them the most theoretically challenging research questions. Thus in Mrs Thatcher's Britain it is no accident that our Centre features the language of corporate strategy and change. Topic choice, funding, the selection of sites, and realizing access are all interconnected.

Another feature of long-term planning relates to the settings where it is hoped particular access will be sought. In which sectors, public or private is the research to be pursued? Is the geographical focus to be the UK, Continental Western Europe, or the Pacific Basin? Relationships have to be built to underpin research topics which require new settings. Network building is a critical activity for any serious group of empirical researchers. All reserch centres need a foreign policy. Everyone working in the Centre is a critical actor in the foreign policy. Research performance is a confluence of topic selection, intellectual creativity and surefootedness, entrepreneurial energy, the quality and nature of a Centre's networks, skill in negotiating access to critical sites, and a broadly based and well-executed dissemination strategy. The short-term planning aspect of site selection is more easily linkable to what we call research design. Here again a judicious mixture of forethought and intentions, chance, opportunism, and environmental preparedness play their part. However, experience suggests the following decision rules may help to guide choice.

Go for extreme situations, critical incidents and social dramas

The rationale here is straightforwardly pragmatic. If the phenomena to be observed has to be contained within a single or relatively small number of cases then you have to choose your case or cases where the process is transparently observable. Dramas have to be studied alongside the relative routine that intersperses them. The point of studying a sequence of social dramas longitudinally is that they provide a transparent look at the growth, evolution, transformation, and conceivably decay of an organization over time. In an earlier publication (Pettigrew, 1979) I noted that:

1. Each drama provides a clear point of data collection, an important practical consideration in such an extended stream of time, events, people, and processes.
2. Each drama can act as an in-depth case study within the overall case study and thereby provide a dramatic glimpse into the current workings of the social system.
3. The longitudinal study of a sequence of dramas allows various readings to be taken of the development of the organization, of the impact of one drama on successive and even consequent dramas, and of the kinds of mechanisms that lead to, accentuate, and regulate the impact of each drama.

4. As the point about mechanisms of transformation implies, only dramas can provide consequence and meaning in relation to routines. The quality and analytical impact of the study of dramas can only be as good as the researcher's understanding of the relative routines with which each drama is interspersed. In this sense the routines provide the contextual backdrop for the foreground drama and the researcher becomes interested in the interactive effect between context and foreground and the mechanisms and processes of transformation from routine to drama and new routine and further drama.

5. Examining the dramas affords the opportunity to study continuous processes. In the school study the focus on continuous process related to questions of organizational goals, their emergence and transformation, and to changes in systems of beliefs, power relationships, and culture.

Sometimes social dramas and the public inquiries they produce offer social scientists the first opportunity to look inside a previously shielded social system. Thus the Bank Rate scandal in Britain in 1957 and the published inquiry reports which followed it provided Wilson and Lupton (1959) with an opportunity to research and publish one of the first studies of the interlocking family connections and directorates in the City of London. Perrow (1984) was quick to use the Three Mile Island accident to develop thinking about disasters.

A variant of the critical case is the choice of a highly visible case. By and large social scientists have not studied the elite and powerful groups in the societies where they practise their skills. Access to and publication of significant research results about an elite institution can have significant positive knock-on effects. The publication of the Imperial Chemical Industries study of strategic change (Pettigrew, 1985a) has opened many doors for the CCSC.

Theoretical propositions may also guide the choice of research settings. Thus theoretical writing and empirical enquiry on organizational politics suggests a relationship between high levels of political activity and non-programmed innovative activity (Pettigrew, 1973, Hickson *et al.*, 1986). If you want to observe politics in action choose cases where there are consequential and structurally complex decisions being made.

Go for polar types

If one is interested, as we are, in the links between the capability of firms to manage strategic and operational change and their relative competitive performance then one needs to build in sites which illustrate high and low performance. Measuring relative competitive performance is not a straightforward matter but even treating competitiveness as a multi-level and dynamic phenomenon (Whipp *et al.*, in press) it is possible to structure site selection to pursue the research question in mind.

An important aspect of choosing by polar types is to select cases which disconfirm patterns from earlier case studies. In a programme of research driven initially by a strong series of hunches which in turn are reinforced by early data collection, a sound strategy is to build in space for later cases which can be used for purposes of disconfirmation. Chains of evidence should be challenged by chains of possible falsification (Yin, 1984; Whipp *et al.*, 1988).

Go for high experience levels of the phenomena under study

The pragmatic logic here is similar to that which was explained under the extreme situation decision rule, though there is not the implication here of any necessary transparent drama suddenly revealing a social system. The site selection for our human resources work and our Aids research is guided by this decision rule. Thus in the human resources work we have chosen longitudinal cases where there is evidence of recent business environment and business strategy change occasioning some degree of concern for an activity in changing human resource policies and practices. In the Aids research where the phenomenon under study did not exist as an organizational fact in the UK until 1983, we are choosing research sites where there is experience of either hospital-based services, or community-based services, or health-promotion activity.

Go for more informed choice of sites and increase the probabilities of negotiating access

This last suggestion is not so much a decision rule as a general tactical recommendation which we have developed by learning from doing. Faced with the situation where one wishes to focus in on a particular industry sector; where there is a requirement to choose sites which meet one or other of the three decision rules mentioned above; and where one needs the kind of intensive access necessary for longitudinal work – do a low cost study of the key players in the sector first. In the British context where there are strongly established norms about privacy it is easier to 'cold call' firms for two or three one-and-a-half hour interviews than it is to persuade firms to grant long-term access. A low-cost survey of the key players in a sector can:

1. Provide the researchers with an empirically formed view of the problems, prospects and range of experiences in a sector;
2. Provide early publications at the sector level of analysis;
3. Establish a network of relationships in a sector fairly quickly;
4. Allow more informed choices to be made about sites on the basis of theoretical ideas and empirical trends; and

5. Dramatically increase the success rate in negotiating access into preferred longitudinal sites.

The other critical practical consideration which stands alongside the choice of sites is how many sites? Again there is no absolute answer to this question. An *n* of 1 can be adequate if the treatment of the case material is sufficiently generic (see Miller and Friesen 1982: 1016 for a development of this point), or if the quality and nature of the findings are suitably unique or in other ways strong. In our experience of comparative longitudinal case study work high standards of input and output can be sustained if each experienced full-time research fellow has in the region of four to six cases over a 3-year period. There can be some flexing of these figures and standards maintained if distinctions are made between major (intensive) cases and minor (less-intensive) cases. The significant loss on the minor cases compared with the major ones will be a weakening of the data and interpretation on the how and the why of change (the process and the contexts) whereas there may be approximate equivalence of standards on the what (content) of change.

Data collection and degree of involvement

Skill in the field is critical to the success of an endeavour based on the longitudinal comparative case study method. Yin (1984) and others have commented on some of the kinds of skills required of a good fieldworker. These include asking and interpreting apposite questions, listening, being adaptive and flexible, being knowingly unbiased, and having a firm grasp of the issues being studied. In addition to these requirements the long distance fieldworker needs the social and political skills to develop and maintain credibility with a wide range of respondents from different levels and functions inside and outside the focal organization, and in the case of the Centre's work style, the skills to run research in action workshops – of which more later.

This is clearly too big a subject to dwell on here. I can only highlight some of the key features of our data-collection procedures. General issues of fieldwork in case study research have been adequately dealt with in Van Maanen (1983, 1988), Yin (1984), and Burgess (1984). Our aims are to collect data which are processual (an emphasis on action as well as structure overtime), comparative (a range of studies in various sectors), pluralist (describe and analyse the often competing versions of reality seen by actors in change processes), historical (take into account the historical evolution of ideas and actions for change as well as the constraints within which decision-makers operate), and contextual (examine the reciprocal relations between process and contexts at different levels of analysis). This means producing case studies and not just case histories – going beyond chronology to develop analytical themes. It also means collecting data not only at different levels of analysis (economy, sector, firm, department, and individual) but also pursuing the inter-linkages between levels of analysis (demonstrating how actors mobilize features of economic and sectoral contexts to legitimize or delegitimize ideas for change and continuity).

What does this imply for fieldwork? A triangulated methodology is used to gather different types of data which can be used as cross checks. Thus for example, in our health service work (McKee and Pettigrew 1988) this can involve:

1. *In-depth interviews* with key informants: selected because of their lead position in the organization or in the change process under analysis; those affected by the changes as well as the initiators of change; different elites and interest groups internal and external to the focal organization (on average 50 interviews per case). Interviews are tape-recorded. Interview pro-formas are discussed in each research team, tested in the field and then modified as appropriate.
2. *Documentary and archive data*: including the minutes of relevant meetings, strategy and policy documents, and secondary quantitative material on activity levels, deaths and discharges; and memos and correspondence.
3. *Observational and ethnographic material*: including attendance at formal meetings, planned site visits to meet staff and visit facilities; as well as informal, chance meetings, conversations, and extensive time spent living and working within the organization.

Fieldwork can involve 2 or 3 days a week over a 5-month period with intermittent contact thereafter. The balance between the three sources of data mentioned above varies from project to project. In terms of the sequencing of data collection, the pattern is for the what of change, the chronology to be established first, often using archival data and interviews; and then further interviewing, observation, secondary data collection and informal questioning to reveal the how and why of change, drawing on variables at different levels of analysis.

Managing the degree of involvement with the research site is a crucial issue for any field researcher. It is also an important area for strategic clarity for a research centre. If you are working with a system for three years you cannot play the role of the brusque detached scientist. Research is a social process not just a technical task. Equally one should not get over-involved and 'go native'. Researchers are in the perspective business. The fact that we work in three-person project teams and meet regularly as project teams and as a Centre helps enormously to balance detachment and involvement and inhibit any tendency to over-identify with particular interpretations or interests. Our comparative methodology also helps to achieve perspective on individual case studies.

Research is also a reciprocal activity. People engage in it for a variety of motives. Time spent clarifying motives and expectations at the front end process of negotiating access can save heartache and friction later. We have a standard 'contract' about entry which is explicitly reciprocal. We have access to study the topic we define and all publications are shown to the organization prior to publication. Respondents have an opportunity to correct errors of fact and to ensure we do not divulge commercially sensitive information. Editorial control remains with the research team. In fact the process is not as stark as that. Practices vary from researcher to researcher in the Centre but wiser souls manage the release of interpretations towards the end of the research process so that final case-study reports do not inflict massive surprise. The key mechanism we offer as reciprocity for access is a research-in-action workshop. These workshops are designed to meet the particular requirements of each case but by and large include the following:

1. presenting a full case-study report to key power figures prior to the workshop;
2. preparing an executive summary before the workshop for all the workshop participants; and,
3. running a one-day interactive feedback workshop for 10–15 key people in the organization where an analysis of the past and present development of the organization is explicitly linked to the future strategic concerns of that organization.

Such workshops have achieved the following purposes.

1. They have helped us to secure longitudinal access to upwards of 60 private and public sector organizations. This is unique for a UK-based research centre in the management field,
2. They have been found useful by our respondent organizations and have strengthened relationships for future work,
3. They have provided additional research data for current work; and,
4. They provide validation for the interpretations offered by the research team.

As such the research-in-action workshops are a critical mechanism for balancing detachment and involvement, achieving validation and new data, and deepening relationships and achieving perspective. They also represent an important arena for personal development for the Centre staff.

Research outputs, audience, and presentation

The obvious may be stated at the outset; researchers need to be clear about the varieties of research output achievable within their mode of operation, the sequencing with which those outputs are deliverable over time, the audiences for which the outputs are intended, and the most suitable form of presentation for each audience.

Table 3.1 sets out some of the varieties of research output possible from longitudinal comparative case study work. It also suggests, through the vertical line running from time t_1 to t_n, what forms of output may be deliverable at what points in time in the research process.

Table 3.1 Varieties of research output from longitudinal comparative case study work

t_1

1. ANALYTICAL CHRONOLOGY
   - The Narrative
   - Across levels of analysis
   - With causal linkages
   - Establishing early analytical themes

2. DIAGNOSTIC CASE
   - All of the features mentioned in 1 above
   - Plus a listing and analysis of the organizations current strategic concerns

3. INTERPRETATIVE/THEORETICAL CASE(S)
   - Theoretical placement
   - Narrative and interpretation
   - Stronger analytical themes
   - General empirical placement

4. META LEVEL ANALYSIS ACROSS CASES
   - Broad thematic presentation
   - Theoretical and empirical placement in comparative terms
   - Loss of case integrity
   - Case data used for thematic illustration

t_n

Table 3.1 indicates that clarifying the research output is a non-trivial issue. In an interdisciplinary research centre it is important to have a non-constraining meta level of analysis (in our case the context, content, process formulation), it is also important to be clear about outputs. Conducting longitudinal field research can be an arduous task with motivation seeping away as the volume of inputs increase and the delayed gratification of outputs seems ever in the future. Achieving successful

outputs of the 1 and 2 variety is a very important motivational consideration along the way to the 'higher level' outputs implied in varieties
3 and 4.

Thus far the pattern in the Centre is for outputs 1 to be written for
ourselves as part of the process of sharing, learning, and developing
themes within and across projects. Outputs 2 we produce for the research-
in-action workshops with our case study organizations. Shortened
versions of output 1 have been produced for practitioner journals. Here
we have learnt that publishing a series of short articles in the same widely
read practitioner journal can have a significantly greater impact than
spreading case writing around a series of journals (see, for example,
the *Personnel Management* series Hendry and Pettigrew, 1987, 1988;
Sparrow and Pettigrew, 1988a, b). Outputs 3 and 4 are appearing in
academic journals (e.g. Sparrow and Pettigrew, 1988c; Rosenfeld *et al.*,
in press, Whipp *et al.*, in press) but are only possible to produce alongside
other research demands into the second and third year of a 3-year project.
The major meta level publications will be in book form and will appear
in the fourth and subsequent years, although significant meta level writing
has been completed. In our human resources work within three years
(Pettigrew *et al.*, 1988a, b).

Our research is also being incorporated into documentary programmes for National networked television, for example, Granada TV 17
July 1988, and a Central TV programme on leadership and change shown
on 11 October 1988.

Routes to simplification

Anyone who has carried out longitudinal field research; who has worked
in an interdisciplinary team using the comparative case study method;
or who has sought to assist doctoral students through such a research
process will know that the central problem is dealing with complexity.
For some there is no release from the overwhelming weight of information, from the task of structuring and clarifying, from the requirement
for inductive conceptualization. The result is death by data asphyxiation
– the slow and inexorable sinking into the swimming pool which started
so cool, clear and inviting and now has become a clinging mass of maple
syrup.

Rather than dwelling on the causes of complexity, or the process which
leads to the overwhelming of the researcher by data, I shall use this
section to highlight some of the pathways to avoid data asphyxiation.
I call these routes to simplification and offer them as a source of
encouragement for scholars prepared to take the risk of conducting
longitudinal and comparative field research in organizational settings.
Many of the routes have been implicitly or explicitly mentioned earlier

and they are collected together here to provide summary emphasis. Table 3.2 lists some of the routes to simplification that we at the CCSC have consciously used. This list of 10 routes is by no means complete and I invite colleagues to add to it from their 'learning by doing'. As the list is incomplete it may also be idiosyncratic – research is after all a craft activity, the merging of skills, knowledge, and the person around an intellectual problem. However, the list also has a systemic and generalizable quality about it – the categories are sufficiently broad to be capable of interpretation and application to many particular situations. Crucially the list covers many key activities in the research process – from objectives, the fundamental of the front end of the process, to outputs, the goal of attempts at discovery. I labour this point about the scope of the list to emphasize that the problems of data overload are not reducible just to questions of data reduction and display (Huberman and Miles, 1983).

Table 3.2 Some routes to simplification in longitudinal and comparative field research

1.	Being clear about research objectives
	• Building on strengths
	• Awareness of limitations
2.	Being clear about the unit of analysis and study questions
3.	Coming to terms with time
4.	Making explicit your theory of method
5.	Making explicit your meta level analytical framework
6.	Making explicit the character of the generic propositions you are seeking
7.	Identify analytical themes which cut across data
8.	Use techniques of data reduction and display
9.	Make prescriptive statements as an aid to analytical generalization
10.	Make explicit the varieties and sequencing of research output

Being clear about research objectives, the appropriate unit of analysis, and the vagaries and choices in coming to terms with time have already been mentioned. The contextualist researcher is not interested in change episodes but focuses on continuous processes in context. The quest is for holistic understanding, realism of context and concept and theory building. One has to make explicit and pragmatic judgements about artificial beginnings and artificial endings in a continuous process, about how time frames may open up and close down perspectives on continuity and change, and how processes at different levels of context may have their own pace and direction.

In the first section of this chapter I laid out our contextualist theory of method with its emphasis on time, different levels of context, challenges in dealing with context and action, exogenous and endogenous sources of change, and causal loops and not causal lines. The search for holistic understanding also has to be operationalized into a clear articulated, tested, and refined proforma of research themes and questions.

Our meta level analytical framework – the exploration of change through time by means of the interconnected analysis of contexts, content and process is the critical basis for intellectual coherence in the Centre. Here is a guide well rooted in previous longitudinal research (Pettigrew, 1985a) which offers analytical structure at a broad level but no over-restrictive theoretical web, and certainly plenty of space to adjust research designs and study questions as one moves from one content area of change to another. The study of change processes is a classically interdisciplinary topic. It cannot be reduced to the myopias of any particular discipline (Pettigrew, 1987c). A programme of research on change is best tackled through interdisciplinary teams. Teams of talented people need intellectual space. Analytical space only has meaning if juxtaposed alongside an analytical structure.

The character of the generic propositions in our work are naturally derived from our meta level analytical framework. Does the content of a change influence its process? How does the pursuit of a multiple change agenda influence the progression of each individual change? Are there receptive and non-receptive contexts for change irrespective of variation in the content of change? Will the analysis of the fine shading of the inner context of an organization differentiate between receptive and inhibitory contexts for change or is it always a question of the judicial mixture of inner and outer context shaping the rate, pace and direction of change process?

As Huberman and Miles (1983) argue, techniques of data reduction and data display are crucial mechanisms for structuring and thereby simplifying data. Pattern reduction is a critical intellectual process for all engaged in longitudinal comparative case study work. We use proformas, flowcharts of chronology, matrices, graphs, tables, lists of factors with assessments of relative importance; all the unexceptional sorting and classifying tools of a researcher.

In the dialogue between researcher and researcher over the development of analytical themes and general propositions, requests for prescriptive statements may help simplification. If, for example, the intellectual task is to begin to specify the characteristics of so-called receptive and non-receptive contexts for change, the variables at play may be clarified by asking – what features of intra-organizational context would one have to change in order to increase or decrease the degree of change receptivity in that particular setting?

Finally we try to write clearly in whatever we write. We have a goal to produce meta level articles and books but know we cannot go from chronology to meta level analytical writing in one leap. Persistence and patience is as much a necessity for the long-distance researcher on change as it is for the initiator of change processes.

Lessons for future research on change

Forty years ago in a paper entitled 'The Strengths of Industrial Sociology' George Homans wrote that 'people who write about methodology often forget that it is a matter of strategy, not of morals. There are neither good nor bad methods but only methods that are more or less effective under particular circumstances in reaching objectives on the way to a distant goal' Homans (1949: 330). Homans is, of course, quite right in one respect, the choice of methodology is contingent on the problems and questions under study and the state of development of any body of knowledge. Choices will also be bounded by budget and time constraints, the vagaries of site selection and individual differences between members of a research team and the individuals in research sites to whom they have to relate. Although I am sure Homans never meant to imply as such, it would be wrong to suggest that the contingent and strategic aspect of choice of method indicated that such choices were amoral. There are many ethical considerations posed by the kind of fieldwork advocated in this paper. These ethical questions relate particularly to the front end of the research – how expectations and contracts are set between grant-awarding body and researcher and researcher and respondents. There are also major ethical issues in gathering and using highly sensitive information about long-term processes of strategic choice and change.

Searching for lessons from experience cannot be just a strategic or a tactical exercise, but neither should one be drawn into the kind of moral imperatives Homans was really trying to avoid. A theme of this chapter has been that research is a craft activity. It is not just the application of a formal set of techniques and rules. A craft activity involves the application of skills, knowledge, and the person in varying settings. Within these settings individual judgements are made in the context of a wider system of collective rules and communication. It seems naive and two-faced of us to recognize the now-familiar notions that problem-solving and decision-making processes in organizations include elements of political process, incrementalism, and garbage can, and yet to continue to think of our own research activities in organizations as if they were exercises in technical rationality. As Beveridge (1950) and Mitroff (1974), and others have told us the rationality of scientific activity has its artistic and subjective sides. Even if the methods advocated in this paper had all been codified and written down (and there is much productive work to do in that direction) craft skills would still be required to interpret and apply such codifications according to the particular nuances and subtleties of each research project and site. Researchers are clearly engaged in a craft process with ethical requirements. They are also in the perspective business. They are most certainly not in the business of making moral imperatives and absolute choices about methodology.

Having offered such conditional statements what general lessons are emerging from the Centre's research programme on change? Some of the key areas of learning from doing were well rehearsed in the second section of this chapter. I refer here to the crucial issue of time and perspective; the need to be clear about the beginning and end of change processes under investigation; the precise meaning and use of 'time' and 'change' in research on change process; and, of course, the issue of time and the appreciative system of the researcher.

Site selection has been characterized here as a process of 'planned opportunism'. The Centre is perhaps unique in the British academic business school scene for the high level and high quality access it enjoys. This has occurred neither because of opportunism nor accident. There is an intentional and design component to site selection which strategically is linked to long-term considerations such as academic and practitioner relevance, funding strategies and explicit network building to open up site options. At the level of short-term planning for individual research projects the discussion in section two emphasized the importance of a set of decision rules which included the use of dramas and routines, polar types, and case studies which revealed high experience levels of the change phenomena under investigation.

A key lesson for us has been how to manage and balance the degree of involvement and distance in field sites. It is neither possible nor desirable to play the role of brusque detached scientist in field situations where one is seeking co-operation over a 3-year real-time investigation posssibly combined with a decade or more of historical analysis. In this kind of longitudinal field research on change reciprocity between research team and research site is a critical consideration. Our use of research-in-action workshops to feedback and validate findings and collect additional data has been a critical mechanism in opening up organizations for study on some highly sensitive issues. A crucial area where we still have much to learn is how to deal with the sheer volume and complexity of information collected using the comparative and longitudinal case method. The points summarized in Table 3.2 emphasize that the process of simplification starts with clarification about research objectives, themes, and unit of analysis; crucially involves explicitness about theory of method, and the availability of a meta level analytical framework. Using and developing project-specific techniques of data reduction and display is important to help reveal patterns in processes of change, as is making explicit the character of the generic propositions being sought.

What Table 3.2 fails to make expicit but which I know to be critical is individual differences in conceptual and writing skills among researchers. Some researchers provide their own route to simplification by their superior skills of inductive thinking and conceptualization and by highly developed literary and writing skills. Identifying patterns in processes is, of course, crucially about inductive generalization which involves the easy movement from the particular to the general. Writing skills are not only important in identifying and representing themes within cases they are absolutely essential in representing the often subtle nuances of constancy and variability within and across several longitudinal cases involving in our work several levels of analysis. Inductive skills and writing abilities can be developed through experience but there are clear individual differences between scholars in these competences and they are a major consideration in selection decisions for employment in the CCSC.

Table 3.1 emphasises the importance of research managers clarifying the varieties of research output achievable within a particular methodological approach. Although this issue may be obvious it is certainly not trivial. A lesson I would take from our first generation of research is to produce the analytical chronologies and diagnostic cases as early as possible in the research process. Such case study writing is the essential building block for interpretative and meta level analysis and writing. Stopping the fieldwork at the most efficient time and clearing the decks for within case analysis and writing produces massive gains later on as the demands for pattern recognition, cross case analysis and theoretical development loom larger and larger. There is still much to do in the Centre to synthesize the findings from our first generation of empirical projects. Our highest quality publications may well come in the second phase of our development. In this second phase we might expect to reap the benefits of cross-project analysis at the firm and sector level.

Recognizing that the quantity and quality of research output may vary according to the development phase of a research centre points directly to the central issue of the organization and management of organizational research. There are a number of advantages in creating a research centre composed of full-time, experienced post-doctoral staff. The advantages are:

1. the opportunity to build a distinctive intellectual coherence around a critical mass of scholars from a variety of disciplines;
2. the time to conduct large-scale empirical studies using the longitudinal comparative case study method;
3. the intellectual space to take a longer-term view of research requirements and effectively deliver on those requirements; and,
4. the time to build academic and practitioner networks to communicate

results, receive feedback, and build a positive climate for future funding possibilities and project development.

The field of corporate strategy and change is diffuse and inter-disciplinary in character. Empirical inquiry in this area demands well-motivated teams of experienced scholars from a variety of disciplines. To be effective such teams require a distinctive coherence. They also need a life together beyond the confines of an individual project. Continuity is important not only because of the requirement for time-series data but also to ensure learning acquired in early work is not dissipated and lost. Large research problems ask for a critical mass of resources. Studies of processes of strategic choice and change call for craft skills of a high order. Such craft skills are best learnt and developed in the field with sympathetic colleagues some of whom can carry learning by doing forward into future generations of work.

References

Berg, P.O. (1979) *Emotional Structures in Organizations; A Study of the Process of Change in a Swedish Company*, Lund: Student Literature.

Beveridge, W.I.B. (1950) *The Art of Scientific Investigation*, London: Heinemann.

Boruch, R.F. and Pearson, R.W. (1988) 'Assessing the quality of longitudinal surveys', *Evaluation Review* 12: 3–58.

Brousseau, K.R. (1978) 'Personality and job experience', *Organisational Behaviour and Human Performance* 22: 235–52.

Burgess, R.G. (1984) *In the Field: An Introduction to Field Research*, London: Allen & Unwin.

Burrell, G. and Morgan, G. (1979) *Sociological Paradigms and Organisational Analysis*, London: Heinemann.

Child, J. and Smith, C. (1987) 'The context and process of organizational transformation: Cadbury Limited in its sector', *Journal of Management Studies* 24: 565–94.

Edstrom, A. (1986) 'Leadership and strategic change', *Human Resource Management* 25: 581–606.

Elchardus, M. (1988) 'The rediscovery of Chronos: the new role of time in Sociological theory', *International Sociology* 3: 35–59.

Engwall, L. (1985) 'Organizational drift as a response to resource dependence. University of Uppsala, Sweden', *Working paper, Department of Business Administation*.

Featherman, D.L. and Lerner, R.M. (1985) 'Ontogenesis and sociogenesis: problematics for theory and research about development and socialisation across the lifespan', *American Sociological Review* 50: 659–76.

Feldman, S.P. (1987) 'The cross-roads of interpretation: administration in professional organisation', *Human Organisation* 46: 95–102.

Ferlie, E. and Pettigrew, A.M. (1988) 'The management of change', in

Bloomsbury DHA, Aids and Acute Sector Strategy, Unpublished report: CCSC, University of Warwick.

Goldstein, H. (1979) *The Design and Analysis of Longitudinal Studies*, London: Academic Press.

Greiner, L.E. (1985) 'Response and commentary to Chapter 7 in E.E. Lawler and associates', *Doing Research that is Useful for Theory and Practice*, San Francisco: Jossey Bass.

Hardy, C. (1985) *The Management of Organisational Closure*, Aldershot: Gower Press.

Hendry,C. and Pettigrew, A.M. (1986) 'The practice of strategic human resource management', *Personnel-Review* 15: 3–9.

Hendry, C. and Pettigrew, A.M. (1987) Banking on HRM to respond to change. *Personnel Management*, November: 29–32.

Hendry, C. and Pettigrew, A.M. (1988) 'Multiskilling in the round', *Personnel Management* 20: 36–43.

Hickson, D.J., Butler, R.J., Cray, D.J., Mallory, G.R., and Wilson, D.C. (1986) *Top Decisions: Strategic Decision Making in Organisations*, Oxford: Basil Blackwell.

Homans, G.C. (1949) 'The strategy of industrial sociology', *American Journal of Sociology* 54: 330–9.

Huberman, A.M. and Miles, M.B. (1983) 'Drawing valid meaning from qualitative data: some techniques of data reduction and display', *Quality and Quantity* 17: 281–339.

Johnson, G. (1987) *Strategic Change and the Management Process*, Oxford: Basil Blackwell.

Kervasdoue, J. and Kimberly, J.R. (1979) 'Are organization structures culture free?' in G. England *et al.* (eds) *Organizational Functioning in a Cross-Cultural Perspective*, Kent State University Press.

Kimberly, J.R. (1976) 'Issues in the design of longitudinal organisational research', *Sociological Methods and Research* 4: 321–47.

Ladurie, E.L. (1979) The event and the long term in social history: the case of the Chouan uprising, in E. Leroy Ladurie *The Territory of the Historian*, London: Harvester Press.

Lerner, R.M. and Kauffman, M.B. (1985) 'The concept of development in contextualism', *Developmental Review*, 5: 309–33.

Lucas, R. (1987) 'Political-cultural analysis of organisations', *Academy of Management Journal* 12: 144–56.

Mancuso, J.C. and Ceely, S.G. (1980) 'The self as memory processing', *Cognitive Therapy and Research* 4: 1–25.

McKee, L. and Pettigrew, A.M. (1988) The management of change in the NHS: Bromsgrove and Redditch DHA. Unpublished research report: CCSC, University of Warwick.

Miller, D. and Friesen, P.M. (1982) 'The longitudinal analysis of organisations: a methodological perspective', *Management Science* 28: 1013–34.

Mintzberg, H. and Walters, J. (1982) 'Tracking strategy in the entrepreneurial firm', *Academy of Management Journal* 25: 465–99.

Mitroff, I.I. (1974) *The Subjective Side of Science*, Amsterdam: Elsevier.

Morgan, G. (1986) *Images of Organization*, Beverly Hills: Sage.

Mumford, E. and Pettigrew, A.M. (1975) Implementing Strategic Decisions, London: Longman.

Pepper, S.C. (1942) *World Hypotheses*, Berkeley: University of California Press.

Perrow, C. (1984) *Normal Accidents, Living in High Risk Technologies*, New York: Basic Books.

Pettigrew, A.M. (1973a) *The Politics of Organizational Decision Making*, London: Tavistock.

Pettigrew, A.M. (1973b) 'Occupationalization specialization as an emergent process', *Sociological Review* 21: 255–78.

Pettigrew, A.M. (1975) 'Strategic aspects of the management of specialist activity', *Personel Review* 4: 5–13.

Pettigrew, A.M. (1979) 'On studying organizational cultures', *Administrative Science Quarterly* 24: 570–81.

Pettigrew, A.M. (1985a) *The Awakening Giant: Continuity and Change in ICI*, Oxford: Basil Blackwell.

Pettigrew, A.M. (1985b) 'Contexualist research: a natural way to link theory and practice', in E.E. Lawler (ed.) *Doing Research That is Useful in Theory and Practice*, San Francisco: Jossey Bass.

Pettigrew, A.M. (1985c) 'Examining change in the long term context of politics and culture', in J.M. Pennings (ed.) *Organizational Strategy and Change*, San Francisco: Jossey Bass.

Pettigrew, A.M. (1985d) 'Contextualist research and the study of organisational change processes, in E. Mumford *et al.* (eds) *Research Methods in Information Systems*, Amsterdam: North Holland.

Pettigrew, A.M. (1987a) 'Theoretical, methodological, and empirical issues in studying change: a response to Starkey', *Journal of Management Studies* 24: 420–6.

Pettigrew, A.M. (1987b) 'Context and action in the transformation of the firm', *Journal of Mnagement Studies* 24: 649–70.

Pettigrew, A.M. (ed.) (1987c) *The Management of Strategic Change*, Oxford: Basil Blackwell.

Pettigrew, A.M., Hendry, C., and Sparrow, P.R. (1988a) *Competitiveness and Human Resource Change*, Sheffield: Manpower Services Commission. Available from CCSC, University of Warwick.

Pettigrew, A.M. Hendry, C., and Sparrow, P.R. (1988b) *The Role of Vocational Education and Training in Employers Skill Supply Strategies*, Research report, Sheffield: Manpower Services Commission. Available from CCSC, University of Warwick.

Pettigrew, A.M., McKee, L., and Ferlie, E. (1988) 'Understanding change in the NHS', *Public Administration* 66: 297–317.

Pettigrew, A.M., Whipp, R. and Rosenfeld, R. (in press) 'Competitiveness and the management of strategic change processes: a research agenda', in P.K.M. Tharakan and A. Francis (eds) *The Competitiveness of European Industry: Country Policies and Company Strategies*, London: Croom Helm.

Quinn, J.B. (1980) *Strategies for Change: Logical Incrementalism*, Homewood, IL: Irwin.

Rosenfeld, R., Whipp, R., and Pettigrew, A.M. (in press) 'Processes of internationalization: regeneration and competitiveness', *Economia Aziendale*.

Schon, D.A. (1983) *The Reflective Practitioner: How Professionals Think in Action*, London: Temple Smith.

Sparrow, P.R. and Pettigrew, A.M. (1987) Britain's training problems: the search for a strategic human resources management approach. *Human Resource Management* 26: 109–27.

Sparrow, P.R. and Pettigrew, A.M. (1988a) 'Contrasting HRM responses in the changing world of computing', *Personnel Management* 20: 40–5.

Sparrow, P.R. and Pettigrew, A.M. (1988b) 'How Halfords put its HRM into top gear', *Personnel Management* 20: 30–4.

Sparrow, P.R. and Pettigrew, A.M. (1988c) 'Strategic human resource management in the UK computer supplier industry', *Journal of Occupational Psychology* 61: 25–42.

Tuma, N.B. and Hannan, M.J. (1984) *Social Dynamics*, Orlando, Florida: Academic Press.

Van Maanen, J. (ed.) (1983) *Qualitative Methodology*, Beverly Hills: Sage.

Van Maanen, J. (1988) *Tales of the Field: on Writing Ethnography*, Chicago: University of Chicago Press.

Wall, T.D., Kemp, N.J., Jackson, P.R., and Clegg, C.W. (1986) 'Outcomes of autonomous work groups: a long-term field experiment', *Academy of Management Journal* 29: 280–304.

Wall, W.D. and Williams H.L. (1970) *Longitudinal Studies and the Social Sciences*, London: Heinemann.

Whipp, R. (1988) 'A time to every purpose': an essay on time and work', in P. Joyce (ed.) *The Historical Meanings of Work*, Cambridge: Cambridge University Press.

Whipp, R. and Clark, P. (1986) *Innovation and the Auto Industry*, London: Frances Pinter.

Whipp, R., Pettigrew, A.M., and Sparrow, P.R. (1988) New technologies and firm performance: the management of technological change at the firm and network level. Unpublished research report available from CCSC, University of Warwick.

Whipp, R., Rosenfeld, R., and Pettigrew, A.M. (in press) 'Culture and competitiveness: evidence from mature UK industries', *Journal of Management Studies*

Wilson, C.S. and Lupton, T. (1959) 'The Bank Rate Tribunal: the social background and connections of top decision makers', *Manchester School of Economic and Social Studies* 27: 30–51.

Yin, R.K. (1984) *Case Study Research: Design and methods*, Beverly Hills: Sage.

Chapter four

The case study: a vital yet misunderstood research method for management

N. Craig Smith

In recognition of the case study

Why should the research of management academics have intellectual authority and command the respect and attention of practitioners? An appropriate response to such a question would note the role of management academics as social scientists and that management research is therefore 'scientific'. It is not simply because management academics are usually to be found in universities and other "centres of learning" and often have titles conveying eminence and wisdom! The legitimacy of management research must also be derived from the way in which it is conducted. In other words, the scientific method is employed to ensure that research findings are meaningful, both theoretically and practically too within an applied discipline, accepting that they may not have immediate application.

Einstein said 'The whole of science is nothing more than a refinement of everyday thinking'. The refinement comes from the methods which scientists employ. So it is the use of the scientific method which confers legitimacy on management research (and, as a consequence, much management teaching). However, what does the scientific method amount to in application to management? An examination of the content of many management journals containing empirical papers would suggest that being scientific means quantification within a hypothetico-deductive approach to science. Qualitative and inductive approaches are much less frequently reported, if at all (Bonoma, 1985).

Consideration of the contribution of this management research (the extent to which it is meaningful) is beyond the scope of this chapter. It would raise a number of major questions, particularly about the agenda for management research and who sets it, though these issues should not be ignored. The concern here, however, is with whether in seeking to apply scientific method to management, researchers are using the most appropriate research methods and techniques. This clearly has some bearing on the potential contribution of research in management. The case study, it is suggested, is deserving of greater recognition as a research method. Such a claim has to be made within the context of an appreciation of what management research is trying to achieve.

Within social science generally there has long been criticism of positivist research orientations (Silverman, 1985). This is gradually being acknowledged within the management literature (see, for example, *Administrative Science Quarterly*, 24 (December 1979) or Bonoma, 1985). However, positivism continues to dominate, especially in the United States. Despite the leadership of the United States in management education, the traditional American research model would be a poor one to emulate. Being scientific is not solely or necessarily the result of number-crunching. While this author would not deny a role for quantitative approaches within management research, qualitative approaches, including the use of the case study method, are often more appropriate for tackling the important research problems of management.

In using any research method it is helpful to understand its epistemological underpinnings. By examining the relationship between epistemology and research methods further support can be found for the use of qualitative approaches such as the case study in management research. It should be noted that all references to case study research in this paper refer to the development of case studies for research purposes. Teaching cases are developed to illustrate established theory. Research cases are used to build theory, though this does not preclude their later development into teaching cases.

Epistemology and research methods

Rigby's (1965: vii) observations on the failure of management researchers to address fundamental methodological concerns seem almost as valid today as they were twenty years ago. Such criticism is borne out by the reference above to the positivist orientations found in much published management research. Positivism can be simply defined as 'working as natural scientists are believed to' (Bell and Newby, 1977: 21). It reflects, therefore, a belief that the social sciences can be investigated in the same way as the natural sciences. Many writers on research methodology have argued against positivism; the essence only of these arguments will be necessary here to demonstrate the relationship between epistemology and research methods and, as a consequence, the shortcomings of some of the more commonly adopted research approaches in management.

It should first be noted that positivists only rarely define themselves as such. Positivism is all but a term of abuse; though some would say rightly so, for in extreme cases it amounts to an ignorance of epistemological issues. Yet the waters beyond positivism are dangerous. They are best avoided by the faint of heart. In some respects, to operate

51

within a positivist framework allows the researcher the luxury of not having to question whether the research is meaningful; the methodological concern of such research often focuses on internal rather than external validity. Ultimately, this is dysfunctional if social science is to advance.

There has been considerable debate about the 'scientificness' of the social sciences, including management (for example, Dainty, 1983; Hunt 1976). Science aims to create order, to make sense of facts. It seeks patterns or regularities. In so doing, a process of systematic observation, description, explanation and prediction is employed. At least this much can be agreed on. And all of this may be found within the social sciences. A reasonable position to adopt seems to be one of admitting the limitations to social science achievements while acknowledging the complexities of social science research. It may then be claimed that the social sciences are sciences insofar as they apply scientific method. But one must ask, what form of scientific method (if any) is appropriate to social science?

Consider the nature of this particular human activity known as science. Hughes (1980: 12) notes that 'scientific methods seek deliberately to annihilate the individual scientist's standpoints and are designed as rules whereby agreement on specific versions of the world can be reached: a distinction, in short, between the producer of a statement and the procedure whereby it is produced.' The outcome of these methods is scientific knowledge: 'a systematic body of concepts, theories, principles and laws or law-like statements designed to explain phenomena' (Hughes, 1980: 1). This outcome is achieved where plausibility is recognized or where, as Hughes puts it, there is agreement on specific versions of the world. The problem for the social sciences (and hence some of the complexity of social science research as acknowledged above) is that this involves a human attempt to explain human phenomena. This is problematic because it is doubtful as to whether method can ever 'annihilate' the individual scientist's standpoint. Medawar (1967: 149) admits this problem within the natural sciences; he quotes Whewell: 'Facts cannot be observed as facts except in virtue of the conceptions which the observer himself unconsciously supplies.' Such is the dilemma posed for the social sciences, that Hughes (1980: 124) feels obliged to ask: 'Is a science of social life impossible?'

In reference to Schutz, Hughes (1980: 119) explains the dilemma of the social sciences in terms of the social construction of reality: 'Like all sciences they make objective meaning claims, or at least aspire to do so, but in the case of social sciences these have to be within the context of the human activity which has created them and which cannot be understood apart from this scheme of action.' As Berger and Kellner (1981: 68) put it, in a different context, 'Direct access to facts and laws . . . is never possible, no matter what one's standpoint . . . there is no magical trick by which one can bypass the act of interpretation.' This is the basic epistemological problem of social science. How can the human world be objectively known in subjective, human terms?

One may, indeed, go further, for scientific activity and what is associated with it, including the status of scientists and scientific knowledge is, after all, like the phenomena studied by social scientists, a social construction. As Ford (1975: 5) neatly observes, 'When academics take off their white scientific coats and funny philosophical hats they turn into ordinary people.' This is the problem, and one that social scientists cannot escape. Moreover, to echo an earlier and vital theme, if they didn't have their white scientific coats and other accoutrements of scientific activity – including titles and ivory towers – would the outcome of such activity, scientific knowledge, still have intellectual authority?

Clearly, at this juncture, the analysis of epistemological issues surrounding social science research has reached a point well within the maze of research methodology. The problems facing social scientists seem intractable. One might, therefore, take heart in the following words from the sociologist George Homans, quoted by Denzin (1978):

> You do not have to believe anything about theory and methodology that is told you pretentiously and sanctimoniously by other sociologists – including myself. So much guff has gotten mixed with the truth that, if you cannot tell which is which, you had better reject it all. It will only get in your way. No one will go far wrong theoretically who remains in close touch with and seeks to understand a body of concrete phenomena.

It is very easy to end up in a methodological maze. Providing the researcher has a basic grasp of the issues and remains close to the phenomena studied, meaningful research is likely to be conducted. Yet, within this sensible conclusion, lies a key to some resolution of the problem identified above as well, highlighting the principal weakness of positivist research. The superiority of scientific knowledge, its greater intellectual authority, stems from whether the scientist *qua* scientist was able to 'stand back a bit', achieve some measure of objectivity. Morally at least, there is an obligation on the scientist to do this if claims of superiority are to be made. But even though social science involves human attempts to investigate human phenomena, a natural science, positivist approach to the social sciences often ignores the inevitable act of interpretation by the scientist. It then becomes invalid because the attempt at objectivity is illusory. Moreover, because of this artificial distancing, the researcher is not sufficiently close to the phenomenon under investigation to understand it. So, just as there is a requirement 'to stand back a bit', there is an equal requirement not to stand back so far that the findings are distorted by distance as well as by the act of interpretation.

This argument about distance from the phenomenon under study and its impact on objectivity and whether research is meaningful can be expressed another way. It was earlier noted that science involves a systematic process of observation, description, explanation and prediction. In applying natural science methods and techniques to social science problems, positivist approaches assume that social science is at a point of development whereby methods and techniques appropriate to explanation and prediction may be employed and that much of the complexity of social phenomena can be ignored. For much of social science, observation and description, with possibly limited explanation, are the requisite modes. Certainly, this is true of management. Accordingly, methods appropriate to this phase of development need to be employed.

Bonoma (1985), in one of the few papers in the management literature on the case study method, covers this problem of positivist research orientations by referring to a trade-off between 'currency' and 'data integrity'. Currency pertains to generalizability of results, an amalgam of what is elsewhere termed external validity and pragmatic or ecological validity. Data integrity refers to those characteristics of research that affect error and bias in research results, an amalgam of internal validity, statistical conclusion validity and reliability. Bonoma notes that, ideally, high levels of both data integrity and results currency should be sought, but that it is not possible for any single research method simultaneously to minimize multiple threats to both data integrity and currency. So, for example, laboratory experiments offer high data integrity but low currency, in contrast to case research which offers high currency but low data integrity.

In making the trade-off, choosing the right method, Bonoma suggests the researcher has to consider the purpose of the research and nature of the phenomenon under investigation. On the former, Bonoma, in essence, notes that high data integrity methods (and, therefore, with low currency) cannot be efficiently applied to theory-building research; that is, research at the description end of a research continuum of description, classification, comparison, measurement/estimation, establishing association, and determining cause and effect. This is because 'either the power of deductive methods is underutilized, or theory and/or method are prematurely pressed into service when their underlying assumptions cannot be met'. Of course, the converse applies to high currency, inductive methods. In considering the phenomenon under investigation, he suggests the key issues are whether the phenomenon can be studied outside its normal setting (often requisite for high data integrity) and whether it is amenable to quantification. On the latter point, Bonoma gives the example of good practice in marketing management as a research topic which currently, at least, defies quantification.

In looking at the research conducted in marketing, Bonoma concludes that 'the apparent research bias towards types of investigation that preserve data integrity at the expense of currency results in a methodological one-sidedness that may impair the development and testing of sound theories'. This reiterates the concern earlier expressed about the research agenda for management. Some areas of management can quite legitimately be investigated using quantitative and hypothetico-deductive approaches. In such circumstances one might conclude that positivism is acceptable. However, to what extent are these areas more worthy of investigation than those demanding more inductive and qualitative approaches? One must certainly question a research agenda should it be determined by a requirement to use particular research methods.

In sum, an understanding of the epistemological issues surrounding social science research point to the requirement to use an appropriate method for the research problem; in other words, 'horses for courses'. The debate about positivism has illustrated the limitations of traditional research methods when applied to many social science problems. An alternative and seemingly more potentially fruitful path would employ qualitative and inductive approaches. The case study is included in such approaches.

Epistemological issues as discussed above seem frequently to be considered irrelevant to the practice of research – to be ignored if the researcher can latch on to an appropriate research method, appropriateness usually stemming from prior use in similar circumstances. Yet, they have a direct consequence for the meaning which may be attributed to the research; meaningful research demands a sound epistemological base to the research methods. Epistemology and research methods are inter-related in a complex way. Despite the assumed division between the theory and practice of research, the two cannot be considered in isolation. There is, so to speak, a two-way street. Much of the criticism of the use of case studies in research stems from this misapprehension, the view that the relationship between epistemology and research methods is unidirectional, a one-way street.

In reply to questions of representativeness

The principal criticism of case studies in research is that they are unrepresentative. Theoretical conclusions derived from case studies are not considered to be valid unless the cases can be demonstrated to be 'typical' of the phenomena under investigation. The very word 'representative' implies recourse to survey research methods to demonstrate, via quantitative procedures, that the theoretical conclusions derived from the cases are applicable to the population as a whole. Qualitative research, according to the canons of positivism, is fine for exploratory studies, but quantification is necessary to establish the validity of any findings. But concerns with representativeness may be irrelevant. Some would argue this irrelevance is absolute. Others that it is only temporary, that – for the moment – representativeness can be ignored, but that it must be attended to eventually if generalizations – valid theoretical conclusions – are to be drawn. The next section, in examining theory building and the case study method, is largely concerned with the former proposition that representativeness is absolutely irrelevant. Such a poposition rests on accepting the two-way street concept of the theory and practice of research, that there is an interrelationship between epistemology and research methods and hence concern with whether cases are typical or not is epistemologically erroneous. However, before explaining why this should be so, it is useful to consider the proposition that representativeness is only temporarily irrelevant. In so doing, the more conventional argument for the use of the case study method may be briefly explored.

Perhaps surprisingly, there is not a great deal of literature on the use of the case study method, at least not under that title. Yet, many researchers refer to case studies. This imbalance seems to reflect the low status of case study research (because of the representativeness issue) and the view that it is not a method as such. One can find references to research methods such as repertory grid or comparative analysis which then *produce* case studies, but they are not conceived as forming a part of case study method. Consequently, McClintock *et al.* (1979) refer to case study 'strategies' rather than 'methods'. This would indicate that case studies are an approach, rather than a method. As Goode and Hatt (1952: 331) put it over thirty years ago: 'The case study, then, is not a specific technique. It is a way of organising social data so as to preserve the *unitary character of the social object being studied.* Expressed somewhat differently, it is an approach which views any social unit as a whole.' Clearly, the case study is not a technique, it is not a means for obtaining data. Yet, it may be described as a research method insofar as it is a method of organizing data. One may also refer to case study methods, such as participant observation, content analysis, or repertory grid, by which data for case studies is obtained. (However, it is simpler to distinguish between techniques and the method, particularly as techniques such as content analysis or repertory grid are not exclusive to the case study method.)

Case studies, as qualitative research, may be employed within a positivist perspective. One may seek to involve numbers and counting, as Jauch *et al.* (1980) suggest in advocating the structured content analysis of cases; or as McClintock *et al.* (1979) propose, apply the logic and method of survey research. The latter paper considers some of the literature on the use of case studies and qualitative versus quantitative approaches. It suggests a choice between 'thick', 'deep', and 'holistic', and 'thin', 'narrow,' but 'generalisable'. In response to the question: 'What do you do if you prefer data that are real, deep *and* hard?' McClintock *et al.* favour the invention of research designs that incorporate qualitative and quantitative strategies. They seek (quoting Warwick), 'to wed the qualitative and historically attuned case study with representative coverage and quantification.' By incorporating elements of positivist research design (sampling, quantification, etc.), they absolve themselves from the charge that their cases are unrepresentative.

Theory-building and the case study method

So the problem of representativeness may become temporarily irrelevant either by choosing to view case studies as appropriate to exploratory work only, or by making them representative through the application of quantitative procedures. However, both solutions still accept the epistemological requirement for representativeness. One may, alternatively, view it as absolutely irrelevant.

There are two reasons for this. First, one may have different intentions when using case studies as opposed to survey research. One's purpose, for example, may be with description rather than correlation. Second, and perhaps most importantly, there is the recognition that representativeness is irrelevant because it can be a spurious basis for claiming validity. As Worsley and others (1970: 112) write:

> The general validity of the analysis does not depend on whether the case being analysed is representative of other cases of this kind, but rather upon the plausibility of the logic of the analysis. The generality is of the same kind that enabled Sir Ronald Ross to announce the 'cause' of malaria when he found the malaria parasite in the salivary gland of a single female Anopheles mosquito in 1897.

Clyde Mitchell (1983) has expanded on this argument in a recent article which presents a particularly thorough and convincing submission for the case study method. As he shows, 'Logical inference is epistemologically quite independent of statistical inference.' How he comes to this conclusion is worthy of close consideration. Mitchell starts by referring to an eclipse of interest in case studies as a method of sociological analysis, which he attributes to the tremendous increase in quantitative studies following the development of statistical techniques and powerful computer technology. He suggests there is a consequent confusion about the use of case studies, as indicated by the challenge frequently addressed to those who have chosen to pursue the deviant path of case studies: 'How do you know the case you have chosen is typical?' Mitchell responds to this challenge by explaining the difference between making inferences from statistical data and from cases. In so doing, he provides guidelines for the use of case studies in social investigation and theory building.

Mitchell defines the case study as 'a detailed examination of an event (or series of related events) which the analyst believes exhibits (or exhibit) the operation of some identified general theoretical principle.' He notes that different types of case study may be identified according to their complexity and their use. However, Mitchell's central concern and the 'fundamental problem' in case studies is 'the basis upon which general inferences may be drawn from them'. He asks how obstensibly unique material can form the basis for inference about some process in general. The very word 'case' connotes this uniqueness and the implication of a chance or haphazard occurrence. Yet most social anthropological and much sociological theorizing is founded on case studies. He suggests the difficulties in the practice of the case study method arise out of the common assumption that the only valid basis of inference is that which has been developed in relation to statistical analysis. However, as Mitchell goes to great lengths to explain, statistical analysis merely permits the inference that characteristics within the sample may be expected within the population. Theorized relationships between the characteristics are the result of a separate procedure and not substantiated by statistical analysis.

Mitchell offers an interesting example of a study for which the author claimed validity on the basis of statistical significance, but which was rejected because it was not plausible. The findings were rejected, not because the variables failed to correlate statistically, but because they were not logically (or causally, if one prefers) related. The researcher had linked interpretations of Rorschach inkblots with dietary disorders. It had been found that there was a statistically significant difference between those with dietary disorders and those without, in terms of the former reacting to the blot with a 'frog' response. This the researcher attributed to an unconscious belief in the cloacal theory of birth, which involves oral impregnation and anal parturition. The cloaca of the frog (its excretory and reproductive canals) are common, a biological fact providing, it is assumed, the rationale for this belief. The researcher hypothesized: 'Since patients should be inclined to manifest eating disorders: compulsive eating in the case of those who wish to get pregnant and anorexia in those who do not . . . such patients should also be inclined to see cloacal animals such as frogs on the Rorschach.' The response of other clinical psychologists to this, however, was 'I don't believe it', even after having seen the experimental results. The theory proposed was rejected on the grounds of plausibility, regardless of unimpeachable method. As Mitchell explains, 'While the clinical psychologists may well have accepted that more people with dietary disorders saw the blots as frogs than those without, they could not accept the *explanation* of the relationship between the two characteristics' (his emphasis).

He is not, of course, the first to recognize such a distinction. Glaser and Strauss (1967: 62), for example, make the distinction between theoretical and statistical sampling: 'Theoretical sampling is done in order to discover categories and their properties, and to suggest the inter-relationship into a theory. Statistical sampling is done to obtain accurate evidence on distributions of people among categories to be used in descriptions or verifications.' Mitchell, in turn, recognizes the commonly accepted distinction between statistical inference and scientific or causal inference. The former is 'the process by which the analyst draws conclusions about the existence of two or more characteristics in some wider population from some sample of that population to which the observer has access'; whereas, 'scientific or causal – or perhaps more appropriately – logical inference, is the process by which the analyst draws conclusions about the essential linkage between two or more characteristics in terms of some systematic explanatory schema – some set of theoretical propositions.' Importantly though, Mitchell recognizes that the distinction is often absent in quantitative studies:

> In analytical thinking based on quantitative procedures *both* types of inference proceed *pari passu* but there has been some tendency to elide logical inferences with the logic of statistical inference: that the postulated *logical* connection among features in a sample may be assumed to exist in some parent population simply because the features may be inferred to *coexist* in that population (his emphasis).

More importantly, this distinction paves the way for illustrating the irrelevance of representativeness in case studies, for the analyst, in using this method, is only concerned with logical inference. As Mitchell argues,

> The process of inference from case studies is only logical or causal and cannot be statistical and extrapolability from any one case study to like situations in general is based only on logical inference. We infer that the features present in the case study will be related in a wider population not because the case is representative but because our analysis is unassailable.

So, in summary of Mitchell's position on the extent to which case studies have validity, Silverman (1985: 114) writes, 'The claim, therefore, is not to representativeness but to faultless logic.' As Mitchell puts it, 'The extent to which generalizations may be made from case studies depends upon the adequacy of the underlying theory and the whole corpus of related knowledge of which the case is analysed rather than on the particular instance itself.'

Selecting cases for study will, as a consequence, not therefore rest on how typical the case may be, but on its explanatory power. Indeed, 'deviant' cases may be chosen, as analytic induction suggests, to demonstrate the limits to generalization. The presentation of the case will be limited to that material which most effectively reveals the theoretical principle investigated, for just as the 'best' cases are employed, so are the 'best' elements within each case. This atypical, selective quality to case studies gives rise to their criticism as a basis for generalization, but this is ill-founded. Irrelevant elements, just as irrelevant cases, would merely serve to confuse; providing the analyst meets the *ceteris paribus* criterion they should be ignored. Mitchell explains: 'It is perfectly justifiable for the analyst to operate with a simplified account of the context within which the case is located provided that the impact of the features of that context on the events being considered in the analysis are incorporated rigorously into the analysis.' Much, of course, is left to the analyst, particularly his or her intimate knowledge of the circumstances of the case. Mitchell's observations on the logic of case studies has been usefully summarized in a table by Silverman (1985) (Table 4.1).

Table 4.1 The logic of case studies

	Survey research	Case studies
Claim to validity	Depends on representativeness of sample	Only valid if based on articulated theory
Nature of explanations	Correlations not causes	Logical/causal connections
Relation to theory	Theory-neutral	Theory-dependent

In sum, it should be recognized that epistemology and research methods are interrelated. A position on the former does not simply give rise to the latter. Accepting this two-way street prompts a reappraisal of the accepted wisdom that the case study method is inferior to quantitative methods because it lacks representativeness. Such a charge often prompts the response that representativeness is temporarily irrelevant; either because the case studies are exploratory, implying survey research at some future date, or that quantitative and qualitative procedures may be combined to provide the 'best of both worlds', which, while acknowledging the usefulness of case studies, still assumes the importance of representativeness. Alternatively, representativeness may be viewed as absolutely irrelevant. This position, contrary to accepted wisdom, reflects either an acknowledged difference in purpose, as in the concern of an ethnographer to describe a simple society as part of an anthropological study, or recognition of the epistemological distinction between statistical inference and logical inference.

Conducting case study research

The data collected frequently comes from both primary and secondary sources. Semi-structured interviews, using interview schedules, often provide much of the primary data. The interviews should, with the permission of the respondents, be tape recorded and subsequently transcribed in full. Transcribing interviews is a lengthy process, but worthwhile in enabling the researcher to stay close to the data. Tape recording ensures all data were noted and, in leaving the researcher free from the burden of making notes, allows concentration on the issues of concern and rapport to develop more easily. Data such as copies of letters, reports and so on, may also be obtained from interviewees.

Interviews are problematic in a number of ways, as identified by many sources. These problems must, as far as possible, be controlled for, though the author has much sympathy with Silverman's (1985: 161–2) position that there is no bad way of doing interviews, there is only bad analysis of interviews. As he writes, 'for positivists, interviews are essentially about ascertaining facts or beliefs out there in the world', whereas (as an interactionist would argue) interviews may also be seen as social events in themselves, involving interviewer and interviewee in mutual participant observation. Interviews are not just about asking questions and taking the answer given, but also about interactions, as, for example, how they reveal feelings or fears. So finally, before reviewing the strengths and weaknesses of case studies, this section should make brief mention of the form of analysis which may be employed.

The more sophisticated sources on qualitative data analysis (such as Miles and Huberman, 1984: 49–78, or Glaser and Strauss, 1967: 101–15) refer to explicit coding and analytic procedures, whereby categories (concepts or relationships), and their properties are identified and analysed as they occur within the data. Some advocate quantitative procedures, from simply counting categories to statistical analysis. Ignoring the positivist overtones of coding and its analysis, there is the problem of specifying what to code. If the data alone are to generate theory then clearly categories cannot be specified *a priori*. This suggests either leaving the coding to the end of the data collection, which would deny flexibility such that interesting categories would only be recognized too late to prevent appropriate investigation within the study, or coding everything, a burdensome (if not impossible) task, as Glaser and Strauss (1967) acknowledge. They propose the constant comparative method, which, they suggest, incorporates an on-going explicit coding procedure and permits theory development during the study.

However, on the basis of this author's experiences of case study research, this source and even the 'hands-on' manual by Miles and Huberman (1984), seem remote from the practice of research. Research as lived, where interviews are a process of continual idea development; where theory is the outcome of a combination of studying other works, the data collection and chance occurrences and conversations; where as Latour and Woolgar (1979) comment on the natural sciences, order is brought forth from chaos; research as lived may not have the time or requirement for such fancy procedures. Coding, for this author at least, was satisfactorily achieved intuitively during the data collection. Only on writing up the cases was it thought necessary to code the data in any way, and then only to be certain of conveying key elements within the cases. This may, however, have had something to do with the partly deductive approach adopted or the research problem. However, the usefulness of explicit coding during data collection appears limited. If the researcher is close to the data, analysis and theorizing is inevitably taking place. The value of such procedures may have more to do with making qualitative research appear acceptable and rigorous, than improving the method.

A further consideration is deciding how many cases to present, yet this may be out of the hands of the researcher. This author found that as each case progressed, as each interview was conducted, the data were found to be conforming to a pattern. In other words, a theory was emerging. The content of the data became 'predictable' because they conformed with expectations. This is common to qualitative research and is sometimes referred to as 'saturation' (by Glaser and Strauss, for example). When saturation is achieved, the researcher may claim to have a sufficient number of cases.

Strengths and weaknesses of the case study method

The use of the case study method can lead to charges of anecdotalism. Yet, for many research topics within management, this method is the most appropriate. However, case studies need not be viewed as solely exploratory or tentative exercises in research. Their validity, when correctly understood, depends on how they are used and the logic of their analysis.

Yet, it would be foolish to understate some of the weaknesses of the case study method. As the earlier discussion has indicated, qualitative approaches do bring the researcher closer to the phenomenon under investigation and some might say too close. This raises two distinct problems. First, the problem of the dependence on the researcher's skills of clinical analysis in maintaining objectivity. Yet, as with quantitative research, judgement may still be passed on the validity of research results. (Indeed, this distinction between qualitative and quantitative research may be artificial in many ways. As the earlier discussion suggests, one might agree with Ratcliffe (1983) that '*all* approaches to inquiry are inherently qualitative in nature.') Second, there is the political consideration of the acceptability of case study research. As Bonoma (1985) somewhat drily observes – and this is a fitting conclusion to this chapter – 'Because the major thrust of most published marketing research *is* towards deductive, numerate, and causally directed research, the researcher may have a greater challenge in demonstrating the benefits and necessity of qualitative methods for the problem studied.'

References

Bell, C. and Newby, H. (1977) *Doing Sociological Research*, London: George Allen & Unwin.

Berger, P.L. and Kellner, H. (1981) *Sociological Reinterpreted: An Essay on Method and Vocation*, Harmondsworth: Penguin.

Bonoma, T.V. (1985) 'Case research in marketing: Opportunities, problems, and a process', *Journal of Marketing Research*, xxii.

Dainty, P. (1983) 'Meaningful management research', *Graduate Management Research*, 1 (1).

Denzin, N.K. (1978) *The Research Act: A Theoretical Introduction to Sociological Methods*, New York. McGraw-Hill.

Ford, J. (1975) *Paradigms and Fairy Tales: An Introduction to the Science of Meanings*, London: Routledge and Kegan Paul.

Glaser, B.G. and Straus, A.L. (1967) *The Discovery of Grounded Theory: Strategies for Qualitative Research*, New York: Aldine.

Goode, W.J. and Hatt, P.K. (1952) *Methods in Social Research*, New York: McGraw-Hill.

Hughes, J. (1980) *The Philosophy of Social Research*, London: Longman.

Hunt, S.D. (1976) 'The nature and scope of marketing', *The Journal of Marketing*, 40 (July).

Jauch, L.R., Osborn, R.N., and Martin, T.N. (1980) 'Structured content analysis of cases: a complementary method for organizational research', *Academy of Management Review*, 5 (4).

Latour, B. and Woolgar, S. (1979) *Laboratory Life: The Social Construction of Scientific Facts*, Beverly Hills: Sage.

McClintock, C.C., Brannon, D. and Moody, S.M. (1979) 'Applying the logic of sample surveys to qualitative case studies: The case cluster method', *Administrative Science Quarterly*, 24 (December).

Mitchell, J. Clyde (1983) 'Case and Situation Analysis', *The Sociological Review* 31.

Medawar, P.B. (1967) *The Art of the Soluble* London: Methuen.

Miles, M.B. and Huberman, A.M. (1984) *Qualitative Data Analysis: A Sourcebook of New Methods*, Beverly Hills: Sage.

Ratcliffe, J.W. (1983) 'Notions of validity in qualitative research methodology', *Knowledge: Creation, Diffusion, Utilization*, 5 (2).

Rigby, P.H. (1965) *Conceptual Foundations in Business Research*, New York: John Wiley.
Silverman, D. (1985) *Qualitative Methodology and Sociology*, Aldershot: Gower.
Worsley, P. and others (1970) *Introducing Sociology*, Harmondsworth: Penguin.

Chapter five

Experimentation in reflective practice: a conceptional framework for managers in highly professionalized organizations

Gethin Williams

Perspective and preoccupations

This chapter is written from the standpoint of a senior manager in a higher education institution sensitive to rising expectations of managerial and organizational performance and seeking a well-grounded conceptual framework which will facilitate reflective practice, provide a basis for action and hopefully lead to improved performance. There is no time like the present for testing management theory in action, for taking our own medicine or for practising what we preach in our own parish.

These were the kinds of obligations which I had in mind when embarking, some eight years ago, on participant observer studies of corporate planning in the NHS and Higher Education.

As a member of a health authority and senior manager within a college of higher education I was able to observe at first hand the problems of operating planning systems at the organizational level. My own observations were in line with the findings of a comprehensive literature search which I undertook of corporate planning in the private and public sectors post 1970. The review revealed that there has been a major shift in perspective and a significant change in the currency of ideas on corporate planning since the early 1970s. The shift may be characterized as a change in the prominence given to three aspects of corporate planning: philosophy, technology and context. In the early 1970s the rational comprehensive model provided the most widely accepted ideal towards which organizations were expected to progress but which, it was acknowledged, was unattainable, by definition, in its pure form. There were influential critics of the rationalist philosophy but they seemed at a disadvantage in the face of the enthusiasm of the proponents of planning for the rationalist ideal and their confidence in the systems and techniques associated with it. The importance of context was acknowledged and caveats and cautions issued against adopting an overly mechanistic approach to planning, but systematic analysis of context, particularly its behavioural and micropolitical aspects, was largely, though not entirely, neglected.

Since 1970 the technology has been viewed with increasing scepticism, the philosophy has ceased to enjoy uncritical acceptance and context has claimed increasing attention and interest.

What is striking about the shift of attention to context is the growing interest shown in its cultural and micropolitical dimensions. These were already attracting increasing attention in America in the early 1970s when the managers of American universities were having such a tough time that the Carnegie Commission on Higher Education sponsored a general report on the American college president from Cohen and March (1974). The Cohen and March study and the elaboration on the 'garbage can' theory (March and Olsen, 1976) presented a direct challenge to the rational, analytical perspective and gave a view of anarchic organizations pervaded with ambiguity in which their emergent properties were seen to be far more significant than their designed or intended properties. It prompted a radical shift in perspective in the mid and late 1970s and provided encouragement for research into the political and cultural aspects of educational management.

As so often happens, such radical shifts take time to register. Interest had grown sufficiently in the micropolitics of organizations for the British Educational Management and Administration Society to devote its tenth annual conference in 1982 entirely to the subject. The proceedings of that conference are found in Educational Management and Administration (Pratt *et al.*, 1982) which makes interesting reading. Although full of useful insights, a number of the contributors doubted whether these could be given sufficient conceptual and methodological coherence for the conduct of meaningful research. My own experience leads me to be less pessimistic.

Contextualist research and reflective practice

As the neglect of context has become more obtrusive, so too has the shortage of research into the operation of planning systems within specific organizational settings. The shortage is not difficult to understand given the problems of conducting longitudinal studies, considered to be the most appropriate form of research for the study of social processes in organizations (Pettigrew, 1973: 275). Among those in a favourable position to conduct such studies as participant observers are the senior managers of organizations and I believe that their services could be enlisted in the interests of research and management development. Put another way, senior managers should be encouraged to undertake systematic experiments in reflective practice taking the form of extended conversations with the developing situations in which they find themselves. As Schon points out: 'When someone reflects in action, he becomes a researcher in the practice context.' (Schon, 1983: 68).

The correspondences between reflective practice as advocated by

Schon (1983) and contextualist research as described by Pettigrew are striking, as the latter is quick to point out (Pettigrew, 1983: 4–7). Both expose the limitations of established conventions, particularly those associated with the positivist tradition, and seek to provide an appropriate epistemological and methodological underpinning for the forms of 'artful inquiry' which they favour. Artful inquiry or artistry is a shared characteristic highlighted by Pettigrew and one which he considers present in all forms of research.

Four world hypotheses

Although he makes the distinction between quantitative and qualitative research, thereby highlighting the differences in convention which attach to them, he also points out that 'all research involves the application of skills, knowledge and the person in a variety of differing problems in varying contexts, and in that sense it is a craft activity involving skills of individual judgement within a system of collective rules and communication.' (Pettigrew, 1983: 1). The way in which a researcher practises his craft is seen, therefore, to depend on the academic sub-culture to which he belongs, notably the root assumptions held about the nature of knowledge, the means by which knowledge may be obtained and the nature of the phenomena to be investigated. For the purpose of establishing the context in which qualitative researchers conduct artful inquiry Pettigrew draws on the work of Pepper (1942) reinterpreted by Payne (1975, 1982). The aim is to demonstrate that there are ways other than that favoured by positivists, namely multiplicative corroboration, for validating claims to additional knowledge. Pepper advocates the use of structural corroboration and four world hypotheses. The choice of hypothesis is seen to influence attempts to corroborate claims to knowledge as shown in Table 5.1.

Payne also considers a fifth world hypothesis, 'Selectivism', one later developed by Pepper (1966), which is seen as a radical revision of contextualism. As such it implies a similar research approach. Payne takes the view that its refinements are more philosophical than practical, a view shared by Pettigrew who sticks to the original four hypotheses, with particular attention given to contextualism. Pettigrew demonstrates, with the aid of Payne, how organizational analysis has tended to rely excessively on formism and mechanism and thereby neglect contextualism, regarded for many purposes as a more appropriate choice. Valuable though the work of Pepper and Payne is shown to be in providing an epistemological foundation for contextualism, Pettigrew is less concerned with epistemological maps than with the potential contributions of contextualism to theoretical and practical developments in his chosen area, namely the study of organizational change. I share his

Table 5.1 Structural corroboration and four world hypotheses

World hypothesis and is chief philosophers	Preoccupations	Truth theory	Root metaphor
1. Formism Plato Aristotle	Classification of similar objects and phenomena into categories and types	Correspondence *Test*: Similarity between description and object of reference	Similarity
2. Mechanism Locke Hume	Law-like relationship between classes of phenomena which are divided and linked together according to machine-like principles	Cause and effect *Test*: Whether outcomes match predictions	Machine
3. Contextualism (Pragmatism) James Pierce	Event in its setting	Confirmation/ Falsification *Test*: Qualitiative assessment of hypothesis about event	Historic Event
4. Organicism Hegel Royce	Enduring pattern of events irrespective of time and place	Coherence of Conceptual Structures *Test*: Magnitude of fact	Harmonious unity

Source: derived from Payne (1982: 54) and Pettigrew (1983: 8, 9)

sense of priorities but believe that a further underpinning is available employing the Burrell and Morgan schema.

The Burrell and Morgan schema

The view is taken with Burrell and Morgan (1979) that their schema should be used 'as a heuristic device rather than a set of rigid definitions' (Burrell and Morgan, 1979: xii). Employed for the present purpose, therefore, I would locate the kind of research in which I have a particular interest (i.e. participant–observer studies of organizational process conducted by senior managers) within the Functionalist Paradigm with a strong orientation towards the Action Frame of Reference (Burrell and Morgan, 1979: 30).

Table 5.2 The subjective–objective dimension

| | Limits | |
Element	Subjective	Objective
Ontology	Nominalist	Realist
Epistemology	Antipositivist	Positivist
View of human nature	Voluntarist	Determinist
Methodology	Ideographic	Nomothetic

Taking the Subjective–Objective dimension first, although Burrell and Morgan define its limits as shown in Table 5.2, they allow for intermediate positions. Such latitude is important to the researcher operating within the Functionalist Paradigm who wishes to employ the insights offered by the conceptual frameworks and models located at, and possibly spanning, the boundaries between the Functionalist and other paradigms. The choice of methodology and view of human nature is considered to be relatively straightforward: the research requires an ideographic methodology and an intermediate view of human nature – that is, neither wholly voluntarist nor wholly determinist. The identification of ontology and epistemology is more problematic within the context of the Burrell and Morgan schema given their insistence that the four paradigms should be regarded as mutually exclusive. The main problem as identified by Louis (1983: 154) is that of finding room for an inter-subjective perspective. Coping with intersubjectivity involves rather freer movement between the Functionalist and Interpretive Paradigms than Burrell and Morgan appear to allow. The ontological position favoured, therefore is that reality is conceived neither as purely objective nor purely subjective; rather reality is inter-subjectively defined on the basis of shared meanings. These shared meanings form the basis of an epistemology which, while subjectively orientated, is not 'firmly set against the utility of a search for laws or underlying regularities in the world of social affairs' (Burrell and Morgan, 1979: 4).

Turning to the Regulation–Radical change dimension, the primary concern, given a managerialist perspective, is with regulation. The deep-seated structural forces operating at the macro-level in a modern industrial society are not a prime concern. Even so, at the micro-level, the generation of conflict and its resolution will be a major consideration. Burrell and Morgan consider the micro-politics of organization in the context of Pluralism and the Action Frame of Reference, both of which, though located within the Functionalist Paradigm, appear on the fringe of Radical Organization Theory (Burrell and Morgan, 1979: 30, 209–17).

Taking both dimensions, therefore, the end result, as previously indicated, is a predisposition to operate primarily within the Functionalist paradigm with a strong orientation towards the subjective end of the quadrant.

Whichever schema is employed a convincing epistemological under-pinning is available for the study of organizational process. It remains for me to describe how my own research was conducted.

Research style

The choice of research style – by which is meant the traditions of different methods associated with, or appropriate to, particular subjects or areas of research (Wilson, 1979: 4) was considered straightforward since it was seen to be largely determined by the subject being researched. Such a view is taken by Pettigrew (1973: 52–3, 275) who assembles a number of authorities in support of his position. Their aid is invoked to establish:

1. the need for compatibility between problem definition, study design, the kind of data gathered and the investigator's role; and
2. the appropriateness of participant observation and the value of longitudinal research designs for the study of social processes in organizations.

Given the above, the choice for me of longitudinal research design involving participant observation was seen to be self-selecting.

Since the problems of participant observation are well rehearsed, I propose to neglect them for the present purpose other than to acknowledge that ethnographic research raises serious problems of verification. Even so, there are standards which can be applied to increase the general quality of research findings (see, for example, Pettigrew, 1973: 269) and the ethnographer's 'appreciative setting' (Vickers, 1965) may be made explicit.

'Thick' and 'thin' description

The ethnographer has the task of collecting information to produce a verifiable 'thin' description which is then subjected to interpretive analysis in order to produce a richer 'thick' description (Geertz, 1973: Chapter 1). The quality of the 'thick' description depends very much on the interpreter and the interpretive set which he employs. I believe it to be an essential feature of reflective practice that the researcher/practitioner should subject his own predispositions, perceptions, values and beliefs to close scrutiny and thereby make explicit the 'appreciative setting' which informs selection and interpretation.

It is on the choice of interpretive set, however, that I wish to focus attention. Not only is it employed to convert a 'thin' into a 'thick' description but may also be the means of naming and framing a problem for the purposes of conducting the kind of experiment in reflective practice – involving reflective conversation with a situation, back talk and reframing – advocated by Schon (1983).

For my studies of the introduction and operation of corporate planning systems I employed an interpretive set consisting of the Contingency Approach (Child, 1984; Hinings *et al.*, 1971, 1974, 1981), Contextualist Analysis (Pettigrew, 1983, 1985) and Garbage Can Theory (Cohen and March 1974; March and Olsen, 1976). The chief considerations in making the choice were to encompass both the designed and emergent properties of organizations and to find means of analysing the cultural and micropolitical dimensions of organizational change. The three were chosen to represent both relatively 'hard' and 'soft' approaches to organizational analysis, although the versions employed ensured that they were not mutually exclusive. Indeed, the overlapping boundaries between them were considered to confer synergy upon the set.

Power in application of the chosen interpretive set

I found the set to have considerable power in application and came to the following conclusions about each of the interpretive frameworks.

Contingency

This approach is identified with efforts by managers to regulate organizational performance by intention and design, that is by achieving good fit between the organizational arrangements which determine the way tasks are performed and the realities of context, which may relate not only to task contingencies but also to political contingencies. Considerable responsibility is seen to fall on organizational designers since there are no blueprints available and success hinges on the exercise of judgement in the achievement of good fit. Even so it is assumed that appropriate correspondences and alignments are achievable by design and intention as long as managers are equipped with the requisite insights, skills, authority and influence.

My research (Williams, 1987) confirms the need to take account of both task and political contingencies when designing and introducing a corporate planning system. The achievement of integration, accountability and control is seen with Child (1984) to be problematic and to require the use of a portfolio of strategies rather than reliance on just one. The chosen portfolio needs, in turn, to be compatible with the managerial culture(s) and distribution of power found within an organisation. Cultural control is correctly presented by Child (1984: 163–4) as significant for organizations offering professional services and he shares Pettigrew's interest in the concept of legitimacy. Not only does Child provide a conceptual framework of immediate practical vlaue to the practitioner he is also quick to point out the difficulties which the practising manager needs to bear in mind, namely the problem of causality, the presence of multiple contingencies at the same time and the tendency to neglect political rationality.

Garbage can

Despite the reservations shared with Lutz (1982: 124–5) and Pettigrew (1985: 205–6) I found that garbage can theory provided important insights into the introduction and operation of corporate planning systems. The tendencies to anarchy produced by problematic goals, an unclear technology and fluid participation were very much in evidence as was the tendency for choice opportunities to turn into garbage cans when problems having strong cultural and micropolitical connotations arose. On such occasions decision-making was delayed as time was taken to exercise a problem thoroughly before a solution emerged. The confluence of streams may be fortuitous or regulated. The tendency in the literature to emphasize the former at the expense of the latter is not supported by my studies. Certainly more outcomes emerge by default rather than design and versions of reality are frequently constructed 'post factum' but the confluences are also amenable to regulation by politically aware and tactically astute managers.

The distribution of attention by participants in the planning process I found to be particularly significant. They were likely to be as committed to participation by a sense of obligation and socialization into a role as they were by rational calculation or process pleasures. Viewed from this perspective, standard operating procedures exert their primary influence as standard rules linked to concepts of duty, role and obligation.

Garbage can theorists are also preoccupied with correspondences and alignments and identify the need to match models of choice and leadership styles to context. Although the artifactual or non-decision model was seen to apply some of the time, I found anarchy to be less pervasive than the artifactual model requires. Conditions more often corresponded to the coalition–bargaining model which, for higher education, confirmed the findings of Baldridge *et al.* (1978).

Contextualist

Contextual analysis provided the major interpretive thrust and by relating contingency and garbage can to contexualism the power in application of the set was greatly enhanced. My findings confirmed the view taken by contextualists that managers should not be regarded as heroes or victims and that organizations, even highly professionalized organizations with tendencies to anarchy, are not beyond management. Many outcomes do emerge by default rather than design and versions of reality are frequently constructed after the event. But these features of organizational life simply reflect the complexities confronting managers rather than entirely disable them. What is required, above all, from managers is an awareness of complexity and an understanding of context, notably its micropolitical and cultural dimensions. Armed with such knowledge and an ability and willingness to exploit it, managers may intervene with purpose. Such interventions as they may choose to make are more likely to be successful if they are regarded not so much as the determined enforcement of managerial will but rather as the skilful exploitation of forces latent or already at work in the organization. Managers aware of the interactions between context, process and outcome through time are more likely to be alert to the opportunities created in the internal and external environments, both fortuitously and by design, to nudge the organization in a particular direction.

Contextualist analysis aims to provide managers with an understanding of the iterative relationship between context, process and outcomes. It does so by tracking the interaction between levels through time and by employing a combination of political and cultural process modes to interpret them. Above all, however, contextualist analysis provides the reflective practitioner with a general understanding of the process of change together with recommendations on its management.

Usefulness of research: truth test and utility test

As indicated the approach adopted has been pragmatic and instrumental with a strong concern to internalize and exploit theory for practical purposes. This concern for increasing the usefulness of research is one to which the *Administrative Science Quarterly* devoted two volumes in 1983. Dunbar (1983: 130) advocated the use of two tests of usefulness: a truth test and an utility test. A truth test asks whether:

1. the research is internally consistent;
2. it adheres to accepted standards for empirical research; and
3. its results are compatible with users' experience and expectations.

For research to have utility it is required to:

1. make feasible recommendations for action; or
2. challenge the status quo by proposing alternative perspectives.

I believe that the kind of research which I have described is able to satisfy both tests.

References

Baldridge, J.V. *et al.* (1978) *Policy Making and Effective Leadership*, San Francisco: Jossey-Bass.

Burrell, G. and Morgan, G. (1979) *Sociological Paradigms and Organisational Analysis*, London: Heinemann.

Child, J. (1984) *Organization*, London: Harper and Row.

Cohen, M.D. and March, J.G. (1974) *Leadership and Ambiguity*, New York: McGraw Hill.

Dunbar, R.L.M. (1983) 'Toward an applied administrative science', *Administrative Science Quarterly* 28: 129–144.

Geertz, C. (1973) *The Interpretation of Cultures*, New York: Basic Books.

Hinings, C.R. *et al.* (1971) 'A strategic contingencies theory of intraorganizational power', *Administrative Science Quarterly* 16: 216–29.

Hinings, C.R. *et al.* (1974) Structural conditions of intraorganizational power', *Administrative Science Quarterly* 19: 22–44.

Hinings, C.R. *et al.* (1981) 'Power and advantage in organizations', *Organization Studies* 2/2: 131–52.

Louis, M.R. (1983) 'Review of Burrell and Morgan's "Sociological Paradigms and Organizational Analysis" (1979), *Administrative Science Quarterly* 28: 153–6.

Lutz, F.W. (1982) 'Tightening up loose coupling in organizations of higher education', *Administrative Science Quarterly* 27: 653–69.

March, J.G. and Olsen, J.P. (1976) *Ambiguity and Choice in Organisations*, Bergen: Universitetsforlaget.

Payne, R.L. (1975) 'Epistemology and the study of behaviour in organisations', *Memo. 68, MRC Social and Applied Psychology Unit*, Department of Applied Psychology, University of Sheffield.

Payne, R.L. (1982) 'The nature of knowledge and organizational psychology', *Memo. 445, MRC Social and Applied Psychology Unit*, Department of Applied Psychology, University of Sheffield.

Pepper, S.C. (1942) *World Hypotheses*, Berkeley: University of California Press.

Pepper, S.C. (1966) *Concept and Quality*, La Salle: Open Court.

Pettigrew, A.M. (1973) *The Politics of Organisational Decision Making*, London: Tavistock

Pettigrew, A.M. (1983) 'Contextualist research: A natural way to link theory and practice', Paper presented to conference Conducting Research with Theory and Practice in Mind, Center for Effective Organizations, University of Southern California, Los Angeles, 3–4 November.

Pettigrew, A.M. (1985) *The Awakening Giant: Continuity and Change in ICI*, Oxford: Basil Blackwell.,

Pratt, S. *et al.* (1982) 'Editorial: Enter Politics', *Educational Management and Administration*, 10, 2.

Schon, D.A. (1983) *The Reflective Practitioner: How Professionals Think in Action*, London: Temple Smith.

Vickers, G. (1965) *The Art of Judgement*, London: Methuen.

Wilson, M.J. (1979) 'Introduction to the course and block 1', *DE304 Research Methods in Education and the Social Sciences*, Milton Keynes: Open University Press.

Williams, G.H. (1987) *Corporate Planning in a Turbulent Environment*, PhD Thesis: University of Bath.

Technology and Innovation

Chapter six

Strategic Management in the Innovating Firm

K. Pavitt

Introduction

In this chapter, I shall present what I think we know, and what we need to know, about the strategic management of technology in the business firm. I shall concentrate on the links between technology and business strategy: in other words on those technology-related activities central to the long-term survival of the firm, ranging from the continuous improvement of existing products, processes and services; through the introduction of new ones; to activities designed to enter new fields.

After putting the present spate of interest in the subject in its historical perspective, I shall argue that four of the observed characteristics of technological development — functional and professional specialization, uncertainty, cumulative development, and path dependency — offer important guideposts, both for managerial practice, and for further theoretical and empirical research on the subject. I shall further argue that progress in this research has been hindered by the myths and rituals constructed in various academic subdisciplines. Nonetheless, we can now say with some confidence the following three things about technological strategies in firms.

First, the choices normally presented about the content of a firm's technological strategy — broad front versus specialized, product versus process, leader versus follower — are heavily constrained by both the firm's size and its core business. Technologically active firms that have specialized strategies are typically small and oriented towards products, often developed with strong feedback from large and technically sophisticated users. Large firms typically have broad front strategies, with one major path being horizontal diversification emerging from R and D-based technology, and the other being diversification vertically upstream, based on production and (more recently) information-processing technology.

Second, technology strategy formation in the firm inevitably involves more than the R and D and other technical functions, and is conducted through advocacy and political bargaining. However, given the ultimate constraints of user acceptance, strategic action is necessarily purposive, and central elements are the learning activities that render almost indistinguishable the content, context, and processes of technological change and innovation.

Third, technological discontinuities must not be confused with institutional discontinuities. Firms with strong technological activities — often typified by extensive research and development (R and D) activities — are capable of assimilating radical technological advances into the development of their core technological skills, thereby modifying their paths of technological and business development. As a consequence, one of the main challenges to management research is to explain the co-existence of institutional continuity with technological discontinuity, in terms that go beyond the role of great managers.

Historical context

In the 1980s, research into technology and the firm has been strongly stimulated in the UK through a variety of initiatives by the Economic and Soci:! Research Council (ESRC) and other Research Councils. Given the pressures to make academic research more obviously relevant to practical problems, this is hardly surprising. It is now widely recognized that, in high wage countries, both competitiveness of firms and more general welfare depend critically on the ability to keep up with the world frontier in innovative products and processes, and in their underlying technologies. The best indicator of this recognition is what business firms actually do. In the increasingly turbulent, uncertain and competitive world since 1973, the rate of growth of business-funded R and D activities in the OECD area has actually increased, rather than decreased (OECD, 1983, 1984). In sectors like electronics, aircraft and fine chemicals, companies' expenditures on R and D are greater than those on investment in fixed equipment and plant.

In the UK, it also recognized that, in spite of recent short-term improvements in certain aspects of economic performance, Britain's technological activities and international competitiveness remain unsatisfactory in many sectors — particularly electronics and automobiles (see Patel and Pavitt, 1987b). Similar concerns about technological competitiveness have spread to other countries as a consequence of technological dynamism and competitiveness of Japanese firms, and of the diffusion of information and computing technologies across an increasingly wide range of firms and sectors. For understandable reasons, these concerns have been particularly marked in the United States.

Hence, the increased interest in the 1980s amongst management scholars, consultants and practitioners in the role of technology in such matters as corporate strategy, operations management, global competition strategic alliances, and the like. Whilst this is to be welcomed, it must in my view be put in proper historical context. There is the danger in assuming that — in both managerial practice and scholarly analysis — nothing much of importance can be learned from the past. This is almost certainly wrong.

Thus, in relation to company practice, we know from the research of David Mowery (1983) and other business historians that technology became an explicit element in management practice and strategy at the end of the nineteenth century, with the growth of large chemical and electrical companies particularly in Germany and the USA. Indeed, the industrial R and D laboratories central to such growth can be seen as part of the functional and professional specialization that defines much of modern management practice. Firms in these and other industries had extensive networks of external technological contacts, competed globally, and formed strategic alliances, often as part of world cartels.

More recent developments must therefore be seen within a relatively long historical period temporarily disrupted by two World Wars. What distinguishes the contemporary period is not just the rise of Japan compared to the USA, since earlier periods saw the rise of Germany and the USA compared to the UK. Nor is it simply the diffusion of radical micro-electronics technology, since earlier periods saw the diffusion of other radical technologies, such as families of synthetic chemicals, electricity, mass production and consumer durables. It is also the breadth and depth of technological activities undertaken in the world: there are now three areas — Japan, Western Europe and North America — competing along a world technological frontier that is increasingly fast-moving, long and differentiated.

Parallel to this accumulation of practical experience in the management of technology has been scholarly research related to it. Although the importance of technological change had been acknowledged by earlier writers, it was Schumpeter (1950) who stressed the central importance of innovation in competition amongst firms, in the evolution of industrial structures, and in processes of economic development; and who gave us the most useful definition of innovation, comprising not just new products and processes, but also new forms of organization, new markets and new sources of raw materials. Schumpeter also made the distinction between administrative management of what is well known, and entrepreneurship which is the creation and implementation of the new. He believed that entrepreneurship depends on super-normal individuals with exceptional intelligence and energy, and that innovation is an act of will rather than intellect.

However, my colleague Christopher Freeman (1988) has pointed out that, although he had a theory of innovation and entrepreneurship,

Schumpeter never developed a theory of the innovating firm. He had little to say on the sources of innovation and the importance of continuous incremental improvements. More specifically, he had little to say about the organizational and other characteristics of the major sources of technical change in established firms — that are large in some industries and small in others — and that maintain their existence over long periods by continuously changing their products, processes and markets. As Freeman has concluded: 'The task . . . is to develop a theory of the firm which . . . does not assume as its foundation either hyper-rationality of individual of entrepreneurs or groups, nor yet super-normal intelligence and energy.'

Disciplinary rites

This sets the agenda quite nicely for the rest of the paper, where I intend to summarize what I think we know and we need to know in order to develop such a theory, and also to improve management practice. I believe that substantial progress has already been made through a steady accumulation of empirical and theoretical knowledge, beginning back in the 1950s and continuing into the 1960s and 1970s, in a research field that has been loosely described as 'innovation studies'. I am not thinking only of Freeman (1982), Rothwell (1977) and other colleagues at the Science Policy Research Unit. Over this period, a number of economists have also made major contributions: including Gold (1979), Mansfield *et al.* (1971), Rosenberg (1976, 1982), Nelson and Winter (1982), Schmookler (1966) and Scherer (1984) in the USA; Kay (1982), Metcalfe (1970) and Stoneman (1983) in the UK; and Dosi (1984), Eliasson (1982) and Soete (1982) elsewhere in Europe. Scholars in the management disciplines have also made their mark: including Allen (1977), von Hippel (1988), Roberts (1987) and Utterback (1975) at the Sloane School; Bright (1968), Abernathy (1980), Clark (1985), and Rosenbloom (1983) at Harvard; Rubenstein *et al* (1976) at Northwestern; Pearson (1980) and Grandstrand (1982) in Europe. Their research output has resulted in numerous books, and in papers in refereed journals such as *IEEE Transactions in Engineering Management, Research Policy, Technological Forecasting and Social Change, R and D Management,* and *Technovation*.

And herein lies the danger, now that technology, its management, and its economic and social effects, have attracted attention in the mainstream of the academic social sciences. The above journals often are not scanned, let alone read, by those concentrating their attention on, say, the *Economic Journal*, or *Administrative Science Quarterly*, or *Sociology*. The results of this research may therefore be ignored.

In this context I am struck by the similarities between academics with their disciplines and subdisciplines, and the functional and professional specialist groups in business firms, described by Pettigrew (1985), with their different goals, values, problem-solving styles, and languages. But there is one important difference between the two. In business firms, the external constraint of competition and survival forces groups to negotiate and work together in order to find solutions to problems that are not only internally acceptable, but also externally efficient. For a variety of often very good reasons, the external constraints on academic specialist groups is much weaker, and so consequently is the pressure to work together, to compete, and to come up with better explanations. The result is that each academic specialty can ignore important empirical results and theoretical insights from other specialties, thereby slowing down the general rate of progress of both understanding and action.

The results of innovation research challenge the assumptions of many disciplines, and identify puzzles that they should help solve. How, for example, can economics best model the disequilibrating, uncertain and path-dependent dynamics of technological change (Dosi *et al.*, 1988)? How can the growing sociologists' interest in the 'social shaping of technology' encompass the results of past research on the relative importance in technological change of 'science and technology push', and 'demand and market pull' (see Mowery and Rosenberg, 1979)? However, I shall concentrate here on the implications of the results of innovation research for the management subdisciplines, rather than for sociology or for economics.

Characteristics of technological innovation

Innovation research has helped delineate four key characteristics of innovative activities in the firm.

First, they involve continuous and intensive collaboration and interaction amongst functionally and professionally specialized groups: R and D, production and marketing for implementation; organization and finance for strategic decisions to move into new areas.

Second, they remain profoundly uncertain activities. Only about one in ten R and D projects turn out to be a commerical success, the other nine not meeting technical objectives or (more often) commercial ones. About half industrial R and D funds thus find no direct profitable application.

Third, they are cumulative in development over time. Most technological knowledge is specific, involving the development and testing of prototypes and pilot plant, and experience in the production and use of equipment. Although firms can buy in technology and skills from the outside, what they have been able to do in the past strongly conditions what they can hope to do in the future.

Fourth, they are highly differentiated. Specific technological skills in one field (e.g. developing pharmaceutical products) may be applicable in closely related fields (e.g. developing pesticides), but they are not much use in many others (e.g. designing and buildings automobiles).

I shall now try to show that these characteristics have major implications for theory and action related to the content of technological strategy, to the processes through which they are developed and implemented, and to organizational continuity in the face of technological discontinuity.

The content of technological strategies

The cumulative and differentiated nature of technological developments in firms suggest that the choices about the content of technological strategy, normally presented in the literature — broad front versus specialized, product versus process and leader versus follower, do not take into account the enormous variety between firms in sources of technological opportunities, and in the rate and direction of their development (von Hippel, 1988; Scherer, 1982). In particular, the innovative opportunities open to a firm are strongly conditioned by a firm's size and by its core business (Pavitt *et al.*, 1989a).

Thus, innovating small firms are typically specialized in their technological strategies, concentrating on product innovation in specific producers goods, such as machine tools, scientific instruments, specialized chemicals or software. Their key strategic strengths are in the ability to match technology with specific customer requirements. The key strategic tasks are finding and maintaining a stable product niche, and benefitting systematically from user experience.

Large innovating firms, on the other hand, are typically broad front in their technological activities, and divisionalized in their organization. The key technological strengths can be based on R and D laboratories (typically in chemicals and electrical-electronic products), or in the design and operation of complex production technology (typically in mass production and continuous process industries), and increasingly, in the design and operation of complex information processing technology (typically in finance and retailing).

In R and D-based technologies, the key strategic opportunities are horizontal diversification into new product markets. The key strategic problems are those of mobilizing complementary assets to enter new product markets (e.g. obtaining marketing knowledge when a pharmaceutical firm moves into pesticides), and continuous organizational redesign to exploit emerging technological opportunities (e.g. personal computers cutting across previous responsibilities in computers, office machinery, and even consumer electronics).

In production-based and information-based technologies, the key strategic opportunities are in the progressive integration of radical technological advances into products and production systems, and in diversification vertically upstream into potentially munificent production inputs (e.g. CAD-CAM, robots, and software). The key strategic tasks are ensuring diffusion of best practice technology within the firm, and choices about the degree of appropriation (i.e. internalization) of production technology.

Thus, firms do no have a completely free choice about whether or not to be broad front or specialized, product or process oriented. Similarly, they do not have a completely free hand about being a leader or a follower. In many areas, it is not clear before the event who is in the race, where the starting and finishing lines are, and even what the race is about. Even when it is, firms may start out wishing to be a leader, and end up being a follower. And Teece (1986) has shown that, although there are some advantages in being first, particularly when there are strong regimes of property rights or cumulative learning, it is sometimes advantageous to be second, particularly when product configurations are not fully fixed, so that followers can learn from the mistakes of leaders who find themselves without the required range of complementary assets.

Given the cumulative nature of technological development, technological choices in the firm also depend critically both on the time horizons chosen, and on management's abilities to anticipate future cumulative paths of technological development, and their commerical significance. In particular, longer-term and speculative projects will be down-played, if time horizons are short and cumulative developments ignored or little understood. Thus, left to themselves, accountants are likely to come to different conclusions to those of engineers about investments in, for example, robots, precisely because of such differences. (On the distinctions between myopic and dynamic systems, see Patel and Pavitt, 1988.)

A satisfactory theory of the innovating firm requires further development of understanding of the nature and determinants of paths of technological development in different classes of firm. I am fully aware that, for many social science scholars, any proposition that technological opportunities might in themselves have a major and independent influence on managerial practice (or any other social form) is the methodological equivalent of admitting to strong drug addiction, links with organized crime, or even active membership of the Nazi Party. Nonetheless, the results of past research point to the need for better description, classification and explanation of the following.

1. Strategies and search processes of technical specialists in choosing technological trajectories (e.g. what is the logic that has pushed

continuously towards minituarization in semiconductor technology?):

2. The effects on management organization and practice of specific technological developments (e.g. the emergence of major technological opportunities, the development of which requires resources from a variety of existing divisions; the shift in the chemical industry from large-scale production of bulk chemicals, to product innovation in high value fine chemicals and custom-made materials);

3. The role of corporate R and D laboratories in developing corporate technological strategies, and in identifying and exploiting corporate synergies;

4. The method used in firms for evaluating longer-term and speculative technological activities in firms.

The processes of technology strategy

Another limitation of the 'content' view of technological strategy, described above, is that it neglects the context within which, and the processes whereby, technological strategies are generated, chosen and implemented. These processes are bound to involve more than the technical function. As we have seen, production and marketing are inevitably involved with R and D implementation, finance in setting ground rules for evaluating and monitoring programes and projects, and organization and the strategic function in decisions about entering new areas.

Company structure and company strategy thus play a major role in the formation of technological strategy. As Hobday (1989) has recently pointed out, the ambitious technological strategies of Japanese firms making electronic components depend in large part on their vertical integration with electronic equipment manufacture, and the relatively strong emphasis put on long-term growth compared to short-term profits. More generally, Japanese firms are apparently more likely than those in Europe and the USA to have a member of the main board responsible for technological policy (see Patel and Pavitt, 1987a). Sharp (1989) argues that recent initiatives in European technological co-operation in ESPRIT have taken off rapidly precisely because they involved chief executives rather than R and D directors.

Given that technology strategy involves many functions and professions, as well as major uncertainties, its formation and implementation are bound to be a choice territory for the advocacy, battles and negotiations that analysts in the process school of strategy give such great importance. This was recognized some time ago by Freeman (1974) when, after reviewing the disappointing experience that firms had had with formal, quantitative methods of R and D project selection and technological forecasting, he concluded as follows:

. . . empirical evidence confirms that decision making in relation to R and D projects or general strategy is usually a matter of controversy within the firm . . . uncertainty means that many different views may be held and the situation is typically one of advocacy and political debate in which project estimates are used by interest groups to buttress a particular point of view. Evaluation techniques and technological forecasting, like tribal war-dances, play a very important part in mobilising, energising and organising.

However, the results of past research show that technology strategy cannot be described solely in terms of political negotiation between hostile professional and functional tribes. In the market system, the ability to satisfy user's needs better than the alternatives on offer is the ultimate measure of success and profitability, and consequently the allocation of resources, power and prestige within the firm. Innovation research has come to robust conclusions about the factors associated with successful innovations, thus defined. In addition to the quality of technical work, these include strong horizontal linkages among functional departments, with outside users, and with other sources of relevant technical expertise; and a responsible manager with experience in all the functional activities involved.

Either by conscious choice or by trial and error, successful innovating firms are more likely to evolve 'routines' (or rules of thumb) that reflect these ingredients. Given the high uncertainties involved, trial and error are inevitable in the development and implementation of innovation. In fact, the major importance of development — as opposed to research — activities in industrial laboratories can be considered as a systematic form of trial and error. Theory and computer simulations are not powerful enough to predict the performance of technological artefacts with a high enough degree of certainty to eliminate the costly development and testing of prototypes and pilot plants.

In addition, the ability to learn from experience, whether internally (learning by doing), or from suppliers, customers and competitors (learning by using, learning by failing, reverse engineering), is of major importance in the management of innovation. As Dodgson (1989) has pointed out, learning from experience, thus defined, actually dissolves sharp distinction in the strategy debate between content, process and context. This is because processes of learning about the context help define the content of strategy, the implementation of which in turn helps define both the nature and directions of subsequent learning processes, and changes in context.

Individuals' capacities to learn from their experience depend not only on their personalities but also their training. Comparative empirical research has demonstrated the importance of training for the effective exploitation of technology (Pratten, 1976; Prais, 1987). Particularly in the large firm, learning is also a collective activity requiring frequent communication among specialists and functions. Since knowledge accumulated through experience is also partly tacit, and the tasks to which such knowledge is applied are complex and loosely structured, personal contact and discussions are the most frequent and effective means of communication and learning. Policies for effective learning therefore go beyond training and organization to include those of geogrpahical location. Allen (1977) and other scholars have shown the importance of physical location in influencing patterns of communication, both within the technical function and between the technical and other functions in the firm. And Howells (1989) has shown that decisions about the location of R and D laboratories by firms in the UK pharmaceutical industry have been strongly influenced by the requirements for effective internal communication with other functional areas.

These research results show that further analysis of the processes of technological innovation in the business firm need to go beyond purely political relations between functional and professional groups, to include learning from experience, and communication within and among the firm's functional elements, and with the outside world of suppliers, users and competitors. It is now possible to formulate quite sharp hypotheses and questions about, for example:

- communication, feedback and learning between firms' technical functions and their eventual users;
- links with external sources of relevant expertise;
- the characteristics of managers most likely to integrate the various functions into successful implementation.

In this sense, it is rather disappointing to see the important and ambitious programme of research on processes of innovation, led by van de Ven and his colleagues at Minnesota (1988), using an analytical framework consisting of five elements: people, ideas, transactions, context and outcomes. This may be satisfactory for the development of a general theory of change, encompassing not just innovating firms, but also (say) the Soviet Communist Party, the Roman Catholic Church, local government, or the family. But it is a choice that effectively excludes a rich seam of research on the characteristics and determinants of change specific to technology and the business firm.

Technological discontinuities and institutional continuities

With the present wave of radical technological change in microelectronics and information technology, considerable emphasis is being placed in management theory and practice on the notion of 'technological discontinuities', implying a radical increase in the rate of technical change, and a marked shift in its associated skills and required organizational forms (see Tushman and Anderson, 1987). It is often argued, on the basis of either Schumpeter's notion of creative destruction, or the so-called product cycle theory, that technological discontinuities are associated with the emergence of new small firms to exploit them, given conservatism, obsolescence and bureaucracy in established large firms.

I am very sceptical about this view of the world (although, by way of an academic health warning, I am bound to say that many of my colleagues in innovation studies disagree with me). The statistical evidence available shows that, in electronics (the main sector of 'discontinuity') in the UK since 1945, the proportions of significant innovations made by both large firms (with more than 10,000 employees) and by small firms (with fewer than 1,000 employees) have both been increasing at the expense of the medium-sized firms in between (Pavitt *et al.*, 1989b). Over the longer term, I find that the observation by Mowery (1983) that the growth of industrial R and D in the twentieth Century has been associated with greater stability amongst large firms, is persuasive. Established chemical firms have successfully survived and indeed benefitted from successive waves of radical innovations in synthetic products. In spite of the semiconductor and the growth of new firms exploiting it, such as Intel, Texas Instruments and Motorola, other market leaders like NEC, Hitachi and Fujitsu are long established; and IBM was a world leader in the earlier, traditional electro-mechanical technologies — office machinery — before it moved into computers (Pavitt, 1986).

It is also the case that some of the most revolutionary business applications of information technology today are to be found not in new technology-based firms, but among the longest established, largest and most conservative of capitalists: the money lenders, the merchants and the grocers — in other words, banks, other financial services, and large-scale retailing. Two factors help explain why technological discontinuities can co-exist with institutional continuities.

First, large established firms normally have specialized and professionalized R and D laboratories and other technical functions with accumulated skills and experience in orchestrating and integrating inputs from a wide variety of scientific and technical disciplines. They are therefore experienced in hiring and integrating professionals from promising new areas. Examples from the past include the hiring of computer experts by IBM (Katz and Phillips, 1982), and of aerodynamic and hydraulic engineers by Sulzer for the development of the shuttle-less loom (Rothwell, 1976), whilst we can witness today the strenuous efforts being made by large chemical firms to understand and assimilate

89

the dark secrets of the biotechnology tribe (Faulkner, 1986).

The second reason was identified by Schumpeter in his later writings. Large firms have both considerable resources and oligopolistic power. In some, but not all, countries, they are not subject to a strong, short-term profit constraint. They therefore have both the resources and the time to explore the implications of technological discontinuities for their business, and to link them with core competences within the firm, through learning and incremental change, before deciding whether or not to move into commercialization. One observable feature of innovating firms is precisely that they develop technological capabilities beyond those strictly related to their current output.

Perez (1983) correctly pointed to the dangers of a mismatch between institutional routines and skills, on the one hand, and the effective exploitation of technological discontinuities, on the other. Given its long-term importance, we need to know more about how and why many established business firms successfully overcome any mismatch, and assimilate and exploit technological discontinuities. Recent analyses of information technology in service firms (Richard Barras, 1986, Graham Thomas and Ian Miles, 1989), suggest a process that can be described either as a 'reverse product cycle', or as the equivalent of technical change in production-centred firms that I described earlier. Information technology is first used in such firms to improve processes, and after a sometimes long period of learning, becomes the basis of products sold outside. Further empirical studies are needed to see whether this model can be extended to other sectors, or to other technical areas like biotechnology.

Conclusions

To sum up, I believe that — given the state of the art described above — the development of a satisfactory theory of the innovating firm requires an understanding of the conditions for the coexistence, over a relatively long period, of institutional continuity, coupled with rapid and sometimes radical technological change. Business historians and scholars of strategic management processes can make major contributions, especially when their analyses are related to research findings and concepts emerging from other branches of the social sciences. However, given the varied nature of technical change and of business firms, it will also be necessary to support comparative studies of the key factors determining firms' technological strategies. With recent advances in the quantitative measurement of technological activities, it will not be too difficult to develop reliable data on firms' revealed technological competences. The greater methodological challenge will be to find economical and accurate methods for measuring and comparing firms' organizational linkages, institutional learning, and methods of evaluating technological opportunities. A modest start can perhaps be made by building up systematic information on the organizational and geographical locus of R and D and other technical functions in large firms.

However, scholars and practitioners will rightly be asking what role (if any) is left, after the above discussion, for the discretion, skill and flair of the manager? The evidence shows that management's role is inevitably constrained by the accumulated organizational and technological characteristics of the firm. At the same time, coping with continuous change is not easy, and requires more than a tribal chief organizing war dances, or a charismatic prince playing Machiavellian politics. The results of research suggest that, among other things, the successful management of technology requires:

1. The capacity to orchestrate and integrate functional and specialist groups for the implementation of innovations;
2. Continuous questionning of the appropriateness of existing organizational forms and skills for the exploitation of technological opportunities;
3. A willingness to take the long view of technological accumulation within the firm, together with the skills and flair to form realistic expectations about the implications of future technological developments.

In other words, the management of technology is a professionally demanding and difficult activity. We need a theory that assumes that management is neither a supercomputer (capable of perfectly rational choice), nor superman (overcoming all obstacles to progress), nor simply a bunch of squabbling professionals. Many innovating firms have successfully coped with the messy and murky real world of technological change, over long periods and under different managements. In this context, it is refreshing to read one of the conclusions of the recent study of the introduction of information technology into firms, namely, that important changes are often made by professional managers doing their everday jobs (Buchanan, 1986).

The experience and preoccupations of one group of professionals, namely R and D managers, is reflected in a recent report by the European Industrial Research Management Association (EIRMA, 1986), entitled 'Developing R and D Strategies', and including the results of a survey of 70 of its member companies. Its contents bring into sharper focus many of the issues discussed in this presentation, in particular the following:

– The considerable variation across sectors in product development times and the length of product life cycles;

- The concern to improve links between the R and D function and the operating parts of companies. More than 80 per cent of the firms with more than 10,000 employees had both corporate and divisional R and D laboratories;
- Marked effects, on the level, composition and organization of R and D in the firm, through the development and implementation of R and D strategies;
- The heavy involvement of all functions of the firm in the development of R and D strategies, coupled with a relatively slight involvement of the R and D function in the development of corporate strategy;
- A consequent concern amongst R and D managers to ensure that R and D does not have simply a reactive, but a proactive, role in the determination of corporate strategy, by securing greater representation of the technical function on the main board;
- A recognition that firms have a choice along a spectrum from being 'traders' concentrating on low risk activities with quick but low returns, at one extreme, to being 'investors' undertaking high risk activities with greater possibilities of longer-term growth, at the other;
- A clear awarness of the limitations of the general strategic matrices developed by management consultants;
- Authoritative knowledge of the dynamics of the technologies central to their firm, and their links to firm strategy and market opportunities.

It is encouraging that the research agenda defined above reflects many of these preoccupations.

References

Abernathy, W. and Hayes, R. (1980) 'Managing our way to economic decline', *Harvard Business Review* July/August, 58: 67–77.

Allen, T. (1977) *Managing the Flow of Technology*, Cambridge, Mass.: MIT Press.

Barras, R. (1986) 'Towards a theory of innovation in services', *Research Policy* 15 (4): 161–73.

Bright, J. (1968) *Technological Forecasting for Industry and Government*, Englewood Cliffs, NJ: Prentice-Hall.

Buchanan, D.A. (1986) 'Management objectives in technical change', in D. Knights and H. Willmott (eds) *Managing the Labour Process*, Aldershot: Gower, pp. 67–84.

Clark, K. (1985) 'The interaction of design hierarchies and market concepts in technological evolution', *Research Policy* 14 (5): 235–51.

Dodgson, M. (ed.) (1989) *Technology Strategy and the Firm: Management and Public Policy*, London: Longman (forthcoming).

Dodgson, M. (1989) 'Introduction: technology in a strategic perspective', in M. Dodgson (ed.) *Technology Strategy and the Firm: Management and Public Policy*, London: Longman.

Dosi, G. (1984) *Technical Change and Industrial Transformation*, London: Macmillan.

Dosi, G., Freeman, C., Nelson, R., Silverberg, G. and Soete, L. (1988) *Technical Change and Economic Theory*, London: Pinter.

Eliasson, G. (1982) 'Electronics, economic growth and employment — revolution or evolution?', in H. Giersch (ed.) *Emerging Technologies: Consequences for Economic Growth, Structural Change and Employment*, Tubingen: Mohr.

European Industrial Research Management Associatin (EIRMA) (1986) *Developing R and D Strategies*, Working Group Report No. 33, Paris.

Faulkner, W. (1986) 'Linkage between industrial and academic research: the case of biotechnological research in the pharmaceutical industry', D'Phil thesis, SPRU/University of Sussex.

Freeman, C. (1982) *The Economics of Industrial Innovation*, London: Francis Pinter (first edition published by Penguin in 1974).

Freeman, C. (1988) 'Schumpeter's 'Business Cycles' Revisited', paper prepared for Schumpeter Society Conference, Siena.

Giersch, H. (ed.) (1982) *Emerging Technologies: Consequences for Economic Growth, Structural Change and Employment*, Tubingen: Mohr.

Gold, B. (1979) *Productivity, Technology and Capital*, Lexington Books.

Granstrand, O. (1982) *Technology, Management and Markets*, London: Pinter.

Hippel, E. von (1988) *The Sources of Innovation*, Oxford: Oxford University Press.

Hobday, M. (1989) 'Corporate strategies in the international semiconductor industry', in M . Dodgson (ed.) *Technology Strategy and the Firm: Management and Public Policy*, London: Longman.

Howells, J. (1989) 'The location and organisation of research and development: New horizons', *Research Policy* (forthcoming)

Katz, B. and Phillips, A. (1982) 'Government, Technological Opportunities and the Emergence of the Computer Industry', in H. Giersch (ed.) *Emerging Technologies: Consequences for Economic Growth, Structural Change and Employment*, Tubingen: Mohr.

Kay, N. (1982) *The Evolving Firm; Strategy and Structure in Industrial Organisation*, London: Macmillan.

Mansfield, E. *et al.* (1971) *Research and Innovation in the Modern Corporation*, New York: Norton.

Metcalfe, J. (1970) 'The diffusion of innovation in the Lancashire textile Industry', *Manchester School of Economics and Social Studies*, No. 2: 145–62.

Mowery, D. (1983) 'Industrial research and firm size, survival and growth in American manufacturing, 1921–1946: An assessment', *Journal of Economic History* 43: 953–80.

Mowery, D. and Rosenberg, N. (1979) 'The influence of market demand upon innovation: A critical review of some recent empirical studies', *Research Policy* 8: 102–53.

Nelson, R. and Winter, S. (1982) *An Evolutionary Theory of Economic Change*, Belknap.

OECD (1983) *Research and Development in the Business Enterprise Sector, 1963–1979*, Basic Statistical Indicators, Vol. D, Paris.

OECD (1984) *Recent Results: Selected Science and Technology Indicators, 1979–1984*, Paris.

Patel, P. and Pavitt, K. (1987a) 'Is Western Europe losing the technological race?', *Research Policy*, 59–85.

Patel, P. and Pavitt, K. (1987b) 'The elements of British technological competitiveness', *National Institute Economic Review*, 4: 72–83.

Patel, P. and Pavitt, K. (1988) 'The international distribution and determinants of technological activities', *Oxford Review of Economic Policy*, 4: 1–21.

Pavitt, K. (1986) 'Chips' and 'trajectories': How does the semiconductor influence the sources and directions of technical change?', in R. MacLeod (ed.) *Technology and the Human Prospect*, London: Pinter, pp. 31–54.

Pavitt, K., Robson, M. and Townsend, J. (1989a) 'Technological accumulation, diversification and organisation in UK companies, 1945–1983', *Management Science* 35 (1): 81–99.

Pavitt, K., Robson, M. and Townsend, J. (1989b) 'A fresh look at the size distribution of innovating firms' in F. Arcangeli *et al.* (eds) *Frontiers of Innovation Diffusion*, Oxford: Oxford University Press (forthcoming).

Pearson, A. (ed.) (1980) 'Industrial R and D Strategy and Management', *R and D Management* (Special conference issue).

Perez, C. (1983) 'Structural change and assimilation of new technologies in the economic and social systems', *Futures*, 15: 357–75.

Pettigrew, A. (1985) *The Awakening Giant: Continuity and Change in Imperial Chemical Industries*, Oxford: Blackwell.

Prais, S. (1987) 'Educating for productivity: comparisons of Japanese and English schooling and vocational preparation', *National Institute Economic Review*, No. 119: 40–69.

Pratten, C. (1976) *A Comparison of the Performance of Swedish and UK Companies*, Cambridge: Cambridge University Press.

Roberts, E. (ed.) (1987) *Generating Technological Innovation*, Oxford: Oxford University Press.

Rosenberg, N. (1976), *Perspectives on Technology*, Cambridge: Cambridge University Press.

Rosenberg, N. (1982) *Inside the Black Box: Technology and Economics*, Cambridge: Cambridge University Press.

Rosenbloom, R. (ed.) (1983) *Research on Technological Innovation, Management and Policy*, JM Press: Connecticut.

Rothwell, R. (1976) 'The Sulzer weaving machine: a case study of successful innovation', *Textile Institute and Machinery*, May: 170–3.

Rothwell, R. (1977) 'The characteristics of successful innovators and technically progressive firms', *R & D Management*, 7 (3): 191–206.

Rubenstein, A., Chakrabarti, A., O'Keefe, R., Souder, W. and Young, H. (1976) 'Factors influencing innovation success at the project level', *Research Management* XIX: 15–20.

Scherer, F. (1982) 'Inter-industry technology flows in the United States', *Research Policy* 11 (4): 227–45.

Scherer, F. (1984) *Innovation and Growth, Schumpeterian Perspectives*, MIT Press.

Schmookler, J. (1966) *Invention and Economic Growth*, Cambridge, Mass.: Harvard University Press.

Schumpeter, J.A. (1950) *Capitalism, Socialism and Democracy*, New York: Harper & Row.

Sharp, M. (1989) 'Corporate strategies and collaboration – the case of ESPRIT and European Electronics', in M. Dogson (ed.) *Technology Strategy and the Firm: Management and Public Policy*, London: Longman.

Soete, LK. (1981) 'A general test of technological gap trade theory', *Weltwirtschaftliches Archiv* 117: 638–60.

Stoneman, P. (1983) *An Economic Analysis of Technological Change*, Oxford: Oxford University Press.

Teece, D. (1986) 'Profiting from technological innovation: Implications for integration, collaboration, licensing and public policy', *Research Policy* 15 (6): 285–305.

Thomas, G. and Miles, I. (1989) 'Strategic options for new telecommunications services', in M. Dogson (ed.) *Technology Strategy and the Firm: Management and Public Policy*, London: Longman.

Tushman, M. and Anderson, P. (1987) 'Technological discontinuities and organisation environments', in A. Pettigrew (ed.) *The Management of Strategic Change*, Oxford: Blackwell: 89–122.

Utterback, J. and Abernathy, W. (1975) 'A dynamic model of process and product innovation', *Omega* 3: 639–656.

Ven, A. ven de and Associates (1988) *Progress Report on the Minnesota Innovation Research Programme*, mimeo, University of Minnesota, July.

Chapter seven

Technology, marketing, and culture: the politics of new product development

John Hendry

Recipes for successful innovation

The problem of how to foster and manage technological innovation has long been of primary concern to both academics and executives. Since the late 1960s a large and still-growing body of research evidence has pointed consistently to the conclusion that, for relatively small innovations at least, there is a broad correlation between the success of new product innovations and the extent to which their development is marketing or user led (Marquis, 1976; Mansfield *et al.*, 1971; Utterback, 1971; Litvak and Maule, 1972; Rothwell, 1974; Cooper, 1975; Mansfield and Wagner, 1975; von Hippel, 1976, 1978, 1982; Freeman, 1984; Quinn, 1985; Georghiou *et al.*, 1986; Cooper and Kleinschmnidt, 1987). This is not to say that technology push has no part to play in successful innovation. On the contrary, it has been widely recognized that a purely market-led approach can be every bit as limiting as a purely technology-driven one (Dessauer, 1971; Tauber, 1974, 1975; Imae *et al.*, 1984; Voss, 1984; Little and Sweeting, 1984). The art, as most commentators have agreed, is to combine the two; or, to use a phrase adopted in two of the key studies in the field, to ensure the 'proper coupling of R&D with marketing' (Mansfield, 1971; Freeman, 1984; see also Cooper, 1975; Aram and Javian, 1973; Souder, 1977, 1987; Rubinstein *et al.*, 1976).

A second and largely separate line of research has focused on the barriers to innovation experienced in organizations, and especially in large corporations, and on the characteristics of those projects in organizations in which the barriers are successfully overcome. Here the emphasis has been on two factors, the importance of which has been well demonstrated and is now generally accepted. One is the existence of product champions operating at a senior enough level in the firm to effectively sponsor the innovation and overcome any natural organizational resistance to change (Schon, 1963; Roberts, 1968; Chakrabarti, 1974; Maidique, 1980; Burgelman, 1983). The second is a general commitment of top management to innovation, embodied in the practice

96

of rewarding risk-takers and managing failure as the accepted organizational norm (Roberts, 1968; Quinn and Mueller, 1963; Backus, 1984).

On the basis of these consensus conclusions, a variety of recipes for the successful management of technological innovation have been put forward. Reflecting the research literature these are, broadly speaking, of two kinds. One, based primarily on the literature on R&D and marketing, focuses on the need for co-ordinating structures. In particular it advocates the use of matrix organizations for R&D or, carrying the same principle further, of a project-based organization for new product development in general, with all the main functional divisions of the organization represented in each project team. The other kind combines this prescription, though often with severe qualifications on the use of matrix systems, with a range of 'cultural' imperatives drawn from the general observation of successful innovating firms and linked with the literature on champions and top management support.

Most recent recipes have been of the latter kind, and although the details have varied from guru to guru they have shared a common core of main features. The need for active collaboration between the marketing and R&D functions remains central, even if it is sometimes obscured by the surrounding cultural rhetoric. And a project-based organization is the order of the day. But beyond this there is a call for competing project teams with multiple approaches, skunk works and developmental shoot-outs. Failure is to be managed as the norm, but membership of a successful product development team is to be made into the key employee goal. Champions are to be nurtured and made into corporate heroes. Top management should be visibly committed to the innovation process, which should be a key component of a strongly pronounced corporate image. And they should also have a strong market orientation, which should penetrate and act as the driving force for the whole organization (Peters and Waterman, 1982; Pascale and Athos, 1981; Quinn, 1985; Peters and Austin, 1985; Clifford and Cavanagh, 1985; Imae *et al.*, 1984; Roberts, 1980). The aim, in the phrase coined by Quinn (1985), is 'controlled chaos': an environment in which all the advantages of small entrepreneurial firms are retained at the project level and corporate control is provided by the management of culture and by a pervasive awareness of and deference to the market place.

These recipes appear to work well for the exemplary firms on whose practices they are largely based. They are clearly related to the research traditions mentioned above, and they also tie in well with the recent research results of Souder (1987, 1988) correlating innovation success with the use of organizational commitment in place of formal controls, and with high levels of interaction and communication across traditional task boundaries. However, they leave unanswered two very basic problems. One is how to implement them. Knowing where to go is one

97

thing, but getting there is quite another, and many firms clearly find the recipes almost impossible to enact. The other problem, underlying this practical one, is how the two sets of component prescriptions fit together: how the structural prescriptions for the coupling of R&D and marketing relate to the more general prescriptions on corporate culture.

Barriers to implementation

The overriding problem is in implementing the required co-ordination between the marketing and R&D functions. Many firms would nowadays claim to be doing this effectively, and many now employ some kind of structural co-ordinating mechanism. But recent research results suggest strongly that such mechanisms are not working. There is still a chronic lack of understanding in industry as to how the marketing–R&D interface ought to operate. Even where there is a marketing input to initial project assessments, this is rarely carried through into the crucial engineering design phase. And where the marketing function is given a role in the development process it typically seeks to control that process, withholding its own information from engineers and designers, and rejecting any contributions they might seek to make outside its own imposed specifications or terms of reference (Gupta *et al.*, 1985; Gupta and Wilemon, 1988; Dumas, 1988; Bonnet, 1986). Either way, effective collaboration between marketing and R&D remains elusive.

Underlying this lack of collaboration is a lack of understanding. Researchers have long recognized that the marketing and R&D functions are typically characterized by strongly contrasting organizational subcultures, with different values, motivations and goals, differing status structures and reward systems, and different concepts of procedure and control (Lawrence and Lorsch, 1967; LaPorte, 1967). Given this context, it is scarcely surprising that members of the two functions find it very difficult to understand each other's worlds. Recent research by Souder (1988) has shown that this is indeed the case, that, in particular, they find it difficult to understand and adapt to each other's operational requirements, and that fron this lack of understanding there arises a wide range of grievances and suspicions.

It should not be surprising either, given what we know about the sources of conflict between departments and functional groups, that far from resolving these differences, organizational structures which bring the two subcultures into immediate contact tend also to bring them into open conflict (Lawrence and Lorsch, 1967; Seiler, 1963; Walton and Dutton, 1969; Souder, 1977, 1987). Classic sources of interdepartmental conflict, such as task-related asymmetries and mutual dependencies, become more visible. And while any conflict may be overcome in some cases through the creation of a strong project identity and commitment, anything short of a very strong, and very elusive, degree of cohesion in this respect is likely fatally to compromise the organizational initiative.

Besides this fundamental problem, other interfunctional relationships, such as those between marketing or R&D and operations can also cause problems well recognized in the research literature (Quinn and Mueller, 1963; Burgelman, 1983) but scarcely addressed by the recipes for success. And the use of any project-based organization in which the project teams have a high degree of autonomy faces other serious difficulties too. To advocate the management of failure is all very well, but innovative projects and internal new ventures do have very high failure rates (Roberts, 1980; Little and Sweeting, 1984). And research into executive attitudes to project teams and venture groups has shown that while executives recognize many advantages for such organizational structures their attitudes are dominated by persistent perceived disadvantages. They are worried about the difficulty of imposing financial control, and about excessive autonomy leading to developments that might fit into the company's overall strategy. They anticipate difficulties in finding the right people to head up the teams. In short, they are quite reasonably worried about the danger of losing control, and strongly prefer to stick to a more traditional and tightly controlled organizational structure wherever possible (Hopkins, 1975).

In summary it would appear that, while there is a large measure of consensus on the requirements to be met if a strategy of technological innovation is to be pursued successfully, there are formidable barriers to the implementation of these requirements. And there is relatively little guidance, within the recipes for success, as to how to overcome these. You cannot imitate 3M or Sony by imitating their organizational machinery. Matrix or project-based structures are not universal panaceas. The objective recognition of the need for project autonomy, loose financial controls, and operating flexibility sufficient to allow for skunk works, spontaneously arising high-performance teams and multiple competing approaches, is far from equivalent to a subjective preparedness to accept the loss of immediate control entailed. And above all the call for an integration of marketing with research and development, or for a combination of a strongly marketing-led approach with technological freedom, is far removed from most firms' realities of practice. Underlying all this is a pervasive uncertainty and vagueness about what roles the different parts of the recipes play relative to each other, and what specific functions each part serves.

The politics of innovation

The key to this dilemma is to recognize that the innovation process is, like most organizational processes, a political one. Many writers in recent years have drawn attention to the political nature of organizations, and of the managerial processes within them (Farrell and Petersen, 1982; Gray and Ariss, 1985; Mintzberg, 1985, 1987; Mintzberg and McHugh, 1985; Kotter, 1986; Pfeffer, 1981; Narayonan and Fahey, 1982; Nielsen and Rao, 1987; Hambrick, 1981; Jemison, 1981, 1984). In particular the political nature of decision-making processes, both in general and in the context of technological innovation, has now been thoroughly attested to and explored through a substantial body of empirical research (Fahey, 1981; Hickson *et al.*, 1986; Pfeffer and Salancik, 1974; Pettigrew, 1973; Wilson, 1982; Welsh and Slusher, 1986; Johnson, 1987; Hendry, 1988; Graham, 1986). The importance of political activity in the promotion or hindrance of change processes has also been thoroughly demonstrated (Mumford and Pettigrew, 1975; Pettigrew, 1985; Greiner, 1986; Guth and Macmillan, 1986). And a political perspective is also implicit in the literature on innovation champions and on interdepartmental conflict. The political nature of the processes concerned is not, however, recognized in the recipes for success, and it is here that the difficulties discussed above arise.

From a political perspective, the problem of managing technological innovation is one of how to manage the collaboration between rival interest groups within the organization. Usually this will include interest groups with generally similar cultural backgrounds (and operating within the same functional divisions), but with different personal or social values or goals, different professional backgrounds, or competing political interests. Almost always it will include groups with contrasting cultural backgrounds, radically differing experiences, and different status and reward environments. If a set of prescriptions for solving the problem is to be sucessfully implemented, it must address this political reality, by taking full account of the political relationships between the parties involved.

In those recipes which focus purely on the organizational structure, the aim, in political terms, is to provide a mechanism for the establishment of working relationships and consensus decision-making across some of the principal political divisions of the organization. This prescription relies, however, on a sense of belonging and commitment to a project being sufficient to override the conflict automatically engendered by bringing the rival interest groups into close contact. And it also fails to address the political situation outside the project or venture group, and the barriers to change that are encountered there.

One way of addressing these problems is to focus attention on methods for binding organizations together: for providing project teams with the cohesion to overcome their internal conflicts, and organizations as a whole the cohesion both to limit conflict on a larger scale and to provide an environment of trust in which project groups can be given sufficient autonomy to escape the effect of this wider conflict. And it would appear to be this approach that underlies the relative success of the more recent culturally based recipes for managing innovation. A strong corporate image binds people together. So does a perceived commitment on behalf of top management to the innovation process. A preparedness to allow project teams to form spontaneously and the encouragement of competition between teams both serve to strengthen team bonding. Indeed the encouragement of conflict between groups (i.e. between project teams) is probably the fastest and most effective way of reducing conflict within them (i.e. between functions). And while it imposes its own problems, especially in terms of the management of failure, these are at least manageable. So long as the structure of political conflict separates vital elements of expertise, such as those held by the research and marketing specialists, nothing is manageable for there is nothing to manage.

These binding effects are important. But they are also limited. A strongly proclaimed set of corporate cultural norms informs people what is expected of them, and provides a foundation for bonding in terms of shared perceptions. But it can only act as an effective unifier if it is specific enough to direct people's behaviour, and that brings us back to our original problems. Unless there are other means of co-ordinating research and marketing, for example, proclaimed cultural norms must almost inevitably favour one or the other, or be irrelevant to the innovation process. Within the framework of the existing prescriptions a corporate commitment to innovation *per se* can only work in conjunction with the use of autonomous and competing project teams, and these raise the issues of control discussed earlier. Any organization needs some form of control over its activities, and if this is not to be operated through a tight corporate structure there must be some overriding discipline, be it financially or more broadly marketing based, which will again upset the balance of the innovation process. Or else an organization must be prepared to take genuine risks. Of the exemplary companies used as the basis for existing prescriptions, many are actually market led, and while this approach is reaping short-term harvests, its long-term viability remains open to question (Quinn and McGrath, 1985). Others are actually risk-takers, but while it may be necessary to take risks in order to optimise the chances of survival this is an approach that is unlikely to be widely imitated, at least so long as there appear to be more comfortable options.

Overcoming the barriers

So far as they relate to the politics of the situation at all, the existing recipes for innovation success rely almost entirely on the provision of forms of corporate glue. But this is like taking a set of magnets and, instead of aligning them, trying to glue them together by their repelling poles. If the glue is strong enough they may hold together for a time, but the forces of repulsion will be undiminished. The arrangement will be unstable and instead of being put to useful work the magnetic energy will be wasted. Similarly with organizations, one can glue together rival interest groups so as to neutralize their conflicts, but it may be only at the expense of neutralizing their powers too. The glue can play a very important part, but the first priority should be to remove, so far as possible, the sources of conflict.

Surprisingly, despite the considerable research into the sources of conflict, relatively little has been written about their removal. In the course of some recent research on the management of new product innovations, Souder (1988) has however made some suggestions as to how this might be achieved within an organizational development setting, giving some evidence in support of a procedure which involves alternating periods of nominal (side by side) and interacting (face to face) group activities. And once the right question is asked, our knowledge of the practices of successful innovating firms produces some ready answers. In particular, many of the practices of Japanese technology-based firms appear to relate directly to our problem, without being in any way specific to a Japanese context (Ohmae, 1985; Imae *et al.*, 1984; Pascale and Athos, 1981; Rubinger 1985). Drawing on these practices – all of which are mentioned, though not generally emphasized, in the existing literature – as well as on our own research into the management of technology and design and the work of Souder and others on interdepartmental conflict, a list may be put together of eight ways in which conflict might be reduced, and the barriers to innovation lessened.

1. Group development programmes such as that proposed by Souder, in which the timing and extent of integration and retreat can be managed by development experts, have an obvious part to play.
2. Common socialization processes, and in particular common training programmes for marketing and R&D recruits, should serve both to strengthen the glue of an overriding corporate culture and to reduce conflict through the provision of shared experience.
3. The recruitment of science and engineering graduates to the marketing function, either directly or through a period in the R&D function, should help to overcome one of the major communication barriers between the two functions, and with it a large element of mistrust and suspicion.
4. Job rotation programmes or similar schemes, if sufficiently widespread, should further strengthen interdepartmental understanding, both through shared experiences and through the building of personal linkages.
5. Strong social and recreational programmes have a part to play not

only in enhancing corporate belonging but also in encouraging personal cross-functional links.

6. Common status and reward systems should also remove a major source of conflict. For an organization starting with a mixture of systems (by research ability, management ability, seniority, market shortage, etc.), this will inevitably entail costs as some groups are paid over the previous 'going rate', and may also entail some staff losses. But the costs should be mitigated by improvements in quality- and should be substantially outweighed by the benefits. Moreover, since reward systems provide one of the most visible demonstrations of the values of the organization the careful management of relative rewards should anyway be a top organizational priority.

7. Of crucial importance, but rarely discussed, is the role played by the design function. In some firms the presence of a design department serves merely to complicate the political situation, while in others it is virtually an irrelevance, ignored so far as possible by both marketing and R&D (Hendry and Dumas, 1988). But given the appropriate authority it can play an important co-ordinating role, and indeed must do so if the product design process is to be successful. An autonomous design department, independent of the marketing function and with sufficient internal authority not to be ignored by that function can serve both to improve end-product design and to speed up and facilitate the collaborative new product development process. This is also an area in which external consultants can be used to good effect, their freedom from the organizational structure allowing them to create communication channels and bonds between the different functions.

8. More ambitiously, but not necessarily impracticably so, a range of specific training and organizational development programmes might be used to change the very nature of the functions themselves, and particularly of the marketing function.

There is nothing radically new in these suggestions. All are already implemented to some extent in some firms, in the West as well as in Japan. The Japanese education system does simplify the recruitment of scientifically trained marketing and operations staff and the use of the R&D function as a staff resource pool on which other functions can draw. But there is nothing in principle to prevent Western corporations from adopting similar policies.

What all this points to is a form of organization that is marketing centred, but is nevertheless technologically literate, and more specifically design-literate, through and through. Picking up on point (8) above, this suggess a new role for the marketing function. In a recent paper, Miles and Snow (1986) claim to identify the emergence of a new form of organizational structure designed to cope with the increasingly competitive and rapidly changing markets and technologies characteristic of the present era. These 'dynamic networks' are characterized by vertical disaggregation, with market mechanisms and full information-disclosure systems taking the place of the close linkages and trust characteristic of more traditional organizatioanl forms: a move from heirarchies to internal markets. The key figures in these structures are 'brokers', dealing as in a market place with the four separate constituencies of suppliers, producers, designers and distributors.

How representative, and indeed how desirable, this model is is open to question, but it does provide a provocative extreme representation of an organization in which interfunctional linkages and trust cannot be relied upon, as is often the case in the technology-based firm. And it prompts the question: who are the brokers? They can only be the marketing function, and if that function is to play the central role in a disaggregated organization, it should perhaps do so also in the more closely knit firm to which we are aspiring here. Several writers have recently argued strongly for an internal as well as an external role for the marketing function (Leonard-Barton and Kraus, 1985; Simmonds, 1986), and such a role would provide a natural organizational setting for that most crucial of ingredients for innovation success, the product champion. It would seem in many respects to be precisely what is needed for the management of innovation.

As has already been noted, there are many advocates of a marketing-led approach to innovation, but these generally assume a traditional externally oriented marketing function using its knowledge of the external market to specify development targets. An internal marketing role implies a knowledge of the interior of the organization, including the R&D and operating functions, equal to that of the external environment. It implies, in particular, a detailed knowledge of the technological capabilities, preferences and trajectories existing in the organization, as well as of their cultural settings and political structuring. This in turn would require radically new forms of training and avenues of recruitment for marketing personnel. If the function is properly to exercise the powers it is being afforded in contemporary organizations, however, such changes may well be necessary.

References

Aram, J.D. and Javian, S. (1973) 'Correlates of success for customer-initiated R&D projects', *IEEE Transactions in Engineering Management* EM20(4): 108–13.

Backus, J. (1984) 'In research, failure is the partner of success', *Research Management* 27(4): 26–9.

Bonnet, D.C.L. (1986) 'Nature of the R&D/marketing co-operation: the design of technologically advanced new industrial products', *R&D Management* 16: 117–26.

Burgelman, R.A. (1983) 'A process model of internal corporate venturing in the diversified major firm', *Administrative Science Quarterly* 28: 223–44.

Chakrabarti, A.D. (1974) 'The role of champions', *Calfornia Management Review* 17(2): 58–62.

Clifford, D.K., Jr, and Cavanagh, R.E. (1985) *The Winning Performance. How America's High-Growth Midsize Companies Succeed*, Sidgwick and Jackson.

Cooper, R.G. (1975) 'Why new industrial products fail', *Industrial Marketing Management* 4: 315–26.

Cooper, R.G. and Kleinschmidt, E.J. (1987) 'What makes a new product a winner: success factors at the project level', *R&D Management* 17: 175–90

Dessauer, J.H. (1971) *My Years with Xerox, The Billions Nobody Wanted*, New York: Doubleday.

Dumas, A. (1988) 'Attitudes to design in British and American companies', forthoming working paper, Design Management Unit, London Business School.

Fahey, L. (1981) 'On strategic management decision processes', *Strategic Management Journal*, 2: 43–60.

Farrell, D. and Petersen, J.C. (1982) 'Patterns of political behavior in organizations', *Academy of Management Review*, 7: 403–12.

Freeman, C. (1984) *The Economics of Industrial Innovation* 2nd edn.

Frost, P.J. *et al.* (eds) (1985) *Organizational Culture*, Beverly Hills: Sage.

Georghiou, L., Gibbons, M., and Metcalfe, J.S. (1986) 'Staying the distance: technological development and competition', *International Journal of Technology Management* 1: 425–38.

Graham, M. (1986) *RCA and the Videodisc*, Cambridge: Cambridge University Press.

Gray, B. and Ariss, S.S. (1985) 'Politics and strategic change across organizational life cycles', *Academy of Management Review*, 10: 707–23.

Greiner, L.E. (1986) 'Top management politics and organizational change', in S. Srivastva *et al.* (eds.) *Executive Power: How Executives Influence People and Organizations*, San Francisco: Jossey Bass.

Gupta, A.K. *et al.* (1985) 'The R&D-marketing interface in high technology firms', *Journal of Product Innovation Management* 2(1): 12–24.

Gupta, A.K. and Wilemon, D. (1988) 'The credibility-competence connection at the R&D-marketing interface', *Journal of Product Innovation Management* 5: 20–31.

Guth, W.D. and MacMillan, I.C. (1986) 'Strategy implementation versus middle management self-interest', *Strategic Management Journal* 7: 313–28.

Hambrick, D.C. (1981) 'Environment, strategy and power within top management teams', *Administrative Science Quarterly* 26: 253–76,

Hendry, J. (1989) 'Technological decision making in its organizational context: nuclear power reactor development in Britain', Cranfield School of Management working paper, forthcoming.

Hendry, J. (1989) 'The political anatomy of decision making', working paper, Cranfield School of Management.

Hendry, J. and Dumas, A. (1989) 'What do you do with an industrial designer', Cranfield School of Management working paper SWP 25/89.

Hickson, D.J. *et al.* (1986) *Top Decisions: Strategic Decision Making in Organizations*, Oxford: Basil Blackwell.

Hopkins, D.S. (1975) 'The roles of project teams and venture groups in new product development', *Research Management* 18: 7–12.

Imae, K., Nonaka, I., and Takeuchi, H. (1984) 'Managing the new product development process: how Japanese companies learn and unlearn', Hitotsubashi University Discussion paper no. 118.

Jemison, D.B. (1981) 'Organizational versus environmental sources of influence in strategic decision-making', *Strategic Management Journal*, 2: 77–89.

Jemison, D.B. (1984) 'The importance of boundary spanning roles in strategic decision making', *Journal of Management Studies* 21: 131–52.

Johnson, G. (1987) *Strategic Change and the Management Process*, Oxford: Basil Blackwell.

Kotter, J.P. (1986) 'Why power and influence are at the very core of executive work', in S. Srivastva *et al.* (eds) *Executives Power: How Executives Influence People and Organizations*, San Francisco: Jossey Bass.

LaPorte, T.A. (1967) 'Conditions of strain and accommodation in industrial research organizations', *Administrative Science Quarterly* 12(2): 21–38.

Lawrence, P.R. and Lorsch, J.W. (1967) 'Differentiation and integration in complex organizations', *Administrative Science Quarterly* 12: 1–47.

Lawrence, P.R. and Lorsch, J.W. (1967) *Organization and Environment: Managing Differentiation and Integration*, (Harvard Business School.

Leonard-Barton, D. and Kraus, W.A. (1985) 'Implementing new technology', *Harvard Business Review*, Nov.–Dec. 102–10.

Little, B. (1979) 'New technology and the role of marketing', in M.J. Baker, *Industrial Innovation*, London: Macmillan 258–65.

Little, D.A. and Sweeting, R.C. (1984) 'Business innovation in the UK', *R&D Management* 14: 1–10.

Litvak, I.A. and Maule, C.J. (1972) 'Managing the entrepreneurial enterprise', *Business Quarterly* 37: 47.

Maidique, M.A. (1980) 'Entrepreneurs, champions and technological innovation', *Sloan Management Review* 21(2): 59–76.

Mansfield, E. *et al.* (1971) *Research and Innovation in the Modern Corporation*, New York: Norton.

Mansfield, E. and Wagner, S. (1975) 'Organizational and strategic factors associated with probabilities of success in industrial R&D', *Journal of Business* 48: 179–98.

Marquis, D. (1976) 'The anatomy of successful innovations', in R.R. Rothberg (ed.), Corporate Strategy and Product Innovation, New York: Free Press.

Miles, R.E. and Snow, C.C. (1986) Network organizations: new concepts for new forms', *Calfornia Management Review* 28(3): 62–73.

Mintzberg, H. (1985) 'The organization as a political arena', *Journal of Management Studies*, 22: 133–54.

Mintzberg, H. (1987) 'Crafting strategy', *Harvard Business Review*, July–Aug. 66–77.

Mintzberg, H. and McHugh, A. (1985) 'Strategy formation in an adhocracy', *Administrative Science Quarterly*. 30: 160–97.

Mumford, E. and Pettigrew, A. (1975) *Implementing Strategic Decisions*, London: Longman.

Narayonan, V.K. and Fahey, L. (1982) 'The micro-politics of strategy formulation', *Academy of Management Review* 7: 25–34.

Nielsen, E.H. and Rao, M.V.H. (1987) 'The strategy-legitimacy nexus: a thick description', *Academy of Management Review* 12: 523–33.

Ohmae, K. (1985) 'Managing innovation and new products in key Japanese industries', *Research Management* 28(4): 11–18.

Pascale, R. and Athos, A. (1981) *The Art of Japanese Management*, New York: Simon and Schuster.

Peters, T. and Waterman, R. (1982) *In Search of Excellence: Lessons from America's Best-Run Companies* London: Harper and Row.

Peters, T. and Austin, N. (1985) *A Passion for Excellence*, London: Collins.

Pettigrew, A.M. (1985) *The Awakening Giant: Continuity and Change in ICI*, Oxford: Basil Blackwell.

Pettigrew, A.M. (1973) *The Politics of Organizational Decision Making*, London: Tavistock.

Pfeffer, J. (1981) *Power in Organizations* London: Pitman.

Pfeffer, J. and Salancik, G.R. (1974) 'Organizational decision making as a political process: the case of a university budget', *Administrative Science Quarterly* 19:K 135–51.

Quinn, J.B. (1979) 'Technological innovation, entrepreneurship and strategy', *Sloan Management Review* 20(3): 19–30.

Quinn, J.B. (1985) 'Managing innovation: controlled chaos', *Harvard Business Review*, May–June: 73–84.

Quinn, J.B. and Mueller, J.A. (1963) 'Transferring research results to operations', *Harvard Business Review* 41: 49–66.

Quinn, R.E. and McGrath, M.R. (1985) 'The transformation of organizational cultures. A competing values perspective', in P.J. Frost *et al*, (eds) *Organizational Culture*, Beverly Hills: Sage.

Roberts, E.B. (1968) 'A basic study of innovators: how to keep and capitalize on their talents', *Research Management* July: 249–66.

Roberts, E.B. (1980) 'New ventures for corporate growth', *Harvard Business Review*, 58: 134–42.

Rothwell, R. *et al* (1974) 'Sappho updated', *Research Policy* 3: 259–91.

Rubinger, B. (1985) 'Technology policy in Japanese firms: decision making, suppliers links and technical goals', *Technology in Society* 7: 281–96.

Rubinstein, A.H. *et al.* (1976) 'Factors influencing innovation success at the project level', *Research Management* 19(3): 33–7.

Schon, D.A. (1963) 'Champions for radical new inventions', *Harvard Business Review* 41 (March–April): 77–86.

Seiler, J.A. (1963) Diagnosing interdepartmental conflict' *Harvard Business Review* 41 (September–October): 121–32.

Simmonds, K. (1986) 'Marketing as innovation. The eighth paradigm', *Journal of Management Studies* 23: 479–500.

Souder, W.E. (1977) 'Effectiveness of nominal and interacting group decision processes for integrating R&D and marketing', *Management Science* 23: 595–605.

Souder, W.E. (1987) *Managing New Product Innovations* Lexington.

Souder, W.E. (1988) 'Managing relations between R&D and marketing in new product development projects', *Journal of Product Innovation Management* 5: 6–19.

Srivastva, S. *et al.* (eds) (1986) *Executive Power: How Executives Influence People and Organizations* San Francisco: Jossey Bass.

Tauber, E.M. (1974) 'How market research discourages major innovations', *Business Horizons* 17: 22–6.

Tauber, E.M. (1975) 'Why concept and product tests fail to produce new product results', *Journal of Marketing* 39(4): 69–74.

Utterback, J. (1971) 'The process of technological innovation within the firm' *Academy of Management Journal* March: 75–88.

Utterback, J. (1974) 'Innovation in industry and the diffusion of technology', *Science* 183: 620–626.

von Hippel, E. (1976) 'The dominant role of the user in semi-conductor and electronic sub-assembly process innovation', *Research Policy* 5: 212–39.

von Hippel, E. (1978) 'Successful industrial products from customer ideas', *Journal of Marketing* (January): 39–49.

von Hippel, E. (1982) 'Get new products from customers', *Harvard Business Review*, (March-April): 117.

Voss, C.A. (1984) 'Technology-push and need-pull: a new perspective', *R&D Management* 14: 157–1.

Walton, R.E. and Dutton, J.M. (1969) 'Organizational context and interdepartmental conflict', *Administrative Science Quarterly* 14: 522–42.

Walton, R.E. and Dutton, J.M. (1969) 'The management of inter-departmental conflict: a model and review', *Administrative Science Quarterly* 14: 73–84.

Welsh, M.A. and Slusher, E.A. (1986) 'Organization design as a context for political activity', *Administrative Science Quarterly* 31: 389–402.

Wilson, D.C. (1982) 'Electricity and resistance: a case study of innovation and politics', *Organization Studies* 3: 119–40.

Chapter eight

Technological change and strategic management: technological transilience and the British automotive components sector

K.J. Clarke

Introduction

The significance of technology and technological change for the strategic position and performance of the firm is increasingly recognized in the literature on both strategy and technological change. Understanding of the mechanisms and processes involved in the interaction between the two is however less well developed. Kantrow (1980) argued that the strategy–technology link needed to be directly researched, and considerations of technology more deeply embedded in the strategy formulation process to enable more effective strategic responses to technological change by managers and firms.

When new or novel technologies confront the firm the range of possible reactions is large and the process by which the firm reacts complex. Cooper and Schendel (1976) pointed out, from a study which covered a range of industries, that firms by no means automatically embrace new technologies, nor in many cases do they effectively exploit their technologies. They suggest a range of possible reactions by the firm which vary from reinforcing the old technology through doing nothing to embracing the new technology. However, little attention has been given to the specific internal and external context of such a decision situation, particularly at the level of the firm. To do that we need to examine both the potential impact that a significant innovation might have for the firm and examine how that potential becomes finally realized in a specific firm setting. Abernathy and Clark (1985) suggest that early work in this area focused on structural chracteristics such as firm size or on administrative practices on innovation. They argue that more recent work, their own included, has focused more directly on the role of innovations in shaping competitive environments and positions.

This chapter follows and builds on their work from a theoretical and empirical standpoint. In three main sections it examines this development from a conceptual standpoint and relates that to an analysis of four of the operating companies of an engineering group with major interests in the automotive components sector. The final section is a discussion of the issues that emerge from the exploration.

Technology and competitive impact – a conceptual framework

A seminal approach by Abernathy (1978) examined the way in which technological change had shaped the US automobile industry and competitive positions within it. He concluded that to understand technological change in this context the appropriate unit of analysis was the productive unit, that is the product line and the production process taken together. Such a unit shows a systematic development over time, in which in the early stages a fluid state of high product innovation, emphasis on product variety and maximizing product performance is coupled with flexible but inefficient production. Through a transition situation, which encompasses the emergence of a dominant product design (e.g. the internal combustion engine) and a switch to an emphasis on process innovation, the productive unit evolves toward a final specific state in which innovation is reduced and radical innovation rare, production systems are systematic and efficient, the emphasis is on cost reduction. Such a final state is described as technological maturity, at which point there is stability in the core technological concepts and often technologies are readily purchasable (Abernathy, Clark and Kantrow, 1983). This 'technology life cycle' is a powerful concept and has acted as the majo.· background for a number of further studies (Whipp and Clark, 1986; Debresson and Lampel, 1985).

It did not, however, provide an adequate description of the automobile industry as that developed in the 1970s. In later work (Abernathy *et al.* (1983) developed the concept of 'dematurity' implying that reversals along the evolutionary path of the productive unit were possible and likely. This development was in part a reaction to the implication that a final state such as maturity lulls the firm into a belief that all is well and unchanging. As Abernathy *et al.* put it: 'As so often happens with attractive schemes of explanation, what was originally intended as description assumes the status of prescription'.

Abernathy and his colleagues reframed the approach in a more significant way by adding an examination of the Japanese automobile industry on productivity and their relative success in penetrating US markets. They then develop the concept of 'transilience' to describe the impact of an innovation on the competitive structure of an industry and position of a firm.

Abernathy *et al.* (1983) and later Clark (1987) argue that an innovation can be assessed for its significance on two major axes. Those are its effects on production systems and its effects on market linkages. An innovation can be assessed on the extent to which it either (i) disrupts/creates or (ii) conserves/entrenches the firm's market linkages or production and operations competencies. Such competencies are the basis of the firms competitive advantage. The factors by which these axes are created is shown in Table 8.1 (taken from Clark, 1987). The first set cover the equipment, knowledge and organization associated with the design,

Table 8.1 Innovation and firm competence

Domain of innovative activity		Range of impact of innovation
I. *Technology/production*		
Design/embodiment of technology	Improves/perfects established design	→ Offers new design/ radical departure from past embodiment
Production systems/ organization	Strengthens existing structure	→ Makes existing structure obsolete; demands new system, procedures, organization
Skills (labour, managerial, technical)	Extends viability of existing skills	→ Destroys value of existing expertise
Materials supplier relations	Reinforces application of current materials/suppliers	→ Extensive material substitution: opening new relations with new vendors
Capital equipment	Extends existing capital	→ Extensive replacement of existing capital with new types of equipment
Knowledge and experience base	Builds on and reinforces applicability of existing knowledge	→ Establishes links to whole new scientific discipline/ destroys value of existing knowledge base
II. *Market customer*		
Relationship with customer base	Strengthens ties with established group	→ Attracts extensive new customer group/creates new market
Customer applications	Improves service in established application	→ Creates new set of applications/new set of customer needs
Channels of distribution and service	Builds on and enhances the effectiveness of established distribution network/service organization	→ Requires new channels of distribution/new service, after market support
Customer knowledge	Uses and extends customer knowledge and experience in established product	→ Intensive new knowledge demand of customer; destroys value of customer experience
Modes of customer communication	Reinforces existing modes/ methods of communication	→ Totally new modes of communication required (such as, field sales engineers)

Source: Clark 1987: 59–81.

111

production and materials competencies of the firm. The second set cover the marketing operations, customer linkages and customer abilities and how those relate to the firms competencies. Transilience is the term given to the overall impact of the innovation. Transilience then is the capacity of an innovation to influence production systems *and* market linkages (Abernathy *et al.*, 1983), its capacity to influence the firm's existing resources, skills and knowledge (Abernathy and Clark, 1985; Clark, 1987). Such a transilience map of the impact of an innovation is shown in Figure 8.1.

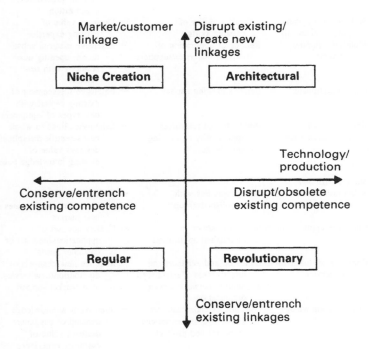

Figure 8.1 Transilience map (1)

Abernathy and Clark argue that the separation of the impact into market effects and technology/production effects allows a description of the different phases and characteristics of industry and firms' innovatory patterns. Innovations which are disruptive on both axes are those in which the industry Architecture (Figure 8.1) is created or developed. Here basic production and market parameters are developed and the shape of many subsequent tehcnological issues and directions emerge. The low impact of, probably incremental, innovation on both axes represents the Regular phase of innovation in the bottom left of the map. Although the impact of individual incremental innovations may not be great, the cumulative effect of many innovations over time can be substantial on say productivity, whilst the overall effect is to entrench market linkages and production competencies. Innovations which offer or exploit new market opportunities but have little effect on production systems are Niche Creation. Here opportunities develop or are created which are met largely within the existing, stable production and design competencies of the firm. Innovations which disrupt productive systems and competence but are applied to existing markets and customers are labelled Revolutionary. Here new designs, materials and production competences develop, perhaps from the push of technology. Such shifts have little immediate impact on market linkages but may be an important source of competitive advantage over time.

The transilience framework was used by Abernathy and Clark to re-examine the development of the US automobile industry. They use it to map industry changes, for example the Model T is evaluated as an architectural innovation, the closed steel body as revolutionary, sports cars such as the Mustang as niche creation, and electric starters as regular. They also develop a map of innovations for the Chrysler organization which they argue illustrates how, in the 1930s, the firm made significant revolutionary innovations to compete successfully against Ford but, in the 1940s, lost ground as it confined itself to regular innovations (Abernathy and Clark, 1985). Clark (1987) uses the framework to evaluate the competitive significance of innovations in the steel industry and develops the approach to emphasize the managerial and competitive differences each mode of innovation implies. Whipp and Clark (1986) use a modified approach in which they argue that the UK automobile industry developed in a different pattern to that of the US, the latter shifting from Architectural to Regular from 1910 to the 1970s then shifting toward the revolutionary in the 1980s, whilst the former maintained higher levels of market ferment through to the 1970s before a revolutionary shift in the 1980s.

The concept of transilience and the mapping of the impact of innovations offers a useful route to evaluate the potential impact of innovations on industries and specific firms. In contrast to the approach which relies on the life cycle and maturity concepts it implies no 'end state' for technological change but emphasizes its continuing potential impact at many times and places. The reduced emphasis on time as the core driving concept in the evaluation of technology change is useful to the extent that no mature 'backwater hiding places' can be inferred from such an analysis of technological change. The shift to an emphasis on unravelling the impact of technology in a somewhat more complex way aids the analysis of its competitive effects.

The empirical study

The work described here is of an investigation into the cases of four of the operating businesses of a large engineering group, principally in the automotive components industry, and how the senior managers of the businesses perceived and coped with technological changes in their business.

The cases are based on interviews with fourteen senior managers (including the Managing Directors) from four of the companies operating businesses. They were interviewed for about two hours each in a semi-structured format to elicit views on the technological development of the industry context, and on the technology-related elements of the strategy that had been pursued, both for the content of the strategy and the processes which had influenced its formation. The research reported here is part of an on-going research study so the results here are the partial results of this work.

The group as a whole has a range of interests but those in the automotive components sector are dominant in the firm's financial well-being. Like much of the industry the early 1980s were traumatic, both for the level of activity and for the specific rundown of the British car industry in the form of Austin-Rover. The firm has enjoyed a high reputation for engineering and has, in its longer-term development, achieved generally successful transformations in the face of changing markets and technologies.

This section of the paper discusses each of the specific cases investigated and evaluates them from two standpoints. The first is how the case can be considered on the transilience map outlined earlier. The second is the factors that led to the realization in practice of the positions and the transitions implied by the analysis. The final section of the paper surveys the lessons to be drawn from the cases.

Case A

Case A is of a business that is concerned with high-precision fuel-injection equipment, principally diesel fuel equipment for the agriculture and

commercial vehicle market. The product is sophisticated and specialized, entry by others using existing technology is unlikely. Much
technological change is currently focused on changes in the management
of the manufacturing system, though such changes are not changing the
basic manufacturing processes involved. Product development is related
to the engine development needs of the engine manufacturers, product
developments are incorporated at such times as engine development takes
place and is strongly temporally linked to engine development. Such
development has led to greater variety in the product line than was
expected and planned for several years ago. In development of new products, new incremental improvements may be incorporated which achieve
a temporary advantage in supplying that manufacturer. Such advantages
are, however, only transient and temporary. The new products features
are quickly learned by others and emulated, often through a process of
reverse engineering. There is considerable professional openness between
the technologists of competing firms, and some of the competition's
developments can be inferred from the developments and buying effects
of the machine industry which commonly supplies most competing firms
and on whom some of the basic technological skills rest. Attempts by
this firm to develop products for substantially new market niches which
have developed rapidly in the last decade have met with limited success.
They attempted a marginal modification of their existing product that
proved less capable than Bosch, the major continental competitor, who
went through a process involving closer co-operation with a significant
customer. Currently under development is a product incorporating a
substantial amount of electronics, but there is no clear agreement that
this represents a new product for the business. The expectation is that
developments by anyone in the industry along these lines are unlikely
to lead to a permanent or sustainable competitive advantage. Such a
development would be additive rather then disruptive to the bulk of the
existing production skills. Engineering interests are seen to prevail in
many of the decision situations facing the firm, the function is strong
and represents the linking function with the wider organization and the
outside world for this business. Marketing as an activity is generally
underdeveloped.

Overall the pattern is one of largely incremental changes to the
production system coupled to largely transient impacts on the marketing
linkages for the firm. The business could therefore be placed in position
A on Figure 8.2, with low transilience on production systems but some
on the marketing linkages.

This business' successes or problems in facing that position depend
on a number of factors. Substantial new market niches have been slight
and slow to develop in the British market, particularly when set against
their continental competitors. Product development is tightly coupled to

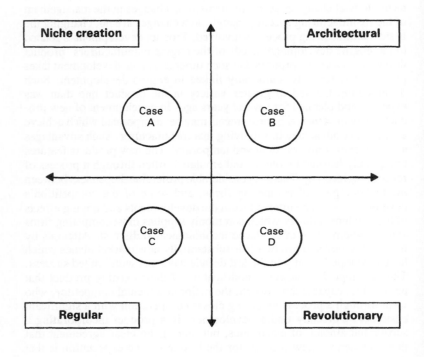

Figure 8.2 Transilience map (2)

that of engine manufacturers, the firm is to some extent dependent on them for evaluation of final user needs and expectations. The degree to which the problem of increasing product variety and reduced volume expectations was led by the customer is significant for this firm. Widespread direct emulation of incremental improvements, and some transfer of technology through machine suppliers means that windows for significant strategic technology advantage are few. The firm has become focused on production technology to the extent that far greater risks are perceived in product developments than in process developments, the latter being significantly easier to formulate and justify for the firm.

Case B

This business is built on the overall group skills in semiconductor technology which is allied to and particularly applied to the business' knowledge of engine fuel and ignition systems to produce electronic engine management systems. The business has now been developed as a distinct business activity and separated as a discrete productive unit. The knowledge and skills related to the application of semiconductors is, however, not seen as only applicable to the products produced by this business.

The application is small but expected to grow rapidly with the increasing use of semiconductors in automotive uses. Customer and user needs are by no means yet well defined for the products of this firm however, there remain a number of technological solutions to meet what are seen as customer and regulatory needs. This firm produced a significant breakthrough in the field which it protected with a patent now widely licensed in the industry. The firm now plans development of a technological breakthrough which would give it a strong position in future markets should it be successful. There are also a number of technologies which are cross licensed in the industry, a feature of new industries in which technologies are changing fairly rapidly. Technological development has also allowed the entry of new competitors who have developed significant strategic positions. Much of the basic technologies lie outside the automotive components industry hence there have been signs of entry by semiconductor manufacturers directly into the industry and the development of agreements and joint ventures between existing industry members and semiconductor suppliers. For this business the main source of these technologies is its own experience in them stretching back over many years. As a result many of the technologies now being developed are being developed by the firm themselves or by the group's central research and development facility. This business' use of this facility is among the heaviest in the group. In that way much of the current development is led by the firms, and groups, research and engineering activities.

This business, therefore, faces a poorly defined market at this stage of its development. Product design remains largely open and major design improvements could prove to be the source of significant competitive advantage. Whilst a number of production technologies are defined and in place many are not or are still the source of future development. This business can, therefore, be located for its transilience in area B on the transilience map in Figure 8.2.

The management of this business do not necessarily see the business as 'high tech', but it is seen as among the most-advanced technologically of the group of companies. On the whole a narrow view is taken of the market opportunities thrown up by technological change. This business does not see its role as developing external new product/markets or new market niches on the basis of the technologies it possesses outside the automotive field. It does, however, forsee the development of an internal market as the 'electronics house' for the group, in that way the technology ferment that might be directed externally is being redirected internally. The managers see possibilities for technological leadership but in this situation the ability to exploit that through market power would be limited. Car manufacturers are shy of single suppliers for these products at present (and market leadership lies with Bosch, the major continental competitor). Given the power car manufacturers possess over the component suppliers, the manufacturers are likely to act as a channel for the transfer of technology between suppliers. So, whilst the 'architecture' of the industry might still be partially open the ability to shape it through technological strength is limited: exploitation methods such as the 'Pilkington approach' are seen as more likely modes of development.

Case C

This case concerns a business which manufactures lighting, a significant component recently dominated in its manufacture by the styling and aerodynamic needs of the motor manufacturer. The business comprises in effect two productive units. In the one, signal lamps, technology is seen to have become mature and essentially uninteresting, though recent developments (not led by this firm) have opened up the possibilities of technological development. In the other, the main one considered here, the business has gone and is undergoing a number of significant developments.

In the early 1970s the product was regarded by the business as virtually completely standardized. The main design, a sealed beam unit, was manufactured in large volumes by a company set up as a joint venture with an electrical company. The product design had, however, never been extensively accepted in Europe and proved not to be flexible to the design needs of the car designers as they developed through the 1970s. The firm was faced in the early 1970s with the problem of being poor at the traditional method of manufacture (still largely in use with Continental manufacturers) and with an inflexible production unit for the emerging design needs. At that time the search for wholly new materials for the manufacture of the product started. At the same time new materials being investigated by the group research facility produced the possibility of a switch to plastic materials for the production of lighting. The new material made possible new designs for the product and required production methods that were completely different from the 'traditional' metal working techniques in use. The transilience of this development can therefore be located on Figure 8.2 in position C. The new production technologies produce significantly different designs for the product but do not require significantly different skills on the part of the customer. The transilience is based around new materials largely developed by the group research facility with the active co-operation of the suppliers of the basic plastics materials supplies. The design and manufacturing process is being actively licensed to other manufacturers. Competitors are, on the whole, more reluctant than this firm to switch to the use of plastic.

The development of the use of this material has however not significantly improved the competitive position of the business. The translation of the technologies from central research has been difficult and time consuming, only partially being solved by the transfer of personnel from the research activity into the operating unit. Customers, the car manufacturers, are regarded as conservative and prefering evolution to radical change. The car manufacturers, reluctant to be dependent on one source, have in effect been the pressure by which a transfer of technology has been made necessary. The customers will accept the new material but are reluctant to accept a mix of materials from different suppliers and have therefore pressured the firm into sharing its technology. This business feels that much of the net benefit to the innovation therefore does not accrue to them but to the car manufacturers. the new material has opened up possibilities of new product designs but other methods of lighting technology adopted by other manufacturers still offer sufficient scope for development. So the new material and designs from this company have not produced a significantly improved market position.

Case D

This is a business concerned with the supply of fuel injection equipment to the industrial engine market. The firm has essentially been following in the technological development of the industry, in the wake of a continental competitor who has in general been more successful at reading and adapting to customer needs. The business and the industry are all pursuing essentially the same underlying technology to meet customer needs but there is increasing difficulty pursuing this technological trajectory (for higher fuel pressures) which is producing more difficult design and material problems for the business. Managers speculate how far it is possible to pursue this technology as further minor advances are increasingly difficult to accommodate. Technological change on product design is incremental but this business has not been as successful as its major competitor at exploiting the market niches that develop with these incremental changes. The recent focus in the business is now on manufacturing management technologies, substantial product redesign and the incorporation of electronics into the product has been slowed in the interests of ensuring that existing product and production technologies are well understood and exploited.

The pattern here then is one of largely incremental development in production systems coupled with a limited development of market opportunities; at least historically. Such opportunities do exist, however, and have been more successfully exploited by competitors. The pressures from customers on the industry for engine economy and performance have been pursued by all industry competitors along a largely common technological path. This business can be placed in position D on Figure 8.2, that of 'regular' transilience.

The reasons for difficulties experienced in exploiting niche possibilities by this firm are not singular but may lie in fields. Niche development relies on customer contact and customer attitudes to innovation. This firm has not been well served by strong links with British customers through what one manager described as a 'cosy' relationship with an ailing industry. Exploiting niche opportunities requires good market understanding coupled with effective manufacturing. The emphasis in this firm has, however, been strongly on manufacturing to the point where it is seen as much easier to justify expenditure on production process improvements than it is on marketing activities, both at the level of the business and to the wider group. In the words of one manager 'we lost sight of the market'.

Discussion

This discussion is divided into three broad themes. The first is the development and use of the transilience map and the way it can be applied to the cases here. The second is the issues that arise from these cases in applying that usage. The third briefly notes some methodological issues.

Transilience mapping

In discussing each case we evaluated, albeit qualitatively, the overall position of each case on the transilience map. Any firm or productive unit is made up of a large number of linked and clustered technologies. Therefore our attempt to understand the impact of innovations on that overall cluster must carry the caveat of some generalizations. We can assert, however, that the prevailing patterns of innovation do provide an adequate basis for locating the firm, at the time of the case, on the map.

The transilience map provides a basis for unbundling the firm and the prevailing innovatory pattern on more than a simple product/

process basis. The map provides a useful basis for understanding the competitive impact that innovations might have in a variety of ways. In comparison the product/process basis offers too high a degree of aggregation of technology development, and gives little direct analysis of the specific competitive impact of technological change. The transilience map adds to the contribution of the technology life-cyle approach important factors by which we can better assess the impact of innovations, particularly in a 'post-maturity' situation.

The transilience map has indicated that within a group of businesses, ostensibly in the same industry, great variety exists in the businesses transilience map position, and that technological change has widely differing effects on different businesses. This stands in contrast to the view that technological shifts, often given very broad characterization such as the mechanical to electronic shift, have equally broad similarity in their impact. The transilience map offers a partial route to evaluating multi-product, multi-technology situations facing business groups where the individual business situation is defined as much by existing market expectations as it is by the development of new technologies.

Each of the quadrants on the transilience map is likely to have differing management needs for its successful management. The architectural position may require the entrepreneurial approach whereas the regular position implies that, since innovation is incremental and relatively non-disruptive, a degree of uncoupling of functional tasks can be tolerated. In the niche creation area such uncoupling is likely to be counter-productive. Here good sensitivity to market needs must be quickly and effectively transmitted to production systems so as to exploit the potentially short-term benefits that technological innovations produce.

Transilience — the realization in practice

The transilience approach as it is formulated here has limitations. It does not of itself suggest how the impact of an innovation can be gauged when the question of the specific firms existing competences is raised. The extent to which the existing competences, attitudes and routines limit the business' ability to achieve the transitions and transformations implied by movements across the transilience map is not directly addressed by the approach. This must be addressed in a wider context. In practice many of the implications of the transilience position were not realized and the benefits and advantages were only partially fulfilled. The discussion of the issues this raises can be divided roughly into those which relate to the external context of the businesses and those which relate to the internal context.

For the former it is clear that many factors in the environment of these firms act as a limit or brake on the appropriation of the benefits that

121

might have accrued to them. There are strong temporal effects wherein the manufacturers of vehicles operate over design cycles which limit the windows of opportunity for component suppliers. Such cycles are, however, much the same facing all competitors so the differential effect of these is likely to be slight. Their effect will be magnified, however, if part of the cycle for the component supplier is spent on gaining access rather than nurturing an existing relationship.

In this particular industry the attitudes and policies of the customer have had a significant effect on innovatory outcomes for the businesses examined here. The buying policies of the automobile manufacturers have been responsible for the spread of technology between component manufacturers, with the result that the firm's abilities to exploit market niches has been limited. This has raised the question for some of the firms here as to where the benefits of innovation finally appear.

Positions on the right hand side of the transilience map, occupied by firms B and C, are more likely to be sustained by external sources of exogenous technology. This is borne out to the extent that these firms made far greater demands on the central group research facilities. Such a situation requires considerable skills in transferring technologies from the development to the applied commercial stage. The evidence is that this has been a source of considerable difficulty for both these businesses, in case B for development of product technologies, in case C for novel production technologies.

The internal context of these firms is clearly significant in the ease or difficulty they experience in managing or changing their position to match an innovations transilience. In developing the argument outlined in the opening discussion above, Abernathy *et al.* (1983) argued that part of the reason for the relative success of the Japanese automobile manufacturers was their use of an effective 'paradigm for production'. They argue that this paradigm lies only partially in the field of applying new technologies but more substantially in the way automobile production is managed. The failure of the US industry lay partly in the failure to adopt and maintain an appropriate manufacturing paradigm. They later argue for a renaissance of American manufacturing based on a new paradigm. However, such a transition is unlikely to be easy. Whipp and Clark (1986) in their study of the Rover SD1 project suggest that such a change is more than simply assuming a rescripting by the corporate centre; such a change involves substantial relearning and performance of the new script. In another study Clark and Windebank (1985) argue that, in the French context, the pursuit of efficiency at Renault in the 1950s made later re-adaptation in the 1960s and 1970s more difficult for the company. When radical innovations appear the ability of existing companies to respond successfully will be directly related to their technological competencies and the degree to which those are destroyed or disrupted (Tushman and Anderson, 1986)

Managers in the firms described and studied here have not yet fully comprehended or practised the paradigm shift that is implied by their position. For example, firms in which the prevailing mode for success is the use of technological innovations to develop and maintain niches the need is to develop and manage the robust productive unit (Clark and Starkey, 1988; Rothwell and Gardiner, 1988). Such a productive unit, where the volume/variety tradeoff has been largely eliminated or avoided in design, has only partially been achieved and has not been matched by the marketing reorientation necessary to manage innovation successfully in the niche creation setting. Such a unit needs to be capable of stretch and flexibility for both robust designs and robust production systems.

The nature of managerial paradigms or frames of reference has been explored in several ways. From a managerial perspective Spender (1983) develops the notion of industry-wide recipes of 'shared patterns of judgement'. Johnson (1988), in contrasting the organization action approach with that of a rational approach to strategy, argues that paradigms become taken for granted, not seen as problematic, and therefore difficult to surface and change. From a more directly technological standpoint Dosi (1982) uses the concept of paradigm to explore developments in the semiconductor industry. He defines a technological paradigm as a model or pattern of solution of selected technological problems, based on selected principles derived from sciences, and on selected material technologies. The paradigm then sets the pattern for technical progress; this progress defines a technological trajectory (Nelson and Winter, 1982). Nelson and Winter (1982) also develop the concept of 'routine' in explaining firms adaptation (or lack of it) and add 'firms may be expected to behave in the future according to the routines they have employed in the past'. The firms examined here do show evidence that such routines do prevail and persist.

Dominating frameworks will be a function not just of the beliefs of individual managers or groups but of how those become articulated in the political forces within the firm. Miles and Snow (1978) suggested that firms could be grouped into Prospectors, Defenders, Analysers and Reactors according to their adaptive process. The dominant coalition in defenders comprises production and finance interests; in prospectors it is marketing and R&D; in analysers it is marketing, applied research and production; reactors show inconsistent and unstable patterns. So in order to evaluate the approach and response to strategic technological innovation an attempt must be made to pattern the prevailing paradigms, interests and their influence on the innovation 'design space' (Whipp and Clark, 1986).

Much of that design space has been occupied in the case of these firms by engineering and closely related functions. Much of the technological co-ordination is carried out by this function. The recent emergence and strength of manufacturing efficiency as a central focus for these firms has benefit only for some aspects of an appropriate new paradigm for the firms, given their transilience positions.

Clearly management of different positions on the map will require different managerial skills and organization (Clark, 1987). In each situation innovation produces qualitatively different issues for management attention and requires different skills for coping with the uncertainty produced. Williams (1983) argues that in the context of the development of the technology life-cycle model that risk and uncertainty shifts from what is to be produced to how it is to be produced. Risk, both as to the uncertainty and value of innovatory activity, will be specific to the transilience effect of a major innovation (Clark, 1987). In the architectural and niche-creation areas market uncertainty and evolution is unclear; in the architectural and revolutionary areas production technology is an area of uncertainty and risk.

The overall attitude to risk among the firms and managers studied here is that process risk and uncertainty is understood and evaluated; market risk and uncertainty is seen but not well articulated and understood. Such a condition is indicative of the regular transilience position. The strong emphasis on manufacturing changes supports this view as does the prevailing view of the powerful position achieved by the engineering function. These are most strongly developed in cases A, C and D.

A methodology note

This discussion concludes with some comments and concerns on the transilience mapping 'methodology'. It is clear that the scale on which transilience is mapped are complex and at this stage largely qualitative. It is by no means obvious how we might evaluate and weight shifts in the changes required in customer knowledge as a result of innovation against, for example, the degree of raw material change in manufacture and changes in vendor patterns. Such problems do not, however, detract from the essential unbundling and evaluation that the approach implies and develops. The mapping process can continue alongside some development of the map grids! At this stage further refinement of the qualitative meaning and significance of the various factors might be a fruitful source of investigation.

Tracing the influence of paradigms is equally exacting. The approach here offers perhaps a route whereby work which has attempted to trace paradigms using an essentially scientific or technological route, such as in the work of Dosi (1982), can be better combined with work which has traced managerial paradigms from a notably marketing or financial perspective (Johnson, 1987; Spender, 1983).

Summary and conclusion

The transilience framwork was originally developed to evaluate and analyse past innovations and innovating patterns. This chapter has argued that it also offers a useful route for the analysis of the situation and decisions confronting managers and firms as innovators. It does, however, need to be combined with a critical examination of the competences and attitudes at work within a specific context to best understand how the potential transilience impact and competitive advantage offered by technological innovation finally comes to fruition.

References

Abernathy, W.J. (1978) *The Productivity Dilemma: Roadblock to Innovation in the Automobile Industry*, Baltimore; Johns Hopkins University Press.

Abernathy, W.J., Clark, K.B., and Kantrow, A.M. (1983) *Industrial Renaissance: Producing a Competitive Future for America*, New York: Basic Books.

Abernathy, W.J. and Clark, K.B. (1985) 'Innovation: Mapping the winds of creative destruction', *Research Policy* 14: 3–22.

Clark, K. (1987) 'Investment in new technology and competitive advantage', in D. Teece (ed.) *The Competitive Challenge*, Cambridge, Mass.: Ballinger, pp. 59–81.

Clark, P.A. and Windebank, J. (1985) 'Innovation and Renault 1900–1982: Product, Process and Work Organisation', ESRC Work Organisation Research Centre Working Paper Series No. 13, Aston University.

Clark, P. and Starkey, K. (1988) *Organisation Transitions and Innovation-Design*, London: Pinter.

Cooper, A.C. and Schendel, D. (1976) 'Strategic responses to technological threats', *Business Horizons* February 61–79,

Debresson, C. and Lampel, J. (1985) 'Beyond the life cycle: organisational and technological design. I. An alternative perspective', *Journal of Product Innovation Management* 3: 170–87

Dosi, G. (1982) 'Technological paradigms and technological trajectories: a suggested interpretation of the determinants and directions of technological change', *Research Policy* 11: 147–62.

Johnson, G. (1988) 'Rethinking Incrementalism', *Strategic Management Journal*, 9: 75–91.

Kantrow, A.M. (1980) 'The strategy technology connection', *Harvard Business Review*, July–August.

Miles, R.E. and Snow, C.C. (1978) *Organisational Strategy, Structure and Process*, New York: McGraw-Hill.

Nelson, R.R. and Winter, S.G. (1982) *An Evolutionary Theory of Economic Change*, Cambridge, MA: Harvard University Press.

Rothwell, R. and Gardiner, P. (1988) 'The strategic management of re-innovation', Paper to the State of the Art in R&D Management Conference, Manchester Business School, 11–13 July.

Spender, J.C. (1983) 'The business policy problem and industry recipes', in R.B. Lamb (ed.) *Advances in Strategic Management*, vol. 2, Greenwich, Conn: JAI Press 211–29.

Teece, D. (ed.) (1987) *The Competitive Challenge*, Cambridge Ma: Ballinger.

Tushman, M.L. and Anderson, P. (1986) 'Technological discontinuities and organisation environments', *Administrative Science Quarterly* 31: 439–65.

Whipp, R. and Clark, P. (1986) *Innovation and the Auto Industry: Product, Process and Work Organisation*, London: Pinter.

Williams, J.R. (1983) 'Technological evolution and competitive response', *Strategic Management Journal* 4: 55–65.

Chapter nine

The implications of electronic point-of-sale technology on the marketing/operations interface in UK retailing

J.E. Lynch

Introduction

It has become an analytical cliche to refer to the increasing pace and complexity of twentieth century change and to the subsequent turbulence in the operating environment. Nonetheless, in many major business sectors, change (particularly technological change) is the major issue confronting management. This is nowhere better exemplified than in the UK retail sector where the rapid diffusion of Electronic Point of Sale technology (EPOS) is already producing important impacts not only for retailers themselves but for the whole of the supply chain. This article considers the EPOS development in the context of the wider evolution of the UK retail market and examines its possible impacts on the operations management/marketing interface.

The UK retail sector

Greenley and Shipley's (1988) excellent overview of the literature on the UK retailing environment has pinpointed six major significant trends. These are shown in Table 9.1 and discussed below.

Table 9.1 Major trends in the UK retail environment

– Increased concentration
– Intensified competition
– Improved productivity
– Increased retailer power
– Growth of own-label
– Industry maturity

Adapted from Greenley and Shipley (1988).

Economists (Utton, 1970) and business analysts (Lidstone, 1977; Holmes, 1982) have frequently noted the tendency in developed markets towards increased industrial concentration. This tendency is fuelled by

127

many elements, including the desire for market dominance and its benefits and the impact of recession-led shake-outs of the weaker or less-efficient performers (Lynch and Jobber, 1986). Such a process of concentration can be seen at an advanced stage in UK retailing. Davies *et al.* (1984) have drawn attention to the growth of the large multiple chains and the consequent closure of large numbers of smaller independents. Davies *et al.* note that, in the retail sector as a whole, the number of outlets has dropped by 42,000 (− 11 per cent) since 1976 and that a trend towards large multiple dominance has produced increasing concentrations of trade. Akehurst (1983) similarly observed that, between 1970 and 1978, the share of overall retail trade held by the largest ten companies rose from 16.6 to 21.7 per cent. In the grocery sector, where most concentration has taken place, Burns (1983) calculated that the top ten retailers accounted for over 40 per cent of total sales by 1980. Van Mesdag (1988) estimated that this figure had advanced to almost 60 per cent by 1985. In the important London market, for example, it has been suggested that two chains (Tesco and Sainsbury) together possess a 53 per cent market share of all packaged goods sales (Thames Television, 1982).

This concentration trend is driven by and in its turn increases the intensity of retail competition. Hardly surprisingly, therefore, the UK retail sector is characterized by a movement towards ever-increasing levels of productivity (Livesey and Hall, 1981). The competitive dynamic has also been reflected in the increasing use of scale buying power by retailers to demand from their suppliers better margins, better service and greater promotional support (Caulkin, 1987). One further illustration of the competitive intensity in retailing can be found in the rise of retailer own-label products which are now estimated to account for around 25 per cent of all retail sales (Oddy, 1987). These products were initially introduced primarily to produce lower on-shelf prices but they are now increasingly being used by retailers to establish their own store-related brand franchise with consumers. This trend has serious implications for the suppliers of traditional branded goods who to some extent have seen their control of the branding weapon shift to the major retailers (Caulkin, 1987).

This scenario of fewer but larger retailers who are locked in an intensely competitive battle reflects a mature industry in which opportunities for competitive advantage are scarce and eagerly sought. It is the competitiveness of the retail arena which has generated the pressure to introduce EPOS technology – initially for improved productivity reasons but, increasingly, for the strategic benefits produced by superior information (Piercy, 1984). EPOS technology and its implications are discussed below.

EPOS technology

Although retailers have been using computer technology for some years

(Jones, 1985), it can be argued that the advent of EPOS takes technology's impact on retailing into a new dimension. Parkinson and Parkinson (1987), for example, suggest that the arrival of EPOS is 'possibly the most significant computing development in the retail environment' of recent times.

The EPOS concept

Wolfe (1988) has defined EPOS as 'the collection in real-time at the point of sale, and storing in a computer file, of sales and other related data by means of a number of electronic devices. The most common of these is the bench scanner, but data can be input by hand-held guns and wands, scales and keypads on the till'. Wolfe goes on to observe that the essential nature of an EPOS system is that the data input device interacts with a Price-Look-Up file which holds the complete list of items stocked by the retailer and their current selling prices. From this interaction the customer receives a full printed record (which is duplicated in the store's computer memory) of exactly what and how many items were purchased, the prices paid for each, the total amount and how paid along with the date, time and place of the transaction. (For a more detailed account of the technology of EPOS which requires the bar-coding of all products at source, see Jones, 1985 and Wolfe and Cook, 1986). Perhaps the most significant long-term implication of the EPOS development is that the detailed information from a retailer's EPOS checkouts can provide the basis for a comprehensive retail business information system (Jones, 1985).

Typically retailers have introduced EPOS in order to pursue what have become known as 'hard' (direct) and 'soft' (indirect) benefits (Dawson *et al.* 1987). Hard benefits are those which are relatively easy to quantify and cost (Retail Business, 1986). These include quicker checkout throughput, the removal of the need for individual product price labelling, quicker shelf-filling and stocktaking, reduced shrinkage and the more consistent and accurate handling of pricing and price changes. The soft benefits relate to the strategic and tactical potential of the EPOS database – in particular the opportunities created for more efficient use of shelf-space and more rational stocking and merchandizing policies. Additionally, the speed of data availability potentially facilitates the testing of new approaches to store layout, display, promotion and product range. While sophisticated retailers have always sought to produce this kind of management control information, it has often appeared too late to be useful. With EPOS, management information is easier to obtain, up to date and accurate. It is hardly surprising, therefore, that UK retailers have begun to invest significantly in the EPOS concept. The spread of EPOS is discussed below.

The diffusion of EPOS in the UK

EPOS was introduced into the US grocery sector in the 1970s and the UK's first fully operational EPOS store came on-stream in 1979. However, it is generally accepted that the move to EPOS in the U.K. did not begin to assume significant proportions until the mid 1980s (Morris, 1987). For a variety of technical reasons (primarily relating to the required source marking and standardization of products) the main initial UK adopters of EPOS have tended to be food and grocery retailers, although other retail sectors are becoming increasing involved (Retail Business, 1984). As is perhaps inevitable with a concept which is relatively new and still in the process of diffusion, there is no consensus among observers as to the precise extent and likely growth of EPOS in the UK and estimates vary widely (Jones, 1985; Wolfe and Cook, 1986; Morris, 1987). However, a conservative compilation of available forecasts suggests that around 20 per cent of total UK grocery sales are probably now handled by EPOS-based stores. Given that the equivalent US number appears to be well in excess of 50 per cent and rising (Morris, 1987), it seems reasonable to assume that UK EPOS penetration will show further significant increase. Sainsburys, for example, now claim that their own EPOS stores account for over 60 per cent of their business and that their forward installation programme has required them to train around 10,000 scanning cashiers each year (Retail and Distribution Management, 1987).

While precise numbers are difficult to establish, it is hard to disagree with Parkinson's (1987) conclusion from his empirical work in this area that 'EPOS systems are diffusing rapidly in the retailing environment and will have a significant impact on this sector in the future'.

The broad spread of EPOS impacts

It seems reasonable to hypothesize that the impact of EPOS will be felt in a wide range of ways across the whole supply chain. Figure 9.1 below illustrates this likely broad spread of EPOS impacts which spans not only the more obvious retailer–supplier relationships but the wider dimensions of the consumer and consumer protection bodies; the market research industry; advertising and sales promotion agencies and the suppliers of process and packaging machinery.

Recent events in the UK have suggested that the consumer impact of the widespread use of EPOS systems may take unexpected forms. The absence of traditional individual item price labelling (a characteristic of the EPOS approach) will compel retail organizations to develop effective checking systems to ensure that the prices marked on shelf-edges exactly correlate with the price list held in the EPOS computer.

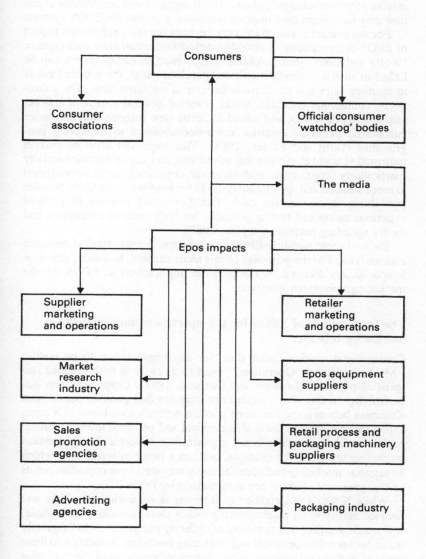

Figure 9.1 Possible impacts of EPOS technology

Evidence presented during a spate of prosecutions against several EPOS retailers for over-charging (Rees, 1988) suggests that insufficient attention may have been paid to price consistency across the EPOS system.

For the market research industry perhaps the most significant aspect of EPOS is its capacity to provide single-source, real-time data capture (Wolfe and Cook, 1986). Additionally, where an EPOS system can be linked to an electronically monitored purchase panel, the potential exists to monitor sales and purchase behaviour at the same time. The subsequent continuous database would combine several forms of market analysis in one source and would facilitate new insights into consumer purchasing patterns, loyalties and responsiveness to marketing programmes (Gorn and Fraser, 1988). This improved level of market information could also mean that advertising and sales promotion activity (particularly programmes with short-run objectives) could be subjected to more-detailed and specific analysis. In the long-term, the likely broader availability of interactive cable facilities could provide heightened experimentation and testing potential for both creative executions and media spending patterns (Staples, 1987).

Each of these possible EPOS impact areas merits detailed research and analysis. For the purposes of this short chapter, however, attention is specifically focused on the possible implications of EPOS for the marketing/operations interface.

The implications of EPOS for the operations management/ marketing interface

Conventional wisdom holds that 'for any organization to be viable, "Marketing" and "Operations" must be as close in both practice and spirit as possible' (Lockyer and Oakland, 1987). Despite the obvious desirability of this ideal, experience suggests that genuine operational closeness between the functions is often difficult to achieve. To some extent this reflects the inevitable political and personal inter-functional conflicts which can occur in any organization. Kotler's (1988) standard marketing textbook, for example, outlines a range of issues over which he suggests marketing and manufacturing may well have important points of disagreement. (These are summarized in Table 9.2).

While Kotler's polarization of interests is somewhat simplistic and focuses narrowly on manufacturing rather than operations as a whole, few would disagree that problems of differing perspectives do frequently occur between the operations and marketing functions. In addition to these perhaps intrinsic differences, other disagreements or problems may arise simply because of a failure fully to appreciate the constraints under which other departments operate. Cowell (1984), for example, rightly notes that 'marketing books rarely describe operations management in any detail'.

Table 9.2 Sources of organizational conflict between manufacturing and marketing

Manufacturing emphasis	Marketing emphasis
Long production lead times	Short production lead times
Long runs with few models	Short runs with many models
No model changes	Frequent model changes
Standard orders	Custom orders
Ease of fabrication	Aesthetic appearance

Adapted from Kotler (1988).

This chapter seeks to suggest that the UK retail sector's shift towards an increasing use of EPOS systems may well prove to be a significant catalyst for advancing discussion and thinking concerning the operations management/marketing interface. Effective retailing demands a distinctive and complex blend of product and service skills which have both marketing and operations implications. Retailing is characterized by the importance, centrality and visibility of operations in the delivery of customer satisfaction. From the customer's point of view, the store itself and the way in which it is operated are inextricable components of the retail 'product'. In retailing (as in most service or quasi-service businesses), the operations and marketing functions combine (either positively or negatively) in the delivery of the customer's total retail experience. For this reason changes in retail operations have inescapable concurrent marketing impacts. Although EPOS is still relatively new in the UK retail sector, it is already possible to hypothesize a wide range of likely impacts on the operations management/marketing interface. Some of these possibilities are reviewed below.

The operations management/marketing interface within retail organizations

The traditional evolution of the retail organization has tended to produce a situation in which a clear organizational separation occurs between marketing and operations. Piercy and Alexander's (1988) study of marketing organization in UK retailing has suggested, for example, that while retail marketing departments have considerable responsibility in the areas of market research, advertising and promotion and planning, they typically have 'a far more limited degree of influence as far as the products themselves and store location are concerned, and perhaps most significantly, even less in relation to the 'hard-edge' areas of the

133

selling or merchandising functions'. Even when the retail marketng department has responsibility, Piercy and Alexander found that this is often shared with other areas. The majority of retail market research units, for example, were not located in the marketing department. This 'separation of powers' effect was also noted by Parkinson (1987) who commented that 'in the sample of retailers, the researcher was often directed to management responsible for the development of information systems rather than to the commercial buying or marketing functions'. While the relative recency of marketing departments in retailing probably helps to explain this situation, (Piercy and Alexander, 1988) the potential inherent problems for effective EPOS implementation are clear. Crucial to the successful use of EPOS at the strategic level is marketing expertise in the analysis and interpretation of data and the establishment of appropriate testing mechanisms. Both Parkinson (1987) and Lynch and Cook (1988) in recent EPOS empirical work found that one of the most significant barriers now emerging to the strategic use of EPOS systems was the sheer volume of data generated and the analytical difficulties of its interpretation. While it is beyond the limited scope of this chapter to propose specific organizational solutions, it is not unreasonable to suggest that retailers who wish to gain maximum benefit from their EPOS investment must address the problem of the traditional separation between operations and marketing. New structures and systems will almost certainly be required. Marketing teachers typically observe that structure must follow strategy (Chandler, 1962). Effective implementation of the EPOS concept may compel reconsideration of this truism in the UK retail sector.

The operations management/marketing interface in supplier organizations

Reference has already been made to the increasing power of major UK retail organizations in relation to their suppliers. Technological advance may have a significant influence on this trend. Several large UK retailers (such as Marks and Spencer, Tesco and Sainsburys) have already begun to pursue the potential benefits provided by Electronic Data Interchange (EDI). EDI has been defined as 'the transfer of structured data, by agreed message standards, from computer to computer by electronic means (Retail Business, 1988). In essence, this means that one company can produce documents on its computer and send them electronically to a trading partner's computer. Clearly EDI in conjunction with EPOS offers retailers the possibility of a fully automatic sales and stock-handling system. The electronic placing of orders could form part of a paperless retail operation. While this development is still embryonic in the UK, the US provides interesting pointers to possible future EDI developments. One major US consulting firm has forecast that by 1990 electronic interchange will 'emerge and grow into the dominant method of exchanging business data for industries in which regular transactions of a repetitive nature take place' (Norris 1984). Significantly, empirical work conducted among US retailers using EDI suggests that a potential supplier's ability to use EDI could become an important factor in the supplier selection process and that, in the future, suppliers may need EDI capability to remain competitive (Emmelhainz, 1987).

Thus even at the basic level of standard operating practice, suppliers to retail may be compelled to ensure that operations and marketing personnel maintain the closest possible working relations. There are other pressures also. If retailers are increasingly possessed of more rapid and detailed EPOS-generated information concerning the performance and profitability of the products they stock, they will have the ammunition to drive for more responsiveness from their suppliers. They will have the potential to test new products more quickly and to experiment with a whole range of new approaches to stocking policy, shelf lay-out and merchandizing. As Caulkin (1987) has observed, the retailer's continuing emphasis on operations will tie suppliers ever more tightly into the whole business system and the supplier's own operations will come under close scrutiny.

One anecdotal example quoted by Young (1988) will serve to illustrate the point. This concerns a UK toiletries company which, for sound strategic marketing reasons, had moved towards a policy of supplying an increasing proportion of retailer own-label products. While this development produced its key objectives of reducing sales and marketing costs compared to the traditional manufacturer branding route, there were significant other effects. Retail customers demanded an increasing pro-liferation of products and product types, many of them at relatively low volumes. The toiletries company's operations had been targetted towards conventional operations objectives such as increased bottling speeds and reduced labour content in the pursuit of lower unit costs. The policy worked — with the high speed bottling lines that were introduced pro-viding 20 per cent lower manning and 50 per cent higher bottling speeds. However, these efficiencies could only be achieved at the expense of a changeover time of up to seven hours. This was obviously only acceptable if each production batch offered several shifts' run-time. However, for many of the own-label products concerned, this represented an unacceptably high three or more months forecast demand. For these reasons the supplier was compelled to transfer some products to lower speed, faster changeover lines and to undertake a critical evaluation of ways of reducing changeover time on its high-speed lines. While this is only one anecdote, it does serve to illustrate the way in which better retail control of market information may well compel suppliers to develop manufacturing systems and processes which are, above all else, flexible and suited to short production runs, quick changeovers and the speedy introduction of new products.

One can also envisage obvious 'knock-on' effects for the suppliers of relevant capital equipment who, in their turn, may feel pressure to supply more flexible machinery capable of lowering production costs. It is probable that suppliers of packaging and packaging equipment may be similarly affected. Wolfe (1988) has drawn attention to the vital role of packaging in retailing. Traditionally, retailers have judged profitability by gross margin per case. However, better EPOS data on the profitability of shelf-space may mean that retailers will be able to calculate a gross contribution to profitability of each unit of floor space or shelf facing. This development would create problems and opportunities in the packaging area and could precipitate a major review of preferred pack formats for retail markets.

In these kinds of ways, new EPOS-generated retail pressures on product development, packaging and the preferred product mix will increasingly create an environment in which both marketing and operations on the supply side will need to work together to develop integrated and mutually acceptable solutions.

There are, of course, many other possible scenarios. The toiletries company anecdote cited above reflects a supplier organization being compelled to review its system by the force of retailer power. Caulkin (1988) has illustrated how a food-processing organization employed an alternative approach in which a more pro-active stance by operations and marketing produced a different end result. This company has pursued an aggressive policy of own-label supply to targetted major retailers, most notably Marks and Spencer. The policy reflects the benefits of extremely close operations and marketing links. The company has evolved complex and sophisticated food distribution systems which make it invaluable to retail customers (and extremely hard to replace). In this way a successful operating system can itself become a source of competitive advantage for marketing exploitation. Additionally, for special retail customers, the company has developed what Caulkin describes as 'man to man marking' — with contacts at every level from chairman to development managers in individual plants. This is a classic example of the 'closeness to the customer' precept ranging across both operations and marketing in an integrated, effective system.

Conclusions

It has been suggested that the increasing spread of EPOS systems in UK retailing may have significant implications for the whole of the supply chain. Since EPOS is still in its infancy as a concept, this is an appropriate time for all the players in the game to consider the strategic implications.

Because of the relative recency of the topic, the illustrations cited have been largely anecdotal in nature. The EPOS subject clearly merits detailed empirical research both to obtain a clearer understanding of the processes involved and the likely routes to possible profitable solutions. However, it is suggested that one important likely outcome will be the need for a review of the operations management/marketing interface and a reconsideration of the most appropriate organizational mechanisms for effecting a higher degree of co-operation, integration and synergy. Christopher (1987) has perhaps stated the ideal when he argues that 'instead of viewing distribution, marketing and manufacturing as largely separate activities within the business, they need to be unified — particularly at the strategic level'. The review presented here suggests that environmental and market forces in the UK retail sector are producing a climate and a context in which far-sighted organizations can begin to approach this corporate Holy Grail.

References

Akehurst, C. (1983) 'Concentration in retail distribution: measurement and significance', *Service Industries Journal* 3: 161–79.

Burns J. (1983) 'A synoptic view of the food industry', in *The Food Industry, Economics and Policies*, J. Burns, J. McInnerney, and A. Swinbank (eds) London: Heinemann.

Caulkin, S. (1987) 'The fall and rise of brands', *Management Today*, July, 45–104.

Caulkin, S. (1988) 'Northern foods' changing recipe', *Management Today*, Feb. 48–52.

Chandler, A.D. Jr (1962) *Strategy and Structure*, MIT Press.

Christopher, M. (1987) 'Distribution and customer service' in *The Marketing Book*, M.J. Baker (ed.) London: Heinemann.

Cowell, D. (1984) *The Marketing of Services*, London: Heinemann.

Davies, K., Gilligan, C. and Sutton, C. (1984) 'The changing competitive structure of British grocery retailing', *Quarterly Review of Marketing* 10. 1–9.

Dawson, J.A., Findlay, A.M., and Sparks, L. (1987) 'The impact of scanning on employment in UK food stores: a preliminary analysis', *Journal of Marketing Management* 2: 285–300.

Emmelhainz, M.A. (1987) 'Electronic data interchange: does it change the purchasing process?' *Journal of Purchasing and Materials Management*, Winter, 2–8.

Gorn, G.T. and Fraser, S.D. (1988) 'Electronic data: marketing answers through behavioural research', *Singapore Marketing Review* III: 7–18.

Greenley, C.E. and Shipley, D.D. (1988) 'An empiricial overview of marketing by retailing organisations', *Service Industries Journal* 8: 49–66.

Holmes, G. (1982) 'Commercial negotiation — ancient practice, modern philosophy', *Journal of Purchasing and Materials Management Autumn.* 2–5.

Jones, P. (1985) 'The spread of article numbering and retail scanning in Europe', *Service Industries Journal*, 5: 273–9.

Kotler, P. (1988) *Marketing Management: Analysis Planning, Control and Implementation*, 6th edn, Englewood Cliffs, NJ. Prentice-Hall.

Lidstone, J. (1977) *Negotiating Profitable Sales*, London: Gower.

Livesey, F. and Hall, R.J. (1981) *Retailing: Developments and Prospects to 1985*, London: Staniland Hall.

Lockyer, K.G. and Oakland, J.S. (1987) 'An operations manager's audit', *Service Industries Journal* 7: 5–13.

Lynch, J.E. and Cook, D.E. (1988) 'The impact of electronic point of sale technology (EPOS) on UK retail marketing', University of Bradford Management Centre, Working Paper.

Lynch, J.E. and Jobber, D. (1986) 'Negotiation: marketing's new priority', in D. Cowell and J. Collis (eds) *Managing Marketing, Proceedings of the Marketing Education Group's 19th Annual Conference*, Plymouth Polytechnic, July, pp. 2–19.

Morris, L.R. (1987) 'The research benefits of scanning' in U. Bradley (ed.) *Applied Marketing and Social Research*, London: John Wiley.

Norris, R.C. (1984) *Business Data Interchange*, Auerbach Publishing.

Oddy, P. (1987) 'The growth in private brands', *Retail and Distribution Management*, May/June, 9–11.

Parkinson, S.T. (1987) 'The impact of new information technology on the relationship between retailers and their suppliers', ESRC END OF AWARD REPORT (No F24250029).

Parkinson, L.K. and Parkinson, S.T. (1987) *Using the Microcomputer in Marketing*, London: McGraw-Hill.

Piercy, N. (1984) 'Is marketing moving from the manufacturer to the retailer?', *Retail and Distribution Management*, Sept/Oct, 25–8.

Piercy, N. and Alexander, N. (1988) 'The status quo of marketing organisation in UK retailing: A neglected phenomenon', *Service Industries Journal* 8: 155–75.

Rees, J. (1988) 'Trouble in store over D.I.Y. pricing says trading chief', *Daily Telegraph*, 5 Oct. 9.

Retail Business (1984) 'Progress in scanning at the checkout', No 316, June.

Retail Business (1986) 'Data from scanning', No 337, March.

Retail Business (1988) 'Electronic data interchange for retailers', No 364, June, 4–8.

Retail and Distribution Management (1987) 'EPOS/EFTPOS 87 at the Barbican', Nov/Dec, 12–26.

Staples, N. (1987) 'Scanning based services and the Nielsen contribution', Admap, April, 47–50.

Thames Television (1982) *The Thames Shopper: a Study of Purchasing and Shopping Behaviour*, London.

Utton, M.A. (1970) *Industrial Concentration*, Harmondsworth: Penguin.

Van Mesdag, M. (1988) 'Europe's brand squeeze', *Management Today*, March, 70–114.

Wolfe, A. (1988) 'Information technology and the retailing of packaged goods', European Marketing Academy Annual Conference, University of Bradford Management Centre, April.

Wolfe, A. and Cook, L. (1986) *The Electronic Revolution in Store*, London: Ogilvy & Mather.

Young, S. (1988) 'Manufacturing under Pressure', *Management Today* July 103–7.

Chapter ten

Interfirm collaboration and innovation: strategic alliances or reluctant partnerships?

Keith Dickson, Helen Lawton Smith, and Stephen Smith

Introduction

Most management studies of the innovation process are essentialist in outlook. That is, they search for the essential or 'key elements' of the innovation process in the belief that it is largely a coherent, rational process which can be modelled in some linear or other form. The underlying assumption is that the articulation of a definitive model will lead to more effective innovation management.

Innovation modelling is something of a refuge: an attempt at clarity in the face of severe disorganisation. Despite extensive state intervention in domestic economies, innovations take place in the context of 'disorganized [Western] capitalism' (Lash and Urry, 1987). With the exception of Japan (and possibly France and Germany) national innovation strategies are absent or ineffective at controlling the uncertainties of global market restructuring. At a micro-level on the other hand, innovation researchers face a Byzantine maze of diverging patterns. The plurality of arrangements for innovation devised by different managements reflect and underscore global disorganization.

Simplistic innovation models thus offer a degree of spurious reassurance in the face of chaos at global and managerial levels.

The refuge is nevertheless reinforced by the enduring image of innovation as a singular entrepreneurial activity, historically associated with great inventors and Noble Prize winners. As R & D has become more institutionalized/corporatized, the perception of a coherent, rational innovation process is now associated with the enterprising firm, as if a bureaucracy can act as a kind of collective entrepreneur.

The progressive bureaucratization of innovation confuses the essentialist quest by introducing organizational issues which present us with a more complex set of factors (e.g. personnel conflicts, informal creative activities, 'invisible colleges' etc.). Essentialist descriptions of innovation blur the distinction between on the one hand, innovation as a craft, and on the other, innovation as a mechanistic institutionalised activity.

Indeed, enough case studies have shown that technological innovation is often a much more 'messy' affair that does not readily fit the prescriptions of 'organizational science'. Worse, many unforeseeable external factors present themselves – factors which cannot easily be integrated into the essentialist models – yet which innovators seem somehow to deal with effectively. There is every indication that innovation is not as coherent nor rational as so often implied. Clearly a more modest approach is called for – there is certainly the need for more flexible models.

These comments apply with even greater force to the collaborative innovations on which our research concentrates. Interfirm collaboration in innovation introduces another set of permutations. While many innovation studies have discussed the benefits of collaboration (Freeman, 1982; von Hippel, 1976; Haklisch, 1986; Shaw, 1986; Rothwell and Zegveld, 1982; Hakansson, 1987; and Harrigan, 1984, to name but a few), they also provide plenty of evidence for the remarkable diversity of collaborative arrangements.

There are clear reasons why collaboration is advantageous in principle. First, there is often a technological necessity for collaboration. Given the complexity of many new product areas, few firms can be expected to possess all the required resources, and skills for the development of a new product or process. Furthermore, the fact that many new product ideas occur at the interface between different technologies suggests that co-operation at the interface could be productive.

Second; collaboration between firms could generate complementary business advantages. Exchanges of different market expertise, the extension of one firm's network through access to the other firm's and shared funding of the R & D, are all found in our sample.

The variety of collaborative types evident in the literature and the many possible reasons for justifying collaboration suggests that a wide choice is available to firms for pursuing collaborative activities. We also argue that firms, particularly small specialist firms, often do not realize the scope of choice available to them.

To summarize, the choice is greater than firms realize, we believe, because:

1. in practical experience, innovation is not as straightforward nor as economically rational as 'essentialist' models suggest. Yet firms may have taken on board intolerant models which have then limited their perception of the scope for collaboration;
2. the business/innovation infrastructure of this country is not well organized or co-ordinated (e.g. by government agencies and industrial associations) so that little effort has been made and few mechanisms exist, to generate, encourage and support inter-firm collaborative ventures;

141

3. differing corporate cultures impose styles and views of the world which, consciously and unconsciously, may inhibit an organizations's scope for collaboration;
4. firms discover that they and their partners are 'culturally incompatible' and retreat from further advances from quite possibly better suitors;
5. more inevitably, firms' starting points in new product development are often widely divergent. Sectoral, market and technological differences may limit firm's sensitivity to the benefits of collaboration with others;
6. the competitive model of competition breeds suspicion.

If the choice is wider, then this suggests to us that the 'space' surrounding collaborative innovative activity (i.e. the variety of effective paths to innovation success) is larger than is realized. Hence, our interest in the nature and conduct of collaborative activities between firms. By investigating how and why managers make decisions about collaborative R & D, we hope to describe how firms begin to explore that 'space' in practice. As we cannot promise straightforward prescriptions for innovation and are not innovators ourselves, our final step is to represent the entire range of models to all the participating companies, in the hope that it may expand their strategic options.

Methodology

In order to examine all the facets of inter-firm collaboration discussed above, we are compiling a number of case studies of recent or current product developments in which significant technical co-operation between two firms has occurred, or is still occurring. These will reach about twenty-five to thirty cases by the end of the project. The collaborative episodes are, primarily, instances of two or more non-competing firms informally combining their complementary skills to develop a new product or process.

The organizations selected are mostly industrial firms producing 'high tech' products such as scientific instruments, process equipment and biotechnological products. In a few cases, it was quickly apparent that there is one dominant partner 'leading' the collaborative activity. But in other cases, we sought and found instances of relatively equal and complementary inputs from both partners in their endeavour to develop entirely new products or processes. Some partnerships turned out to be unexpectedly difficult; others surprisingly successful.

Most of the firms are small to medium sized, though there are a few exceptions where very large and well-known firms are involved with much smaller partners. Firm size differences and geographical locality play a part but are only two of several factors to be kept in mind.

For each case study, semi-structured interviews take place with both collaborating firms, covering all the same issues. In this way, different accounts of the same activities and events are gathered, enabling us to compare and contrast the perceptions, motives and assessments of the two partners. Where possible, this is extended by interviews at different levels within each firm, such as with senior managers and the project engineers involved with the collaborative exercise. Both these techniques – paired firm interviews and internal hierarchal interviews – should serve to highlight both the consistencies and inconsistencies between the various actors, and so provide a richer and more realistic story.

The semi-structured questionnaire used in the interviews, defines the major topics of interest. For example, the firm's recent history and the educational/professional background of the main actors are noted, in line with our belief that historical circumstances and past experience are important influences on the type of collaboration undertaken. Similarly, organizational and operational information is collected, especially that relating to employment, production and market issues, in the belief also that they influence the conduct of the collaborative exercise.

Obviously, R & D issues are covered both at the policy level and at the operational level, to indicate the degree of formal planning involved and the variety of technological inputs. Of particular interest here, is the influence of personal research networks and the mechanisms employed for technical intelligence gathering.

The main thrust of the interviews, however, is to detail each collaborative episode from its inception to its conclusion. Particular issues of interest here include the motives and objectives of each firm, the decision-making arrangements, the conduct and control of the exercise, and the ownership of the outcome. Finally, each firm is asked to assess its experience in terms of perceived strengths and weakness of the relationship, the difficulties encountered and the comparison between anticipated and actual benefits.

From the interviews, a case history of each collaboration is prepared and it is from these case histories that our general analysis is being developed. This could be enhanced by return visits to firms still involved in continuing collaborations and from discussions etc., arising from planned feedback seminars with all participating firms.

Included below are several examples of our initial round of completed case studies which already exhibit some of the diversity of collaborative arrangements and influences discussed above.

Case studies

Case 1 RORA Ltd and STAR Ltd

The actors RORA is a small independent research-based electronics firm producing customized semi-conductor processing equipment. It was founded about ten years ago by Dr Ro, whose strong personality and entrepreneurial style pervades the firm's activities and is a facet of all its collaborative ventures. He certainly views collaboration as a strategic objective of the firm, not just out of technical and financial necessity, but as a mechanism for accelerating commercial development.

Dr Ro has, over many years, assiduously cultivated a strong network of research links and claims to be well-read in the latest research literature (he spends two or more nights a week scanning the technical literature in the Bodleian Library). In this way, he often finds that his firm is better informed about recent research than other, often much larger, firms in the same field.

Dr Ro adopts an organized approach to establishing contact with other firms. He said,

> You've got to mature a relationship over a period of years. Its very delicate. If you formalize things, you get forced up the hierarchy, which in itself, makes it risky. It might then be torpedoed. You have to home in on the product champion.

He identifies key individuals such as senior researchers and project engineers in these firms and solicits their scientific interest in his firm's activities, by sending copies of scientific papers (not just his own), as a means of impressing the contact that RORA is abreast of the latest research. 'Its all part of gaining the dialogue . . . keep them informed . . . keep them nibbling.' He estimates that one in five of these 'feelers' ultimately results in some work for his firm, after preliminary discussions with the contacts.

STAR is a small, scientific analytical firm providing a variety of highly sophisticated testing facilities and material analyses to mainly electronics firms. Such facilities are usually beyond the resources of most electronics firms, and usually reside in university or research laboratories only. Indeed, STAR's origins can be traced back to research at the University of London from whence several researchers spun off into commercial analysis work. The equipment demands high skill input so most of STAR's employees are post-doctoral scientists.

Recently, STAR has sought to diversify its services, not only into other industrial sectors, but also by looking for new opportunities to exploit its expertise. Thus the staff are encouraged to do research with the analytical equipment if and when slack periods arise.

The collaboration   RORA has been developing a new semiconductor processing device which, at a late stage of its development, required testing facilities to check its operational reliability and to characterize scientifically the device's output. RORA therefore looked to firms like STAR to provide testing facilities. However, Dr Ro also saw an opportunity for possible collaborative research with possible commercial benefits to both firms. This is because the device could operate as an add-on to STAR's analytical machine and enhance its capabilities by performing unique and novel analyses.

Dr Ro needed proof that the device could work. Through discussion with the senior researcher, an informal arrangement was reached in which RORA would loan its new device to STAR in return for which STAR would perform a certain amount of free analysis. A measure of STAR's confidence in the new development's potential is the commitment by the senior member of staff (acting as a product champion) to fit this extra research into the firm's work schedule, even though it is not mainstream work, nor has it been formally approved or funded.

Although technical problems were encountered with the trials, both sides persevered with the informal arrangement. The respective research cultures in both firms helped significantly in this respect, so that, for example, no financial issues arose, and professional/scientific trust carried the day.

There is, as yet, little demand for this new analysis, but both partners anticipate that a market will develop. In order to bring the new development to the attention of potential users, the partners intend to publicize the development through joint scientific papers and conference presentations, etc.

Case 2 DISCAT and DESTECH

The actors   DISCAT is a leading beverage equipment manufacturer, and is a wholly owned subsidiary of a world-wide food processing company, whose products it delivers in its vending machines. It was set up in 1970, as a separate entity, as a result of 'intra-preneurship', by the present MD. At the time when DISCAT was set up, the parent company was not interested in new forms of development, but the success of DISCAT is now seen as a model for future spin-offs.

The founding father of DISCAT has been outstandingly successful in creating a business organization which is the market leader. This is in spite of resistance in the parent company to 'entrepreneurial managers', and a constraint on its head count, which means a maximum of nine full-time development staff. As a result of this constraint, DISCAT is obliged to employ contract engineers, some of whom have been with the company for eleven years; and to find external partners for virtually all significant development work.

Until the MD's track record became established, the relationship with the parent company was a source of constant strain. Even today, a good deal of the projects remain undisclosed to the inquisitive bureaucrats at head office. Thus DISCAT's founding father boasts that he does a lot of 'skunk work'. Indeed, DISCAT bears his unmistakable mark. He is demanding to work for, enthusiastic and hardworking. DISCAT have three main suppliers, but with two of these collaboration is at a low level, dealing with technical matters. Our respondent visits these companies regularly, in order to identify and help solve their own internal problems, and technical problems relating to DISCAT's products.

DESTECH is a well suited and willing partner to DISCAT. The three partners, who have made a positive decision not to grow beyond about twenty-two employees, set up DESTECH after the frustrations of working within a large design consultancy. The partners have designed in several areas, ranging from beverage equipment to railway multiple units. They welcome the cash-flow which DISCAT brings, but they are mildly concerned because this link now accounts for two-thirds of their earnings. In principle, DISCAT strongly encourages DESTECH to diversify but, because of the amount of time that has to be devoted to DISCAT, diversification is harder to achieve in practice.

The designers are quietly spoken, self-effacing and respect each other to bring different disciplines and division of labour to projects. One is a mechanical engineer, another an electronic engineer, and the third a three-dimensional designer. Should they ever generate an innovation to meet a mass-market, they would set up a separate manufacturing company to produce it, freeing them to continue working on innovative designs.

Collaboration DISCAT could use its parent's large R & D division, but avoids this where possible. Food technology is left to the parent, while all equipment work is financed out of DISCAT's profits, and this hard-won independence is prized above all. Two of the sixteen contract engineers taken on by DISCAT to get round the head count problem are seconded to DESTECH to work on projects and to learn new CAD techniques, which have been resisted by the permanent employees at DISCAT. The intention is to re-introduce CAD to DISCAT as a proven technique. The expansion of the development team, has, says its MD, 'depended on my deviousness!' 'As a deviationist myself, I don't think large companies can develop new ideas anyway. Large companies have a serious problem, and in two large companies collaborating, that multiplies the problems no end.' He said of collaboration with DESTECH: 'It is unusual in that its not a sales or marketing consultancy. For us its about the need to innovate . . .'

DESTECH has expanded as a result of the work from DISCAT, and have recruited seven staff who now work on DISCAT's projects. Our respondent from DISCAT visited DESTECH at least two or three times a week, and would often stay all day. He added, 'We go into the workshop and make the thing work'.

According to DESTECH, it was they who made the first approach to DISCAT. Before setting up DESTECH, the partners had worked on several projects on behalf of DISCAT's main UK rival.

> So we thought we'd give DISCAT a ring. We got quite a grilling! But after one very small project, we've had continuous work since then. [It is] a much closer relationship than is normal – we're often in contact on a daily basis working jointly on projects. Whereas normally [with other clients] we divide work up in agreed stages then don't see them from one week to the next.

The DESTECH respondent was clear that DISCAT tried to stay away for a period at the beginning of a project.

> They deliberately don't interfere at an early stage, then they get very involved when the design is coming together. Sometimes he [the DISCAT respondent] is here every morning. It isn't a problem – they just don't expect any pretence – while normally we'd want to tidy up and present an image to a client.

Only occasionally have they,

> Felt we were in a situation where we were acting as technicians when we felt we ought to be advising them. But its always resolved . . . Give and take. They [DISCAT] are flexible and open-minded and very fast at decision making.

DISCAT's sources of information come from membership of trade associations, trade journals and feedback from DISCAT's 350 sales staff. Innovation is driven by 'the need to be different in order to sell or lease our own equipment.'

The borderline between 'development work' and 'innovation' is not clear cut. Collaboration with DESTECH has yielded

1. marked changes in the appearance of vending machines;
2. the use of low pressure air as a transport mechanism inside the machines, and
3. a radically new means of brewing coffee grounds from individual sealed packs.

In one of the cases has DISCAT given up ownership of the techniques to DESTECH, and the latter were quite comfortable in having signed secrecy agreements covering all these areas. Average completed and implemented project time-scales stood at about eighteen months to two years.

Case 3 PHOENIX SWITCHGEAR and MATSCI

The actors PHOENIX SWITCHGEAR is a long-established UK supplier to the power generation and distribution industry. A private company, PHOENIX is constituted in a way that makes it fairly safe from takeover and this has given it stability. The company is strongly attached to the maxim 'if we can make it: we make it'. In development work which is 'technologically complicated' they are prepared to collaborate.

The company operates in the field of oil-insulated switchgear technology, pioneered in the UK several decades ago and exported to the Middle East and other countries which have adopted the British system – usually former colonies. Other markets use other insulating technology: 'air' insulated/limited oil insulation (Europe), 'vacuum' and 'inert-gas' are seen as future world standards, though in the UK, area electricity boards were described as being 'extremely slow to change'. This induced complacency in the five major manufacturers in this sector who have been slow to adapt to changing circumstances, allowing the electrical division of this company to be treated as something of a 'cash-cow' by the major shareholders.

Nevertheless, PHOENIX has a world-wide reputation for producing competitive light and heavy switchgear, ferrous and non-ferrous coatings, and other components to form a wide range of assembled products. The MD modestly dismissed these as a, 'bog standard unit with umpteen variations', and had pursued several avenues to introduce innovative products.

Government standard-setting, notably in France, was leading to the long-term decline in oil-filled switchgear. If PHOENIX were to break into new world markets, and preserve their existing market within the traditional British field of influence, then they must innovate in order to survive, said our respondent.

MATSCI are a younger, but very much larger multinational company supplying components in seventy countries. It manufactures in eight countries, has marketing outlets in another thirty two, and sells in another thirty. The company's base is in material science, especially polymer science. Most of the company's business draws on a particular treatment of polymers which affects their physical properties to a highly controlled degree. Although it has been a public company for many years, its ethos and practical day to day running is still in its founders image. His innovative work in the late 1950s has culiminated in a wide range of high value added, customized components in aerospace, telecommunications, power generation and distribution, and oil exploration and distribution.

MATSCI is inherently reluctant to divulge technical knowledge to its customers and will strongly resist 'innovating in public' with another company's engineers, preferring to withdraw to think in private how to solve a client's problems. Though this has served them well over the years, their public reputation as a leading materials science company has brought stock market pressure to break into a new round of technological innovation. Over the last four or five years, the founder had concentrated on setting up, or purchasing, around fifty subsidiary high-technology companies in which MATSCI had taken a large minority shareholding with other venture capitalists. Though still essentially secretive, they were coming round to the notion that, 'the only way to run innovations is as small businesses.' This they were seeing as an alternative strategy for innovation. Ten per cent of all sales go into R & D, and around ten per cent of this is 'blue-sky'.

Collaboration Probably due to a secrecy agreement imposed by MATSCI, PHOENIX and MATSCI were separately reluctant to divulge much to us. According to MATSCI, a third party had originally seen the potential of applying a variant of their polymer technology to a particular high-voltage switchgear component (MATSCI has mostly supplied to low-voltage users). The first attempt at applying the modified polymer as a high-voltage insulator resulted in an explosive failure, but more development work identified the correct polymer treatment. At this point, MATSCI approached several British switchgear manufacturers with an invitation to manufacture and take the technology further. Collaboration was sought because switchgear companies had a knowledge base that MATSCI lacked. Most of those approached either rejected the innovation out of hand ('It'll never work!') or threatened to copy it ('Nice idea – we're going to compete with you'). In the event, none have gone any further with this technology except PHOENIX who have entered a collaborative agreement with MATSCI.

Long and delicate negotiation ensued between one or two MATSCI engineer–salespersons and the MD of the electrical division at PHOENIX. The PHOENIX manager is above all an entrepreneur, and at this one-to-one level the relationship has gone well – MATSCI engineers are socialized into being project champions in any case. Both parties have had to remain sensitive to the fact that the two companies have other, more standard, less secretive, user-supplier links involving less-innovative senior managers at PHOENIX. This is a source of potential embarrassment, and mild suspicion. MATSCI emphasized that, 'Each product innovation is a different story, and this one looks like a classic good news story.'

The 'right' collaborative relationship had been struck. In return for its engineering expertise, PHOENIX is set to meet the UK market, while MATSCI will supply the rest of the world, with PHOENIX's permission and field support. Said MATSCI,

149

We can get into areas of the world which PHOENIX can't. They should be delighted, and we couldn't stop them selling it anywhere they wanted to. The sole UK manufacturing rights are theirs but we could get it manufactured anywhere else.

It was not clear how this announcement squared with PHOENIX's search for new world markets through innovation identified above.

Case 4 PHOENIX and LECNET

The actors PHOENIX has already been described. However, it is worth mentioning that they felt that the current UK government's policy on leaving innovation to market forces would acerbate the inherent conservatism of British switchgear design.

LECNET is a British electricity distribution board. The respondent, a chartered engineer, emphasized the role of an intensive, if closed circle of contacts which made up the British power generation, cable and switchgear manufacturing 'mafia'. In the UK, the shift towards SF6 – the French government-inspired technology standard – had arrived as an external 'technology-push'. The inert-gas system was not the result of any organized movement on the part of the electricity 'mafia'. Indeed, the objectives of increased reliability, reduced maintenance costs and perceived safety (met by SF6) were tempered by a marked reluctance within the UK electricity industry to pay anything other than the lowest price for components.

Although the respondent can make a technical case for higher-cost equipment, the overall decision-making structure in which he works constrains him towards 'value engineering', that is cost reduction. Again in the case of switchgear, the industry inspectorate (ESI) determine which companies reach approved manufacturer status, reducing the available options still further.

Smaller suppliers are very much fewer in number today, again as a result – we think – of the absence of central planning. The last few years have seen a reduction in capital spending, which has been endemic in the country as well as in the electricity supply industry, squeezing out many of the smaller companies. Now that spending limits have been relaxed, there are not enough small companies to supply particular needs. Orders now have to be subcontracted to Norway because UK suppliers can't make enough. There is, therefore, a problem of finding suppliers; but there is no financial constraint, governing the number of relationships.

The respondent anticipated that privatization would lead to reduced information sharing among the competing boards. This might undermine the 'mafia' particularly as collaborative partners were often furnished to LECNET on the recommendations of professionals in other area boards.

PHOENIX have supplied LECNET with switch fuse ring-main units for several years, accounting for some twenty per cent of LECNET's annual switchgear expenditure. Routine contact is therefore inevitable. However, specific collaboration has been spurred primarily because of failures in PHOENIX's units. LECNET have seen these failures develop a pattern over time, arising from what they see as basic design faults.

LECNET approached PHOENIX for a design for a security device to stop the theft of electricity. PHOENIX were asked because this involved 'cut-outs' which PHOENIX already supply. After some months, PHOENIX came up with a drawing which LECNET found incomprehensible, and of little value. There has been no further progress.

LECNET continue to collaborate with PHOENIX on new products, especially as they have confidence in its electrical division managing director. This underlined the importance of professional-to-professional links in a UK context of largely disorganized innovation infrastructures. Indeed the same managing director had progressed several innovations from other sources, one of which had reached the pre-production stage.

Case 5 RORA and EXIGEN

The actors RORA is the same company as described in case 1, only in this example, a quite different product is involved. Dr Ro, the MD/founder of RORA was still the guiding light and initiator for this collaboration. He was well aware of the dangers inherent in the firm size disparity, but felt confident that his unique device and his careful preparation in gathering specialist information would be of interest to the much larger firm. His tactic of carefully identifying the most appropriate person within the other firm, both in terms of seniority and scientific expertise, must be noted.

EXIGEN is one of the largest electrical/electronics firms in Britain, and operates many product divisions as well as an autonomous central research division, which we shall call ERC. Exigen's board has established a strong and distinctive corporate culture within the many divisions, together with a strong emphasis on short-term profit maximization.

ERC employs over 500 graduate researchers within a well-defined hierarchy of assistant directors, laboratory managers, section leaders, group leaders, etc. It obtains its funding predominately from the other divisions within EXIGEN (approximately 60 per cent), but also significant amounts from government sources (mainly MOD and ALVEY), EEC (under such programmes as ESPRIT) and, for more speculative research, direct from central EXIGEN's funds. ERC's size and past reputation has given it a pre-eminent position in UK electronics research but this is declining, partly due to cutbacks in government and central

151

EXIGEN funding, and to relocation of the more applied research back into the production divisions.

In spite of its size, ERC undertakes a vast array of collaborative research projects, though mainly only under such externally funded programmes as ALVEY and ESPRIT etc. ERC recognizes that it has to collaborate in order to secure access to facilities and expertise, but only under well-defined commercial arrangements which ensure that both partners contribute equally (or more cynically, when a third party pays the largest share).

The role of governmental agencies in such collaborative ventures is very significant under such circumstances. Recent cut-backs in government research funding have killed off a number of ERC's collaborative projects, and the heavy hand of the MOD funding inhibits more commercial spin-off. Small electronics companies, not confident perhaps, in obtaining their own government research grants, may well look – and often do – to ERC as a potential collaborator in order to obtain government or EEC funding. ERC is not unwilling to co-operate in these situations! But ERC tends not to get involved formally with small firms on their own, especially when the financial burden is carried by ERC. Although collaborative decisions are initially taken at a technical level, they will eventually have to be approved by the commercial management, whose criteria are strictly commercial and legal, and include such issues as patents, intellectual property rights, and publicity etc.

At the research front, however, a less formal practice is followed and section leaders are able to make fairly long-term, technical decisions about the type and direction of research. A section leader, therefore, is able to initiate and develop informal collaborative research links, though eventually, the cost and time for this research will have to be accounted for and hence formal approval sought. Delays in declaring any informal work, collaborative or not, will occur until sufficiently promising results are obtained to ensure approval. One section leader suggested that this type of 'skunk work' accounted for between 5 and 10 per cent of his group's research. Personal contacts, via former university colleagues, conferences, etc., formed the basis for most of these informal, collaborative arrangements.

The collaboration Dr Ro sought out an individual at ERC who would be both interested scientifically in RORA's technical developments and, if and when necessary, would be senior enough to agree to collaboration. He initially sent some technical publicity material to the selected section leader, which described RORA's previous collaboration with another large electronics firm. This material impressed the section leader, who contacted Dr Ro several months later when he needed some specialist microelectronics processing work to be done.

Dr Ro's immediate response was 'yes but why not also do this', suggesting a line of research on which RORA were currently engaged. Dr Ro visited ERC taking his special device which, when linked up with ERC's ion-implantation equipment, produced some very interesting results. One outcome was that the section leader gave free samples of an advanced prototype 'chip' to RORA, for further analysis. Up to this point, the relationship was very informal and for ERC, the effort involved was kept at a very low profile and 'hidden' within the normal research work of the section leader's laboratory.

The next stage of the relationship, currently under negotiation, involves experimenting with the equipment over a longer period of time, establishing its accuracy and reliability. Such an arrangement may involve a financial deal, but more likely, an exchange of equipment and information. Either way, the collaboration has reached a stage for ERC at least, where a formal contract needs to be drawn up. Meanwhile, 'skunk work' continues at ERC on this project.

A number of possible outcomes may arise for RORA: the research could become a very big project for RORA which will need financing; and RORA may be able to use ERC's name in marketing the device further. The situation is now that ERC is continuing to assess the device informally, at no cost to RORA; and RORA will always retain some leverage over the relationship because of the need to use his original, patented device. Dr Ro has established a good professional relationship with a senior scientist with ERC.

However, in view of ERC's large size and predatory nature, RORA are in danger of being swamped, and may well be 'shut out' if the section leader should leave ERC.

Case 6 CHIC and WEDIS

The actors WEDIS was formed in 1981 by two ex-naval officers interested in microprocessor technology who were asked by business friends to develop a computerized data-handling system for chromatographic analysis.

Now, with 25 staff and over £1 million turnover, the firm primarily produces instrumentation for chromatographic applications in medical research laboratories. The use of chromatographic techniques for chemical separation and analysis is, however, spreading into other business sectors, and WEDIS, aware of this trend, is looking for new products in these areas and is employing more specialist staff to develop initiatives.

The firm's focus has been on applications – specific development work, with all manufacturing subcontracted to a local firm. With this emphasis, WEDIS has primarily been involved in customer-initiated, problem-solving activities with little on-going research in spite of the number of highly qualified staff. Their reputation and visibility, therefore, is mainly via highly satisfied customers, former university contacts and trade exhibitions. While standardized analysers are increasingly available, WEDIS is still often sought out by medical laboratories and other firms to provide technical solutions to unique chromatographic problems. Indeed, it was an enquiry from a previous buyer of a custom-built analyser that indicated this current collaborative example.

CHIC is a medical research laboratory linked to a major London hospital that only performs fundamental research but also provides commercial blood testing services for other organizations. It is run like a private research firm having to generate its own funds and, for example, takes out patents to protect its work commercially. CHIC's director and senior researcher, has a remarkable (for a British researcher) entrepreneurial emphasis to his research which he attributes to his Scandinavian medical research experiences, where industrial collaboration is prevalent. It was he who initiated the current collaboration.

The collaboration The collaboration between the two organizations arose out of the need for appropriate technology to be developed to diagnose and treat metabolic diseases. A technique for diagnosis had been developed by the senior researcher, who approached several large UK companies with a view to commercializing it. It was not until he approached a small company with which he had some previous contact that he found an interested party. At this time he was acting very much as a product champion in the face of opposition from colleagues from within CHIC.

He found that the small company (WEDIS) was more open-minded and flexible in their approach. WEDIS at this time, were on the look out for new projects and, as this was in their field, were interested in seeing if this presented a suitable opportunity for investment.

The collaboration between the partners was made easier because of previous good relationships. WEDIS wanted to undertake a market investigation of the potential offered by the new product. This was effected by CHIC giving WEDIS a list of ten authorities in the field who would be able to give an informed view of market potential. The message came back that there would be a large market for the product.

On the basis of this, WEDIS applied for DTI funding and received a small grant. Some development money also came from the DHSS. WEDIS took out patents on the general principles and contracts were drawn up between CHIC on what would happen if the project were to be successful, and what percentage of sales CHIC would take. WEDIS undertook not to deal with other companies. The agreement did not tie up any further applications of the product, but WEDIS will have first option on any further commercial applications.

It took six months of negotiation and investigation before a document was signed. Until that point, the only commitment was on the basis of a 'gentleman's agreement'. During the six months, there were many meetings to discuss product development issues, what it would look like, where the components would be manufactured and what sort of testing would be necessary. A separate limited company, with both the senior researcher and the head of WEDIS on the Board, has been set up to manufacture the consumables which are needed in the operation of the product.

The advantage to CHIC is that they gain a financial benefit from the commercialization of the product, and the kudos from having been in the forefront of the development of a major new technique. CHIC will be involved in ensuring that the quality of the products is maintained, especially through the production of the consumables. CHIC retains some influence in the relationship because they believe that WEDIS still depend on them for technical knowledge. WEDIS have commercial power, in that they have patents and access to markets, and have been able to move ahead of competitors by this new development.

The future danger to the relationship is that the market potential is so great that the small company will not be in a position to supply market need. A consequence could be that a larger company buys out WEDIS, which would leave CHIC in a position to re-assess their position in an entirely different environment. CHIC could also lose control in this relationship if the technology already handed over is sufficient for significant market penetration, or further development solely by WEDIS.

In this collaboration, the development came about through a small company being able to spend time investigating the possibility of developing a product which might need considerable modification before a standardized product would be available for the market. It is possible that the wrong large companies were approached by CHIC who did not have the right kind of knowledge of which companies would be most suitable. The alternative is that those companies did not perceive that it would be worth their while to invest resources in the project.

Case 7 FABMAC and METACON[1]

The actors FABMAC is a highly advanced consumer product manufacturer, and a wholly owned subsidiary of a multinational. At both FABMAC and its parent company, the corporate culture is distinctive, and largely explains the company's tendency towards co-operation and collaboration in all its dealings. A key element in the corporate culture is an open management system which is best described by FABMAC's managers themselves.

We can criticize each other without fear: we're our own policemen. I can talk to the MD when I want to. That sort of access is probably the most advantageous thing of all. We set Team Objective Meetings as opposed to 'boss and guy'. It knocks all the corners off politics. We've done TOMs for eight years. Having to justify your objectives openly is a very cleansing process – you can't say I'm doing it 'cos I hate that bastard over there!. . . At any time at least half a dozen are going on . . . You have to have a good rational argument otherwise you get shot down in flames . . . It has to be justifiable for the whole team to go for it.

The results of 'frantic inter-relating' is that frequently managers could not locate where decisions come from. Unlike other organizations studied, managers here could often not answer questions on where authority for particular decisions lay. Yet when we asked them about decision-making generally, all managers insisted that their particular function was 'really at the heart of things': 'Everybody here believes that they are at the heart of things'. Decisions then, are organic and spontaneous, rather than contrived and imposed. As another manager pointed out, '. . . by the time you do anything, people have all moved with you. The corporate conscience will have changed'.

In marked contrast to all the other case study firms, FABMAC specifically discouraged 'entrepreneurs'. Innovations are always the result of internal (and external) collaboration involving a wide and changing field of individuals. Entrepreneurs are put in their place. Said the managing director,

. . . the people below you are more expert than you – so from time to time you have to act against expert advice. When a senior manager says that he is the expert, then I know he's not really a manager . . . FABMAC breeds people who will react to a situation with a long-run view.

As we shall see, the absence of entrepreneurs is no barrier to collaborative innovation.

METACON are a medium-sized manufacturer of metal components and containers, wholly owned by a large, multinational corporation. In management style and structure it is much more akin to the British companies we have already described above.

The collaboration   The approach from FABMAC bemused METACON initially, as they had become accustomed to the ruthlessly competitive supplier market which larger UK manufacturing companies had imposed on smaller component suppliers. They had clearly not got used to the idea of charging more than the absolute minimum – and then paying the price in terms of underinvestment in production systems.

Although there was a clear benefit to the supplier of having their tooling-up costs underwritten by the guaranteed purchaser of an innovative product, the full implications of the collaboration only emerged in the final stages of the meeting. Having framed the whole discussion on a 'me OK, you OK' basis, FABMAC presented a serious of significant conditions. Remarkably, the METACON managers asked FABMAC to talk a little more slowly so that they would be able to copy down these 'instructions'. A period of dictation ensued.

Our knowledge of the company is, however, restricted to an afternoon's observation of a discussion between two directors and a senior manager from FABMAC. The meeting was one of a series involving the finalization of the design and tooling of a new metal container. The meeting progressed on the following lines. The representatives of both companies distributed themselves around an oblong table, FABMAC in shirt sleeves, METACON in brown suits and regimental ties. Both sides produced agendas and these were quickly amalgamated. Early discussion centred on recent progress at METACON towards the planned production of innovative enclosures. The financial position of the company was also reported and discussed. METACON had originally sought to sell to FABMAC on a least cost/least price basis; however, the discussion made clear that FABMAC policy was to pay higher than necessary prices in return for certain long-term gains. The argument was being rehearsed for at least the third or fourth time. FABMAC sought the highest specifications in all the materials it purchased, and paid a price which would enable its supplier to invest in advanced manufacturing techniques. This would ultimately lead to the greater efficiency of its suppliers, and a long-run reduction in purchasing costs to FABMAC.

FABMAC also stressed that they hoped METACON would manage to sell the enclosure to as many other users as possible, including FABMAC's principal competitor. This would produce economies of scale, and finance the next round of process innovation within METACON.

The METACON managers gave a strong indication that they found these suggestions helpful and would probably act on them. Thus it became clear that a 'collaborative' relationship can, paradoxically, give a purchasing company a far greater degree of *de facto* control over a supplier than the orthodox 'competitive bargaining' model of inter-firm behaviour.

While the principal enclosure design did not originate with either company, its modification, and the tooling required to produce it, was innovative. At the time, few, if any container manufacturers were prepared to produce it, and METACON and FABMAC were starting from a relatively low base point in terms of technical knowledge.

The innovation has been successfully implemented.

Discussion

The rich pattern of similarities and differences which the case study approach brings, is both a curse and a blessing. Moreover, we have yet to reach the point at which the nth. case begins to add fewer and fewer novel features to the already accumulated data.

The 'messiness' and largely unique character of each case confirms the experience of many other British researchers in the area of innovation, who have adopted a similar case approach. The reader will find that the differences among our cases outweigh their similarities. Thus what they ironically have in common is that each collaborator was confronted by a more-or-less novel set of circumstances in terms of size, product markets, organizational idiosyncrasies and in terms of whoever happened on the scene at the moment when collaboration was sought.

Perhaps three common features were first that timescales for projects were rather short (18 months to 2 years); second that there were important informal networks of contacts; and third, the relative absence of state, trade or other third party involvement, unlike more corporatized political economies.

This third point can probably be explained by the disorganized nature of capitalism in the UK which creates an uncertain environment in which innovating firms have to survive. Even when there is a powerful coherent business elite, as in the case of the UK power switchgear generation and distribution 'mafia', this does not always result in more dynamic innovative activity. The electricity elite were in any case accused of being wedded to conservative design, unlike their French or Japanese counterparts, and had made little apparent attempt to envisage alternative strategic options. For this reason, the UK switchgear industry is being pushed by technological standards already chosen and developed elsewhere, after it had instead aimed at low-cost mechanisms.

The existence of informal, personal networks among the scientific and engineering elite was found to be a key factor in the establishment of collaborative links. As a consequence, these links were often based on professional, 'scientific' trust at the early research stages, but were then formalized when commercial/production possibilities arose. Such 'professional to professional' respect makes it easier to enter into collaborative ventures.

According to Hayek (1960) reliance on individual judgement is both inevitable and desirable in the face of incomplete knowledge and the uniqueness of all conjunctions. Paradoxically this view is compatible with Lash and Urry's (1987) Marxist inspired view of Western capitalist economies. Given that outside Japan, economies remain disorganized, it may well take an individual sense for what may be possible in the extreme particularity of circumstances.

However, one should not be tempted into believing that Hayek's prescriptions for innovation are in any sense the only ones. As our final case study shows, corporations may (unusually) reject the competitive model of the firm and its markets altogether. In a notably 'Japanese' fashion it has opted for what Aoki (1984) has described as a 'co-operative model of firm behaviour'. Instead of acting as an individual unit, Fabmac seeks collaboration and co-operation at all levels – interpersonal, interfirm and at an industrial scale. Entrepreneurs are the last thing they want! Innovations are planned and directed at the net expansion of the industry as a whole, and the rule and importance of the individual is much reduced.

The reader will recognize a characteristically British or perhaps Anglo-American free-market setting which has marked much innovation here. In such a setting collaboration brings gains and threats.

Among the gains, smaller companies, might get their innovative ideas financially underwritten by larger companies. On the other hand, large bureaucratized firms might only find themselves able to innovate, when linked to smaller, and more imaginative entrepreneurs. A clash of 'corporate cultures' must remain a strong likelihood for both sides.

In order to manage these relationships successfully, personal trust has to be established – and this in the face of a temptation on the part of larger corporations to simply rip off the small-scale entrepreneur/scientist. The short-run incentives to do this are high, and there was some evidence of this in our sample. Yet given the remarkable number of issues over which a collaborative link up could collapse, it is perhaps surprising that our six sets of collaborators were managing to get on as well as they were. We nevertheless gained a strong impression from our visits to the various partners, that some were 'natural' partnerships in a way which others were not. The most compatible relationship seemed to be between DISCAT/DESTECH, and WEDIS/CHIC. The actors trusted each other implicitly and drew complementary but different gains from the collaboration. Any mild tensions such as arose were soon dealt with person to person. These collaborators had the advantage of proximity to one another, although other collaborators were managing to work together at some distance.

In the cases of RORA/STAR, and LECNET/PHOENIX, collaboration has yet to prove successful. In the former, this is because the project is still in its infancy. In the latter, however, it is possible that the wide geographical separation of the collaborators contributed to this relative failure; but we feel that the problem centred more especially on the bureaucratic conservatism of both organizations. In this setting 'the intrapreneur' is often eyed with a degree of suspicion by his or her own organization, and we certainly sensed this to be the case here and elsewhere in our field work.

Among the smaller collaborators, e.g. RORA, CHIC, WEDIS,

159

collaboration alone does not overcome the power of the market, where larger enterprises are dominant, though the product uniqueness achieved can provide a surer footing.

Standing back from the field work, one searches for a model or analogy to describe what we are seeing. Certainly, aspects of our cases fit various models of innovation to some degree or other. Fitting individual cases to parts of individual models seems, however, less constructive than developing a typology of interactive behaviour which more adequate accommodates the wide range of choices which the collaborators explore with greater or lesser degrees of naivete. While there must be some kind of limit on what collaborators can choose to do, these limits remain, ice-berg like . . . unseen, but painful on discovery.

Note

1. Original case research conducted by Stephen Smith and Barry Wilkinson (now at Cardiff Business School).

References

Aoki, A.M.A. (1984) *The Co-operative Game Theory of the Firm*, Oxford: Clarendon Press.

Freeman, C. (1982) *The Industrial Economics of Innovation*, 2nd edn, London: Frances Pinter.

Hakansson, H. (ed.) (1987) *Industrial Technological Development: A Network Approach*, London: Croom Helm.

Haklisch, C. (1986) *Technical Alliances in the Semiconductor Industry*, Centre for Science and Technology Policy. New York University Mimeo.

Harrigan, K.R. (1984) *Managing for Joint Venture Success*, Lexington Books.

Hayek, F.A. (1960) *The Constitution of Liberty!* London: Routledge and Kegan Paul, pp 426–7.

Lash, S. and Urry, J. (1987) *The End of Organised Capitalism*, Polity Press.

Rothwell, R. and Zegveld, W. (1982) *Small and Medium Sized Manufacturing Firms: Their Role and Problems in Innovation*, London: Frances Pinter.

Shaw, B. (1986) *The Role of the Interaction Between the Manufacturer and the User in the Technological Innovation Process*, DPhil Thesis, University of Sussex.

Von Hippel, E. (1976) 'The dominant role of users in the scientific instrument innovation process', *Research Policy 5*.

Strategy and Organization

Chapter eleven

The linkage between strategy, strategic groups and performance in the UK retail grocery industry

Pam Lewis and Howard Thomas

This chapter examines the strategy-performance consequences of strategic group membership for firms in the UK retail grocery industry. Indeed, a focal theme in the strategic groups literature (Caves and Porter, 1977; Caves, 1984; Cool and Schendel, 1987; McGee and Thomas, 1986; Porter, 1979) is that there is a theoretical relationship between strategic groups and financial performance. In particular, it is argued that profitability may differ systematically among groups in an industry because of mobility barriers, market factors and firm specific asset profiles.

However, the empirical evidence linking performance differences with strategic groups is not extensive and is conflicting. Cool and Schendel (1987) studying the US pharmaceuticals industry found performance differences in terms of market share but differences in profitability between groups were not observed. Further, differences were not found for risk and risk-adjusted performance. It has been shown that, in the UK brewing industry, within-groups variations in performance were greater than between-groups variations and it was concluded that 'differential firm strategies and asset endowments outweigh interfirm commonality of strategic characteristics in accounting for performance differences' (Johnson and Thomas, 1987: 31). In contrast, Fiegenbaum and Thomas (1987) found some support for the strategic group-performance linkage. In their study of the US insurance industry they found differences between groups for certain measures of economic performance, also for risk measures for returns and market share, and for a risk-adjusted measure associated with economic performance.

Where the linkage appears absent or equivocal, it could be because there is no such linkage; or it could be that the relationship has not been shown because the groups identified within existing studies have used a wide range of approaches (McGee and Thomas, 1986) which have generally not adequately captured the differences in the strategies adopted by firms in competitive environments. Taking the latter argument, we examine whether performance differences (using multiple indicators of

163

performance) exist when groups are formed using the more commonly accepted grouping techniques, namely, first, 'using the relative size of a firm in an industry as a proxy for strategic group membership' (Porter, 1979) and, second, more correctly, forming strategic groups from key strategic dimensions reflecting firms' scope and resource commitments (Cool and Schendel 1987; Hofer and Schendel, 1978).

We then reverse the procedure and question whether we can explain actual performance differences through a discriminant analysis model based on the key competitive strategic dimensions. In essence, we divide the firms into 'high', 'medium' and 'low' performers using actual performance results over the study period and then examine whether we can discriminate among these performance groups using the key strategic dimensions as predictor variables.

We discuss the results of our procedures and conclude that performance differences (in terms of ROS) do exist across some strategic groups defined in terms of key scope and resource commitments but there are no such differences across groups defined in terms of size. Further, we confirm the value of our strategic dimensions by showing, through our discriminant analysis model, that they have predictive validity in explaining performance differences identified in the study.

We speculate that further careful longitudinal studies of the strategy-performance linkage should be undertaken and should include competitive effects in the modelling of industry structure.

Theoretical development

The term 'strategic groups' was originally coined by Hunt in his doctoral dissertation (1972) to contribute to his exploration of the performance of the white goods industry in the 1960s. Porter (1980: 129) provides the accepted definition of a strategic group in terms of the similarity of competitive behaviour:

> A strategic group is the group of firms in an industry following the same or a similar strategy along the strategic dimensions . . . Usually, however, there are a small number of strategic groups which capture the essential strategic differences among firms in the industry.

The main studies in the area are summarized in McGee and Thomas (1986), Cool (1985) and Fiegenbaum (1987). The relationship between strategy strategic groups and performance has been documented in Caves and Porter (1977), Caves (1984), Cool and Schendel (1987), McGee and Thomas (1986) and Porter (1979). The burden of these writings is that it is not clear, based on empirical evidence, whether performance differs among strategic groups.

From a theoretical viewpoint, the main contributions to the explanation of intra-industry performance differences are found in the work of Caves and Porter (1977) and Porter (1979, 1980). They argued that profit rates may differ systematically among groups in an industry and offered explanations ranging from mobility barriers and market factors to firm-specific factors in order to explain such differences. Indeed, Porter (1979, 1980) concentrated more attention on firm than on group performance and emphasized the role of firm-specific factors including asset profiles and execution ability in strategy implementation to explain intra-industry performance differences. Two theoretical possibilities may, therefore, be advanced in researching intra-industry performance differences. First, that there may be performance differences across groups but second, that the uniqueness of firm strategies directed to achieve distinctive sets of assets (capital, financial, human) may better predict within-industry performance differences.

Studies within retailing have been concerned more with the structure of retailing and retailer strategies than the relationship between strategy and performance. Killen and Pattison (1987) detailed the structure as consisting of major supermarkets, medium-sized supermarkets, small independents and co-operatives. Lewis and Killen (1987) and McGee (1987) analysed retailer strategies in the UK. Building on this work to progress towards the linkage between strategy and performance, this chapter addresses the following propositions.

1. Although the UK retail grocery sector is dominated by a small number of large multiples, they differ from each other along a number of merchandise, store portfolio and service dimensions. We would therefore expect to be able to identify a number of distinct groups. For example, we might expect to observe firms operating superstores offering a wide range of merchandise clustered in one group and firms operating a large number of small, limited-range stores in another group.
2. Hatten and Hatten (1987) argued that asymmetric barriers are a necessary condition for growth in concentrated markets, like grocery retailing, where growth is a zero sum game. Further, they argued that the markets of the weaker firms are 'virtually contestable' in Baumol's (1982) sense. Thus entry into and out of some groups is easier than others. This would lead us to expect that some groups would be better defined and more highly defended than others. We might therefore observe a core of stable groups.
3. Economies of scale and scope are important drivers in this industry, both at the firm (buyer-power) and store level. This would lead us to expect to find performance differences between groups.
4. Lippman and Rumelt's (1982) concept of 'uncertain immitability' indicates that it is hard to replicate other competitors' successful

165

strategies even with full knowledge of their strategic choices with respect to scope and resource deployment. This would lead us to expect that firms within strategic groups will not necessarily achieve the same level of profitability. We would therefore expect to observe some performance differences within groups.

Methodology

The aim of the research was to examine the linkage between strategy and performance by examining strategic groups within the UK retail grocery sector. In the following paragraphs we discuss the rationale for focusing on that sector. We discuss the sample, the strategic dimensions and the methodology employed in forming strategic groups and testing the linkage.

Sample

The UK retail grocery sector is a static market where considerable consolidation is continuing to take place. Competition is for market share and the major players are moving to large out-of-town stores where they can offer a 'one-stop' shopping proposition to the car-owning population. The sector is dominated by a small number of large multiples, with the largest five businesses accounting for over 50 per cent of the market. In addition to these, the sector contains a large number of independent and co-operative societies which, jointly, account for approximately 30 per cent of the market. Positioned between the market leaders and the small independents and co-operatives are a number of medium-sized multiples. This research concentrates on the sixteen largest store groups, which account for more than 60 per cent of the sector. Table 11.1 gives a list of these stores.

Table 11.1 Stores in sample

Argyll
Asda
Bejam
Budgen
Dee Corporation
Fine Fare (acquired by Dee in 1986)
Hillards (acquired by Tesco in 1987)
Iceland
J. Sainsbury
Kwik Save
William Low
Marks and Spencer
Morrisons
Safeway (acquired by Argyll in 1987)
Tesco
Waitrose

Consolidation within the industry continued throughout and after the study period (1982–1986). In 1986 Fine Fare was acquired by the Dee Corporation and, in 1987, Safeway was acquired by Argyll and Hillards by Tesco. Thus the original sample of 16 has by now (1987) been reduced to 13 store groups. Future consolidation will be influenced by the regulation of monopoly and the possibility of overcapacity in the sector.

Despite the relatively small number of major players in the sector, they differ along a number of product, store, site and service dimensions. It would not appear unreasonable, therefore, to expect that a group structure would be discernible. This structure, encompassing major supermarkets, medium-size markets, small independents and co-operatives, is discussed in detail in an earlier paper (Lewis and Killen, 1987), which presents an in-depth analysis of the industry (see also Killen and Pattison, 1987).

Choice of strategic dimensions

Hofer and Schendel (1978) and Cool and Schendel (1987) argue that the key strategic dimensions discriminating between businesses and, therefore, forming the basis of strategic groups are those associated with scope and resource commitment decisions. Indeed, Cool and Schendel (1987: 1106) define a strategic group as: 'A set of firms competing within an industry on the basis of similar combinations of scope and resource commitments.'

Table 11.2 Variables

Strategy variables	
STORNO	Number of stores
STORSIZ	Average size of stores
ADVSALES	Advertising expenditures/sales
NFL	Number of food lines
POL	Proportion of own label lines
FAPSS	Food sales as a proportion of supermarket sales
SAGS	Supermarket sales as a proportion of group sales
Performance variables	
ROS	Return on sales
ROCE	Return on capital employed
PER	Weighted index of growth in the price/earnings ratio

The key dimensions in the present study included variables reflecting both of these commitments (see Table 11.2). The resource variables consisted of a store size variable and advertising. Economies of scale at the store level are an important source of competitive advantage

167

within this industry. Average store size is therefore included as a proxy variable to reflect firms' strategy and ability to exploit these economies, since other adequate proxies for scale economies (e.g. degree of capital intensity) were not readily available. Advertising to sales was the other differentiating resource commitment variable, included because it reflected the importance of promotional expenditures in generating store traffic in supermarkets.

The scope variables included a mix of store portfolio, merchandise strategy and focus variables. Supermarket operators are increasingly becoming managers of significant property portfolios and one of the major areas of competition is in the acquisition and development of out-of-town sites for large superstore developments (Segal-Horn, 1987; Killen and Pattison, 1987). The number of stores is included to reflect this crucial competitive dimension. It encompasses both the geographic spread and the store policy of the major players. Food sales as a proportion of super-market sales measures the extent to which stores are moving away from selling mainly food items. Given that expenditure on food is not rising significantly, diversification into non-food, higher value-added items offers both an avenue for expansion and a possible competitive advantage. The number of food lines differentiates between limited range stores (e.g. Kwik Save) and others which offer a wide range of food items (e.g. Safeway and Waitrose). The proportion of lines which are own label lines indicates another form of differentiation. Further, own label products offer a guarantee of quality and increase the retailer's power *vis-à-vis* the food manufacturer. Finally, supermarket sales as a proportion of group sales reflect the firm's focus on supermarket activities.

These seven strategy variables outlined above formed the basis of the grouping procedures.

In order to examine the existence of a linkage between strategy and performance, it was also necessary to derive performance measures for the companies concerned. Ginsberg and Venkatraman (1985) argue that multiple linkages exist between strategy and performance. It was desirable therefore to employ more than one measure of performance. As in a number of earlier studies (Cool and Schendel, 1987, 1988; Johnson and Thomas, 1988), accounting data were the initial source of performance data. ROS (return on sales) was a measure which was particularly relevant in the retail sector, where trading margins are small. In addition, there is significant capital investment taking place within the UK retail grocery sector as store groups change not only their store locations but also their store formats. Some measure of capital efficiency was therefore required. ROCE (return on capital employed) was used here because it appeared to be the most sensible among a number of alternatives and it is a commonly employed measure of capital efficiency in the retail industry. It was decided that a market measure of performance was also required. An index of the growth in the price/earnings ratio over the study period (PER), weighted by the ratio of firm's PE to industry PE, was considered to be an appropriate measure for this sector. The PE index was employed for two reasons: first, because it is used as an indicator of firm's performance by industry analysts and second because other market measures were inappropriate. Specifically, growth in share price and growth in market valuation were both rejected because of the distortions caused by the significant amount of acquisition activity in the sector.

Finally, it should be noted that, while risk-adjusted performance measures were considered worthwhile, none was introduced in this research because of the small time period and the instability of the standard deviation of the returns as a measure of risk. However, the risk exposure across different firms was examined in terms of capital structure variables (e.g. gearing or leverage). While individual firm differences were found, the risk exposure was not significantly different across groups.

Methods of analysis

A number of methods were used to test the linkage between strategy and performance. Groups were generated using three generally accepted methodologies (Harrigan, 1985; McGee and Thomas, 1986), namely, grouping on size, grouping on key strategic variables and grouping on strategic factors. The groups generated were tested for performance differences. A discriminant analysis model was then developed to predict actual performance differences among stores, using the strategy variables as predictors. These methods are described in more detail below.

Grouping on size

The first stage in the analysis was the testing of the relationship between groups based on size and performance. Porter (1979) suggested that a link existed between a firm's profits and industry structure, and thus that firms in some strategic groups would be more profitable than others. In essence, higher profits would accrue in groups with the 'best combination of high mobility barriers, insulation from intergroup rivalry and substitute products, bargaining power with adjacent industries, the fewest other members and suitability to the firm's execution ability' (1979: 219). Porter divided his firms into leaders and followers and proceeded to demonstrate that the firms in the leader groups were more profitable than those in the follower groups. Then, because the characteristic of the leader group firms were associated with size, there is purported to be a link between profitability and size. We sought to test this linkage by forming clusters on the basis of sales (that being the most appropriate measure

169

of size) and then testing whether there were performance differences between groups.

Cluster and factor analysis approaches

The grouping of stores on the basis of the strategic variables proceeded in two stages. In the first stage, clusters were formed directly, using the key strategy variables as the discriminating variables. Clusters were formed on the basis of the seven strategy variables described above and also on the basis of a reduced set of five variables. Food as a proportion of supermarket sales and stores sales as a proportion of group sales were highly correlated with the other variables and it was appropriate to test whether their exclusion would impact on the results. In fact the clusters derived from using seven and from using five variables were substantially the same. Further, since it was desirable to reduce the number of variables *vis-à-vis* the cases, the five variables case is preferred and those are the results reported here. Due to the intercorrelation of some of the key strategy variables, in the second stage varimax rotated principal component analysis was employed to produce factors on which to base the cluster analysis of stores. Because of the potential instability of factor scores with sixteen firms and seven strategy variables, the factor analysis was performed n ($=16$) times to ($n-1$) cases in order to test whether a changing sample composition would alter the factor loadings. In the event, these were the same or similar to the 16-case loadings in 15 out of the 16 runs. It was therefore established that the sample was acceptable for this analysis.

The factors generated by the 16-case analysis were then used as input to a cluster analysis to produce further groupings against which to test performance differences.

Discriminant analysis model

Cool and Schendel (1987) report on the equivocal nature of the evidence on the linkage between strategy and performance and this was supported by Johnson and Thomas (1988). In order to test the linkage fully, a discriminant analysis model was developed to reverse the testing procedure. This involved observing the distribution of the performance variables across the firms over the 1982–1986 study period and dividing them into suitable groups. In the case of all three performance variables the distribution divided into a small number (3 or 4) of well-defined groups.

Discriminant analyses were then used to test whether we could discriminate between the performance groups using the key strategic dimensions as predictor variables. This analysis would, first, further test the linkage between strategy and performance and, second, it would indicate whether the strategy variables used in the previous analyses were valid as predictors of performance differences and whether they could be regarded as key strategic dimensions.

All analyses were carried out using the SSPSPC (1986) package. Ward's hierarchical technique using squared Euclidean distances was chosen to form clusters. The decision rule for choosing meaningful clusters was based on two criteria: the overall variance explained and the incremental change in variance as a result of adding another cluster. The overall variance criterion was set at a minimum of 80 per cent of total variance and a further cluster was added if there was a gain of at least 5 per cent in the total variance. However, if the incremental change was very close to but slightly below 5 per cent, it was a matter of interpretation whether an extra cluster was added.

ANOVA and Scheffe tests were used to test the existence and significance of performance differences between clusters, 0.05 per cent being the critical point for significance. The Discriminant Analyses proceeded stepwise by minimizing Wilks' lambda. The Factor Analyses employed varimax rotated principal components analysis to reduce the number of factors (eigenvalues over 1 determined the appropriate number of factors).

Results and discussion

We discuss the results of the cluster analyses first by discussing the similarity of cluster membership across methods and we find that there is a core of clusters which retain a relatively stable membership pattern. Second we discuss the performance differences across differently based groups. We then discuss the results of the discriminant analysis.

Cluster analysis results

The groups produced by the various clustering approaches are shown in Table 11.3. The clusters on size produced three clear groups: large, not so large and small. The first two clusters contain the five dominant multiples plus Marks and Spencer. These clusters do not demonstrate significant commonality with the clusters produced by the analyses based either directly or indirectly on the strategy variables, as would be expected (Cool and Schendel, 1987: 1106) from the inadequacy of the model specification for groupings based on size. However, the groups based on strategy variables do show distinct patterns of group membership. Thus, while a number of stores appear to change their group membership according to the clustering method used, a core of stores occupying clearly distinguishable groups is discernible. These groups are described below.

171

Table 11.3 Cluster analysis groups

Strategic groups on size (sales)	
1	Marks and Spencer, Tesco, Sainsbury
2	Dee, Argyll, Asda
3	Waitrose, Safeway, Kwik Save, Fine Fare, Iceland, Budgen, Low, Hillards, Morrisons, Bejam
Strategic groups based on 5 strategy variables	
1	Marks and Spencer
2	Argyll
3	Kwik Save, Dee, Budgen
4	Iceland, Low, Bejam
5	Hillards, Tesco, Sainsbury, Fine Fare
6	Safeway, Waitrose
7	Morrisons, Asda
Strategic groups based on factors	
1	Marks and Spencer
2	Dee, Argyll
3	Bejam, Kwik Save, Iceland
4	Budgen, Fine Fare, Low
5	Hillards, Tesco, Sainsbury, Morrisons
6	Safeway, Waitrose
7	Asda

Note: The average annual sales for the three groups based on size were as follows: large, £2.5m–£3.0m; not so large, £1.4m–£1.9m; small, £0.04m–£0.88m.

The first stable group is Marks and Spencer which occupies a group by itself. This store has a maximum value (100 per cent) on its own label strategy and a minimum value for advertising to sales spend. It also takes relatively large values on the variables representing the number of stores and store size. Further, it has a much lower concentration on food items than other stores. It is, therefore, differentiated from other large stores by its concentration on own label products, its low advertising spend and its broad non-food diversification.

The second clearly differentiated group is that containing the Dee Corporation and the Argyll Group. These stores take below average values on all strategy variables except the number of stores, where Argyll, in particular, has twice as many stores as other firms. Further, they are less focused on the supermarket business and they do not differentiate themselves significantly on own label lines.

Hillards, Tesco and Sainsbury form the core of the third stable group, with Morrisons occupying the same group in one set of clusters. These stores are differentiated from the others by their focus on large superstores which offer a wide range of food lines. Asda, the other superstore operator, remains by itself in one case, being differentiated from the other superstores by its relatively small number of stores and its low focus on own label lines. However, in one case, Asda is joined by Morrisons. Thus, the superstore operators occupy two well-defined groups.

The only other clearly defined group which remain stable is the Waitrose/Safeway cluster. The major differentiating factor of these two stores is their very wide range of food lines. They offer twice as many food lines as most of the remaining stores and more than twice as many as some.

The remaining clusters contain the less well-differentiated stores, which cluster together in relatively ill-defined ways. In all cases the store sizes are small and they offer a medium to small number of food lines. The groups into which they fall depend upon relatively marginal differences in some of the strategy variables.

We conclude that the cluster analyses based either directly or indirectly on the strategy variables produce a number of consistent and stable groups. The less well differentiated stores move between two clusters while the rest of the stores fall clearly into groups which are well differentiated along the chosen strategy dimensions. The groups based on size are clearly different. Further, the groups based on the factor analysis are better defined, in terms both of the strategy variables and industry experience, than those resulting from the cluster analysis. Specifically, Dee and Argyll appear together; Asda appears by itself and the other superstore operators occupy one group.

Strategic groups and performance

We now discuss performance differences between groups. Table 11.4 shows the results of the ANOVA and Scheffe tests for the three sets of groups on the three performance variables, ROS, ROCE and PER.

First, for groups based on size there are no significant differences in performance (measured either by ROS, ROCE or PER) between the groups, that is, within-group variance dominates between group variance. It would appear, therefore, that there is no evidence to support Porter's (1979) thesis, thus indicating that size is probably an inadequate surrogate for the key strategic dimensions which drive competitive strategy in this industry. Furthermore, for the clusters based on the strategy variables, there is little evidence to support the strategy-performance linkage. For ROS, the between-group differences in performance are significant for the clusters based on the factor analyses and for the clusters based directly on the strategy variables. However, we should note that the significant results were for differences between the group consisting of only Marks and Spencer and the other groups. There were no significant results for differences between groups excluding Marks and Spencer. We conclude that there is little evidence supporting the proposition that profitability differs systematically between groups.

173

Table 11.4 Results of the ANOVA and Scheffe tests

	Clusters on size	Clusters on 5 strat vars	Clusters on factor analysis
		ROS	
ANOVA	F=2.1065	F=6.1343	F=13.1939
	(0.1613)	(0.0083)	(0.0005)
	N.S.	S.	S.
Scheffe	N.S.	S. *	S. **
		ROCE	
ANOVA	F=0.5080	F=0.4350	F=1207
	(0.6132)	(0.8388)	(0.9846)
	N.S.	N.S.	N.S.
Scheffe	N.S.	N.S.	N.S.
		PER	
ANOVA	F=0.3995	F=0.5337	F=1.0608
	(0.6820)	(0.7462)	(0.4632)
	N.S.	N.S.	N.S.
Scheffe	N.S.	N.S.	N.S.

Note: Figures in parentheses are the level of significance at which the null hypothesis is not rejected.

S. indicates results are significant and N.S. indicates results are not significant.

* Marks & Spencer significantly different from: 1 Argyll; 2 Bejam, Dee, Kwik Save; 3 Fine Fare, Hillards, Sainsbury, Tesco; 4 Safeway, Waitrose.

** Marks & Spencer significantly different from: 1 Argyll, Dee; 2 Bejam, Iceland, Kwik Save; 3 Budgen, Fine Fare, Low; 4 Hillards, Sainsbury, Morrisons, Tesco; 5 Safeway, Waitrose.

Discriminant analysis results

In the discriminant analysis ex-post performance groupings derived by inspection of the distributions of the performance variables were 'predicted' by the strategy variables. For ROS and ROCE the strategy variables classified all groups correctly, but for PER only 76 per cent of firms were allocated correctly.

In contrast to the cluster analysis and analysis of variance, these findings tend to support the hypothesis that strategy is linked with performance and also that the key dimensions chosen to reflect strategy within the sector are likely to be the correct ones.

Conclusions

This chapter set out to examine the relationship between strategy and performance. Specifically, strategic groups were formed on the basis of both size and key strategy dimensions. It was found that, although the strategic groups based on size were different from those based on strategy variables, there was considerable commonality between the groups based directly on the strategy variables and those based on the factor analysis approach. Further, it was found that there were some limited differences between groups' performance in the case of ROS but not for ROCE or PER but that this was not the case for the strategic groups based on size. A discriminant analysis model revealed that the discriminant function calculated from the key strategy variables was a very accurate predictor of performance for ROS, ROCE and PER.

It would appear that the discriminant analyses yield better results than the cluster analyses in terms of testing the linkage between strategic groups and performance. This apparent contradiction can be explained in terms of the differences between clustering and discriminant analysis procedures. The cluster analysis produces groups which are based on clustering in terms of the similarity of strategies and strategic posture as identified by the chosen variables reflecting scope and resource commitments. These may not lead in general to performance differences as indicated in our prior tests and also by the possibility of equifinality of performance across different strategies as suggested by Harrigan (1985). On the other hand, the discriminant analysis specifically links strategy and performance by trying to find that discriminant function (measured across the strategic variables) which identifies good versus bad performers.

It should be noted that the findings of the present paper are substantially supported by some recent work carried out by different authors on the same data set (Carroll and Pandian, 1988). In their work on mobility barriers, these researchers used canonical correlation to identify the strategy variables most closely associated with performance differences between firms. The advantage of this approach is that the analysis of the linkage between strategy and performance takes place prior to a grouping process and therefore takes account explicitly of both within and between group performance differences. Their results indicate that the variables identified in the research reported here as being significant strategy variables are indeed important predictors of performance differences. While the present study uses the strategy variables as predictors of group structures and then tests for performance differences, the Carroll/Pandian study tests the link first and thus confirms that the strategy variables used here are important predictors of performance differences, thus supporting the present findings.

In general, therefore, the findings provide some support for the propositions that performance differences exist across strategic groups and that strategic groups are constructs which have predictive validity in understanding performance consequences and their relationship to industry and competitive dynamics. We believe that the study adds to the similar findings of Cool and Schendel, and Fiegenbaum and Thomas because the research paid attention to two important issues in forming strategic groups. First, the research used an in-depth industry analysis to specify carefully the key strategic scope and resource committments (see also Hatten and Hatten, 1987). This led to an accurate specification of the strategy components in this industry. Indeed, the use of size to specify strategic groups was shown to be invalid. Second, multiple performance indicators were used to test performance differences in accordance with the suggestions of Oster (1982), Dess and Davis (1984) and Cool and Schendel (1987). Thus, market measures of performance were added to the more usual economic measures to try to capture the multifaceted nature of performance. And, like Cool and Schendel's research, performance differences were found for some (in this case, relatively few) but not all performance measures. In addition, the use of a discriminant analysis approach to test for performance differences is relatively novel in research in this area.

The research should, however, be extended longitudinally. The period 1982–1986 was chosen because it represented a stable strategic period over which much prior detailed research has been carried out by the authors. However, the longitudinal dimension is important for several reasons.

First, it should throw light upon the difficulties which firms may face in shifting strategic group membership. Firms may need to develop additional managerial and implementational skills in successfully repositioning their strategies. Indeed, Lippman and Rumelt's (1982) concept of 'uncertain imitability' indicates that it is hard to replicate other competitors' successful strategies even with full knowledge of their strategic choices with respect to scope and resource deployment. Dee Corporation's difficulties in repositioning following its acquisitions of Fine Fare and other grocery retailers show the 'learning by doing' character of strategic repositioning – even though retailing research had (like this research) emphasized the consistent strategic patterns adopted over time by its major protagonists – particularly, Sainsbury and Tesco. Dee attempted to take over a group of stores and transform them into a 'me-too' version of its major competitors. This involved a change of format and image, and a move into a quality sector where it was not already operating. In contrast, Argyll's acquisition of the Safeway chain to augment its up-grading involved acquisitions but will not involve the transformation of the newly acquired stores. There is thus less learning involved in Argyll's strategy. Argyll's strategy for moving up-market appears to be more soundly based than Dee's.

Second, longitudinal analysis should provide richer evidence of the extent of intra-group rivalry. For example, by monitoring competitive patterns in terms of key strategic variables among strategic group members over time, it should be possible to understand the dynamics of competitive strategy. For example, would Dee Corporation always follow the strategic leadership patterns of a Sainsbury or a Tesco?

Third, rivalry across groups could also be examined. For example, different strategic group members may compete in particular segments or niches, reinforcing the need to examine multiple point competition and overlapping groups (Fombrun and Zajac, 1987). There is evidence of this occurring at the local/regional level when supermarket groups monitor the activities of their competitors and focus their competitive strategies accordingly. Thus, while we would expect corporate level strategy within the major players to involve a monitoring of the activities of all other major players, at the local/regional level, with assets temporarily fixed and therefore the competitive arena reduced to a small subset of the major competitors, competitive strategy focuses on the immediate competitor group (Gripsrud and Gronhaug, 1985).

In conclusion, this paper has shown that there is some very limited evidence to support the strategic groups-performance linkage but that, in common with other researchers, the link is equivocal. Indeed, the main findings of this research indicate that the large within-group variation in performances dominates the between-group variation and that the firm may be the important unit of analysis for explaining performance differences. We argue that firm differences in asset endowments and resources (i.e. some firms may have a more appropriate set of strategic assets), market power and skills to implement strategies effectively (Rumelt's (1982) uncertain imitability concept) may dominate group level effects. Furthermore, we find evidence that a core of groups each with a distinguishable set of strategies is discernible. Thus, while some groups are not well defined in terms of their members' strategies, there is a core of groups, in this case five, which remain stable across the two major clustering techniques and which have well-defined strategies. This is in line with the findings of Fiegenbaum and Thomas (1987) who found a core of three groups which persisted across an extended time period.

References

Baumol, W.J. (1982) 'Contestable markets: an uprising in the theory of industrial structure', *American Economic Review* 72(1): 1–15.

Carroll, C. and Pandian, J.R.M. (1988) 'The effects of strategy and strategic change on the performance of retail stores in Great Britain', Department of Business Administration, University of Illinois at Urbana-Champaign.

Caves, R. (1984) 'Economic analysis and the quest for competitive advantage', *American Economic Review* 74(2) 127–32.

Caves, R. and Porter, M.E. (1977) 'From entry barriers to mobility barriers', *Quarterly Journal of Economics*, 91(2) 241–61.

Cool, K.O. (1985) 'Strategic group formation and strategic group shifts, a longitudinal analysis of the U.S. pharmaceutical industry, 1963–82', PhD Dissertation, Purdue University.

Cool, K.O. and Schendel, D.E. (1987) 'Strategic group formation and performance: The case of the U.S. pharmaceutical industry, 1963–82,' *Management Science* 33(9): 1102–24.

Cool, K.O. and Schendel D.E. (1988) 'Performance differences among strategic group members', *Strategic Management Journal* 9(3) 207–23.

Dess, G. and Davis, P.S. (1984) 'Porter's (1980) generic strategies as determinants of strategic group membership and organisational performance', *Academy of Management Journal*, 27(3) 467–88.

Fiegenbaum, A. (1987) 'Dynamic aspects of strategic groups and competitive strategy: concepts and empirical examination of the insurance industry', PhD Dissertation, University of Illinois.

Fiegenbaum, A. and Thomas, H. (1987) 'Strategic groups and performance: The U.S. insurance industry, 1970–84', Working Paper, Graduate School of Business Administration, University of Michigan.

Fombrun, C. and Zajac, E. (1987) 'Structural and perceptual influences on intraindustry stratification', *Academy of Management Journal* 30(1): 30–50.

Ginsberg, A. and Venkatraman, N. (1985) 'Contingency perspectives of organisational strategy: A critical review of the empirical research,' *Academy of Management Review* 10(3) 421–34.

Gripsrud, G. and Gronhaug, K. (1985) 'Structure and strategy in grocery retailing: A sociometric approach', *Journal of Industrial Economics* XXIII: 339–47.

Harrigan, K.R. (1985) 'An application of clustering for strategic group analysis', *Strategic Management Journal* 6: 55–73.

Hatten, K. and Hatten, M.L. (1987) 'Strategic Groups, asymmetric mobility barriers and contestability', *Strategic Management Journal* 8: 329–42.

Hofer, C. and Schendel, D.E. (1978) *Strategy Formulation: Analytical Concepts*, St Paul: West Publishing.

Hunt, M.S. (1972) 'Competition in the major home appliance industry, 1960–1970', Doctoral Dissertation, Harvard University.

Johnson, G. and Thomas, H. (1987) 'Strategic groups and financial performance: A critical examination', working paper, Manchester Business School.

Killen, V. and Pattison, B. (1987) *UK Grocery Retailing*, Retail Strategy Analysis Series, Centre for Business Research, Manchester Business School, UK.

Lewis, P.M. and Killen, V. (1987) 'Understanding the U.K. retail grocery sector', Manchester Business School working paper no. 151, Booth Street West, Manchester M15 6PB, UK.

Lippman, S. and Rumelt, R.P. (1982) 'Uncertain imitability: an analysis of interfirm differences in efficiency and competition', *Bell Journal of Economics and Human Science* August, 13(2) 418–38.

McGee, J. (1987) 'Retailer strategies in the UK', in G. Johnson (ed.) *Business Strategy and Retailing*, Wiley: Chichester.

McGee, J. and Thomas, H. (1986) 'Strategic Groups: theory, research and taxonomy', *Strategic Management Journal* 7(2): 141–60.

Oster, S. (1982) 'Intra-industry structure and the ease of strategic change', *Review of Economics and Statistics*, August 64: 376–83.

Porter, M.E. (1979) 'The structure within industries and companies' performance', *Review of Economics and Statistics* 61: 214–27.

Porter, M.E. (1980) *Competitive Strategy*, New York: Free Press/Collier Macmillan.

Segal-Horn, S. (1987) 'The retail environment in the UK, in G. Johnson (ed.) *Business Strategy and Retailing*, Chichester: Wiley.

SPSS/PC+ (1986) 444 Michigan Avenue, Chicago, Illinois 60611, USA.

Chapter twelve

An integrated approach to global competitive strategy

George S. Yip

Multinational companies are increasingly searching for new models of worldwide strategy. This is a particularly pressing concern for British and other European companies with the 1992 advent of the single European market. 1992 will change the nature of competition both inside and outside the European Community. Academic researchers have recently challenged the old model of multinational strategy, characterizing it as primarily 'multidomestic' in nature. Hout, Porter and Rudden (1982) defined a 'global' industry, in contrast to a multidomestic industry, as one in which a firm's competitive position in one country market is significantly affected by its competitive position in other country markets. The recommended response (developed in Porter, 1986) is a combination of concentration and co-ordination of value-added activities. Bartlett and Ghoshal (1987) used a somewhat different definition – a 'transnational industry' is one in which businesses are driven by simultaneous demands for global efficiency, national responsiveness, and worldwide learning.

The framework

This chapter sets out a framework that systematically relates global strategy choices to global industry conditions, building on Porter (1986) and the industrial organization link to competitive strategy (Caves, 1980). The framework is set out in Figure 12.1. Industry globalization drivers create the potential to achieve the benefits of global strategy. To achieve these benefits, a worldwide business needs to set its global strategy levers appropriately relative to the industry drivers, and relative to the position and resources of the business and its parent company. The organization's ability to implement the formulated global strategy affects how well the benefits can be achieved. The most important constructs in this framework are the industry globalization drivers and global strategy levers.[1] This chapter focuses on the interaction between these two sets of constructs.[2]

180

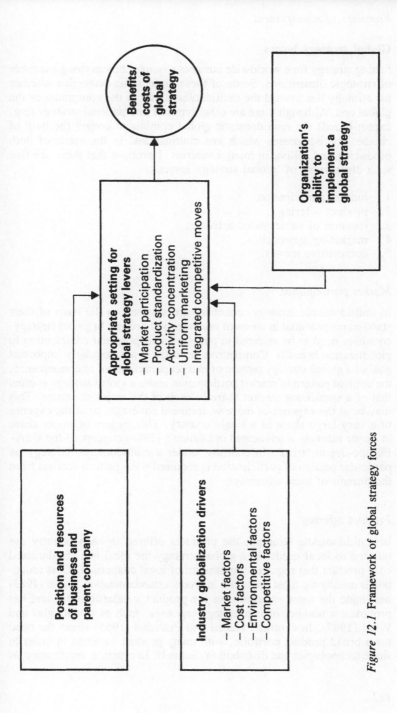

Figure 12.1 Framework of global strategy forces

Global strategy levers

Setting strategy for a worldwide business requires choices along a number of strategic dimensions. Some of these dimensions determine whether the strategy lies toward the multidomestic end of the continuum or the global end. Although there are other types of international strategy (e.g. export-based) the multidomestic-global continuum covers the bulk of choices for businesses which are multinational in the sense of both producing and selling in many countries. I propose that there are five such dimensions of 'global strategy levers':

1. market participation
2. product offering
3. location of value added activities
4. marketing approach
5. competitive moves.

Market participation

In multidomestic strategy, countries are selected on the basis of their stand-alone potential in terms of revenues and profits. In global strategy, countries need to be selected in terms of their potential contribution to globalization benefits. Competitive leverage is a particularly important goal of a global strategy pattern of market participation. In consequence, the optimal pattern of market participation under a global strategy is often that of a significant market share in each of the major countries. This may be at the expense of more widespread coverage, or at the expense of a very large share in a single country. This pattern of major share in major markets is advocated in Ohmae's (1986) concept of the USA–Europe–Japan 'triad'. In contrast, under a multidomestic strategy no particular pattern of participation is required – the pattern accrues from the pursuit of local advantage.

Product offering

In multidomestic strategy, the products offered in each country are tailored to local needs. In a global strategy the ideal is a standardized core product that requires a minimum of local adaptation. Cost reduction is usually the most important in product standardization. Levitt (1983) has made the most extreme case for product standardization, and has provoked a number of countering responses, such as by Douglas and Wind (1987). In contrast, Hamel and Prahalad (1985) stress the need for a broad product portfolio, with many product varieties in order to share technologies and distribution channels. In practice, multinationals have sometimes pursued product standardization to a greater or lesser extent. There is no clear pattern – the varying evidence on its extent has been reviewed by Walters (1986).

Location of value added activities

In multidomestic strategy, all or most of the value chain is reproduced in every country. In another type of international strategy – exporting – most of the value chain is kept in one country. In a global strategy, the value chain is broken up and each activity may be conducted in a different country. The major benefits lie in cost reduction. Porter (1986) views the configuration (i.e. location) and co-ordination of the value added chain as the essence of global strategy. One type of value chain strategy is partial concentration and partial duplication; these combine to provide strategic flexibility (Kogut, 1985) and bargaining power. The key feature of a global position on this dimension is the systematic placement of the value chain around the globe. A few companies are beginning to do this, such as Becton-Dickinson in medical equipment (Cvar, 1986).

Marketing approach

In global strategy, a uniform marketing approach is applied around the world. Buzzell (1968), and Quelch and Hoff (1986) have discussed the possibilities and merits of uniform marketing. The leveraging of scarce ideas is one of the key benefits of a uniform marketing approach. Many companies have tried uniform marketing to some extent, but total uniformity is rare (Walters, 1986).

Competitive moves

In global strategy, competitive moves are integrated across countries, i.e. the same type of move is made in different countries at the same time or in some systematic sequence, or a competitor is attacked in one country in order to drain its resources for another country, or a competitive attack in one country is countered in a different country. Perhaps the best example is the counter-attack in a competitor's home market as a parry to an attack on one's own home market (Porter, 1986). Integration of competitive strategy is rarely practised, except perhaps by some Japanese companies (see Kotler *et al.*, 1985).

Potential benefits of using global strategy levers

There are four major categories of potential globalization benefits:

1. Cost reductions through economies of scale; through exploiting differences in country factor costs; through flexibility (Kogut, 1985); and through enhanced bargaining power with suppliers, workers and host governments (Prahalad and Doz, 1987: chapters 4 and 5).
2. Improved quality of products and programmes through focus and concentration on a smaller number of products and programmes than under a multidomestic strategy.
3. Enhanced customer preference through global availability, global serviceability and global recognition (Levitt, 1983).
4. Increased competitive leverage through having more points to attack and counter-attack against competitors (Porter, 1986).

These benefits cannot be achieved through single country actions, but only through multi-country integrated actions. Table 12.1 summarizes the mechanisms by which each global strategy lever achieves particular globalization benefits.

Industry globalization drivers

To achieve the benefits of globalization, the managers of a worldwide business need to recognize when industry conditions provide the opportunity to use global strategy levers. These industry conditions are the industry globalization drivers. There are a large number of possible drivers. They can be grouped in four categories–market, cost, governmental and competitive. Table 12.2 lists these drivers and summarizes their effect on the potential to use global strategy levers. This section discusses in detail some of the effects. The appendix provides some examples of how companies have used particular global strategy levers to exploit industry globalization drivers.

Drivers are externally given by industry conditions or by the economics of the business, while the levers are choices available to the worldwide business. There can also be feedback whereby the exercise of a lever can change the level of a driver. For example, homogeneity of need (for a type of product) is a driver that allows the use of the product standardization lever. Customer experience of the standardized product can in turn change preferences so that needs become more similar across countries.

Market drivers

Market globalization drivers depend on the nature of customer behaviour and the structure of channels of distribution. These drivers affect the use of all five global strategy levers.

Table 12.1 How global strategy levers achieve globalization benefits

BENEFITS Global strategy levers	Cost reduction	Improved quality	Enhanced customer preference	Competitive leverage	MAJOR DRAWBACKS All levers incur co-ordination costs, plus
Major market participation	Increases volume for economies of scale		Via global availability, global serviceability and global recognition.	Advantage of earlier entry. Provides more sites for attack and counter-attack, hostage for good behaviour.	Earlier or greater commitment to a market than warranted on own merits.
Product standardization	Reduces duplication of development efforts. Allows concentration of production to exploit economies of scale.	Focuses development and management resources.	Allows consumers to use familiar product while abroad. Allows organizations to use same product across country units.	Basis for low cost invasion of markets.	Less responsive to local needs.
Activity concentration	Reduces duplication of activities. Helps exploit economies of scale. Exploits differences in country factor costs. Partial concentration allows flexibility vs. currency changes, and vs. bargaining parties.	Focuses effort. Allows more consistent quality control.		Allows maintenance of cost advantage independent of local conditions.	Distances activities from the customer. Increases currency risk.
Uniform marketing	Reduces design and production costs of marketing programmes.	Focuses talent and resources. Leverages scarce, good ideas.	Reinforces marketing messages by exposing customer to same mix in different countries.		Reduces adaptation to local customer behaviour and marketing environment.
Integrated competitive moves				Provides more options and leverage in attack and defence.	Local competitiveness may be sacrificed.

Source: Yip (1988a).

Table 12.2 Effects of industry globalization drivers on the potential use of global strategy levers

Industry drivers	Major market participation	Product standardization	Activity concentration	Uniform marketing	Integrated competitive moves
MARKET					
Homogeneous needs	Fewer varieties needed to serve many markets	Standardized product is more acceptable		Marketing content needs to be uniform	Allows sequenced invasion of markets
Global customer			Marketing process has to be co-ordinated	Marketing content needs to be uniform	
Global channels			Marketing process has to be co-ordinated	Marketing content needs to be uniform	
Transferable marketing	Easier to expand internationally			Allows use of global brands/advertising, etc.	
COST					
Economies of scale	Multiple markets needed to reach economic scale	Standardization needed to reach economic scale	Concentration helps reach economic scale		
Learning experience effects	Multiple markets accelerate learning	Standardization accelerates learning	Concentration accelerates learning		
Sourcing efficiencies			Centralized purchasing exploits efficiencies		
Favourable logistics			Allows concentrated production		
Country differences in factor costs			Exploited by activity concentration		
High product development costs	Multiple markets needed to payback investment	Standardization reduces development needs	Concentration cuts cost of development		
GOVERNMENT					
Favourable trade policies	Affects nature/extent of participation	May require or prevent product features	Local content rules affect extent of concentration possible		Integration needed to deal with competitive effects of tariffs/subsidies
Compatible technical standards	Affects markets that can be entered	Affects standardization			
Common marketing regulations				Affects approaches possible	
COMPETITIVE					
Interdependence of countries	More participation leverages benefits				Integration needed to exploit benefits
Competitors globalized or might globalize	Expand to match or pre-empt	Match or pre-empt		Match or pre-empt	Integration needed to exploit benefits

Source: Yip (1988a).

Homogeneous customer needs

If customers in different countries want essentially the same type of product or service (or can be so persuaded), then there is the opportunity to market a standardized product. Levitt's (1983) advocacy of standardization is based on the assumption of converging needs. More realistically, the key is to understand what aspects of the product can be standardized and what should be customized. In addition, homogeneous needs make it easier to participate in a large number of markets because fewer different product offerings need to be developed and supported.

Global customers

Global customers buy on a centralized or co-ordinated basis for decentralized use (around the world). The existence of global customers both allows and requires a uniform marketing programme needed to deal with them.

Global channels

Analogous to global customers, there may be channels of distribution that buy on a global or at least regional basis. Global channels or middlemen are also important in exploiting differences in prices by performing the arbitrage function of transshipment. Their presence makes it more necessary for a business to rationalize its worldwide pricing.

Transferable brands and advertising

The nature of the buying decision may be such that successful brand names and advertising require little local adaptation, i.e., brand names and advertising are readily transferable. Such transferability enables the use of uniform marketing strategies. It also makes it easier to expand participation in markets. A worldwide business can also adapt its brand names and advertising campaigns to make them more transferable, or design transferable ones *de novo*.

Cost Drivers

Cost globalization drivers depend on the economies of the business; they particularly affect the use of the activity concentration lever.

Economies of scale and scope

The market of a single country may not be large enough for the local business to achieve all possible economies of scale or scope. Scale at a given location of activity can be increased through participation in multiple markets combined with product standardization and/or concentration of selected value activities.

187

Learning and experience effects

Even if scale and scope economies are exhausted, expanded market participation and activity concentration can accelerate the accumulation of learning (direct manufacturing) and experience (total production) effects. The steepness of the learning and experience slopes is clearly the critical aspect of this driver.

Sourcing efficiencies

The market for supplies may allow centralized purchasing to achieve savings in the cost of production inputs.

Favourable logistics

A favourable ratio of sales value to transportation cost enhances the ability to concentrate production. Other logistical factors include non-perishability, the absence of time urgency, and little need for location close to customer facilities.

Differences in country costs and skills

Factor costs vary generally across countries, and more so for particular industries. The availability of particular skills also varies. Concentration of activities in low cost or high skill countries improves the worldwide costs and productivity of a worldwide business.

High product development costs

Product development costs that are high relative to single-market revenues can be reduced on a per unit basis by developing a standard product for a large number of countries. Standardizing the product and concentrating the development activity also reduce product development costs.

Government drivers

Government globalization drivers depend on the rules set by country governments, and affect use of all global strategy levers.

Favourable trade policies

Host governments affect globalization potential in a number of major ways: import tariffs and quotas, non-tariff barriers, export subsidies, local content requirements, currency and capital flows restrictions, and requirements on technology transfer. The extent of each of these policies makes it more or less difficult to use the global levers of major market participation, product standardization, activity concentration and uniform marketing; and affects the need to use the lever of integrated competitive moves.

Common technical standards

Differences in technical standards among countries affect the extent to which products can be standardized. Often, standards are set with protectionism in mind.

Marketing environment

The marketing environment of individual countries affects the extent to which uniform global marketing approaches can be used. Certain types of media may not be allowed or may have restrictions on their use. There may be limitations on various promotional devices, for example lotteries. These variations have been well addressed in the traditional literature on international marketing.

Competitive drivers

Market, cost and governmental globalization drivers are primarily endogenous to an industry at a particular time. Competitors can play only a limited role in affecting the setting of these factors (although a sustained effort can bring about change, particularly in the case of consumer preferences). In contrast, the set of competitive drivers is entirely in the realm of competitors' choices. Competitors can raise the globalization potential of their industry and spur the need for a response on the global strategy levers.

Interdependence of countries

A competitor may create competitive interdependence among countries by pursuing a global strategy. The basic mechanism is through sharing of activities. Thus a competitor's market share in one country contributes to its overall cost position and, therefore, its share position in another country. Other competitors then need to respond via increased market participation, uniform marketing or integrated competitive strategy to avoid a downward spiral of sequentially weakened positions in individual countries.

Matching and pre-empting competitors' moves

More specifically, there may be a need to match or pre-empt individual competitor moves. These moves include expansion in or into major markets, being the first to introduce a standardized product, or the first to use a uniform marketing programme.

Drivers are not deterministic

There are many ways in which industry globalization drivers provide opportunities to use global strategy levers. Some industries can score high on most dimensions of globalization (drivers), as demonstrated by Yoshino (1986) for the civil aircraft industry. In other industry conditions, national competitors with local strategies may be more successful as demonstrated by Baden Fuller *et al.* (1987) in the European major appliance industry.

Furthermore, there are several reasons why the industry globalization drivers are not deterministic (in the sense of allowing only one type of international strategy to be successful in a given industry). First, no industry is high on every one of the many globalization drivers. A particular competitor may be in a strong position to exploit a driver that scores low on globalization. Second, the appropriate use of global strategy levers provides additional competitive advantage that is incremental to other sources of competitive advantage. These other sources may allow individual competitors to thrive with international strategies that are mismatched with industry globalization drivers. Third, resources pose limitations. A worldwide business may face industry drivers that strongly favour a global strategy. But global strategies are typically expensive to implement initially, even though there should be great cost savings and revenue gains downstream. Fourth, the strategic position of the business is also relevant. Even though a global strategy may improve the business's long-term strategic position, its immediate position may be so weak that resources should be devoted to short-term, country-by-country improvements. Fifth, there may be greater returns in investing in non-global sources of competitive advantage, e.g., superior technology, than in global ones, e.g., centralized manufacturing.

Changes over time

Finally industry evolution plays a role. Each of the industry globalization drivers can change over time. The appropriate global strategy will then change also. In some cases the actions of individual competitors can affect the direction and pace of change. Competitors who are well positioned to take advantage of globalization forces will want to hasten them. For example, a competitor with strong central manufacturing capabilities may want to accelerate the worldwide acceptance of a standardized product.

Summary

This chapter has developed a framework for global competitive strategy that focuses on the interaction between industry globalization drivers and global strategy levers. This framework provides a basis for collecting data to test a number of alternative models and hypotheses that have been developed in the literature and in this chapter.[3] The framework can also be used by a company to evaluate systematically whether it should adopt a global strategy for a particular business, and what that strategy should be along key dimensions. Although the framework has been discussed in terms of globalization, it also applies at the regional level. Companies can use it just as effectively to develop Europeanization strategies.

Appendix: examples of how industry globalization drivers allow use of global strategy levers

This appendix (see also Yip, 1989) presents a few examples to illustrate how some companies are using global strategy levers to exploit industry globalization drivers, as follows:

Industry Driver	*Strategy Lever*	*Example*
Market factors	Market participation	Japanese banks
Market factors	Marketing uniformity	Henkel sealant
Cost factors	Activity concentration	Merck drugs
Government factors	Product standardization	Philips TV sets
Competitive factors	Integrated competitive moves	Black & Decker

Market globalization drivers

Market participation lever

A homogeneous worldwide need for a product provides the opportunity to expand market participation. The need of corporations for sources of financing from debt or equity is relatively homogeneous around the world. Financial institutions are beginning to recognize the opportunity posed by this common need. Over the past few years, American investment banks have moved into Japan in a major way. On the other side, the four largest Japanese stockbrokers, Yamaichi, Nomura, Daiwa and Nikko are attempting to become major players in the New York financial market. The Japanese are entering the market by selling the financial equivalent of Toyotas – treasury bills, mortgage-backed securities, corporate bonds and commercial paper. At the same time, they are establishing a presence in the European financial markets.

Uniform marketing lever

A product that serves a common need can be geographically expanded with a uniform marketing programme, despite apparent obstacles of differences in marketing environments. In 1980 Henkel, the German household products company, had a household sealant, SISTA, that was highly successful in West Germany. Henkel wanted to expand the brand outside Germany but found that other markets were individually too small to support the expensive development of a new product marketing programme. The Henkel parent company was able to persuade local companies to accept a standardized product and marketing programme developed in Germany, and partially funded by the parent. This approach allowed Henkel to succeed with programmes, such as a beer promotion, that seemed unsuitable outside Germany. As a result Henkel was able to expand the sealant into fifty-two countries within two years, and doubled worldwide sales.

Cost globalisation drivers

Activity concentration lever

Low transportation costs allow concentration of production. Merck, the American pharmaceutical company, ships bulk powders to their plant in Menuma, Japan, where they are packaged for sale in consumer sizes. Merck has found concentration of production to be cost effective because production savings more than offset the low transportation costs. Furthermore, being slow to perish, pharmaceuticals lend themselves well to this logistical strategy.

Government globalization drivers

Product standardization lever

Government restrictions in terms of technical standards can make or break efforts at product standardization. The Dutch multinational, Philips NV has a centralized manufacturing facility for European television sets at Bruges in Belgium. But, contrary to expectations, this plant is not a model of efficiency. Cumbersome local standards produce different requirements for various countries. For example, the plant makes seven types of TV sets made up of different tuners, semiconductors and plugs. As a result of these differing technical standards, the assembly line has to be revamped every week. The extra cost of these differing standards is about $20 million a year. But thanks to 1992 EEC harmonization, Philips will be able to standardize the television sets it offers. By 1990, Philips will manufacture only two or three types of sets at Bruges.

Competitive globalization drivers

Integrated competitive moves

Attacks by competitors can force a company to globally integrate its competitive moves. Until the mid-1970s, Black & Decker was the dominant producer of worldwide consumer power tools. But in the late 1970s, the Japanese company, Makita began offering Black & Decker stiff competition. Makita was able to do this by taking advantage of economies of scale offered by standardizing its worldwide product offering. To match this competitive threat, B&D adopted an integrated competitive strategy where, 'Black & Decker is now conducting itself not as 50 separate businesses in 50 different countries, but as one company worldwide, with one strategy and one set of corporate goals.' (Farley, 1986: 68)

Acknowledgements

The author thanks Robert D. Buzzell of Harvard University, Bradley T. Gale of the Strategic Planning Institute, Ruth Raubitschek of New York University/Purdue University and Robert J. Thomas of Georgetown University for their helpful comments on earlier versions of this manuscript.

Notes

1. These two constructs were first developed in Yip *et al.* (1988)
2. Further aspects of the framework, and issues of modelling and hypothesis testing are addressed in Yip (1988).
3. The author is conducting a data-gathering effort via the PIMS Global Strategy Program of the Strategic Planning Institute.

References

Baden Fuller, C., Nicolaides, P., and Stopford, J. (1987) 'National or global? The study of company strategies and the European market for major appliances', *London Business School Centre for Business Strategy Working Paper Series*, no. 28.

Bartlett, C.A. and Ghoshal, S. (1987) 'Managing across borders: New strategic requirements', *Sloan Management Review* Summer: 7–17.

Buzzell, R.D. (1968) 'Can you standardize multinational marketing?' *Harvard Business Review*, Nov–Dec: 102–13.

Caves, R.E. (1980) 'Industrial organization, corporate strategy and structure', *Journal of Economic Literature* XVIII: 64–92.

Cvar, M.R. (1986) 'Case studies in global competition: Patterns of success and failure', in M.E. Porter (ed.) *Competition in Global Industries*, Boston: Harvard Business School Press, pp. 539–68.

Douglas, S.P. and Wind, Y. (1987) 'The myth of globalization', *Columbia Journal of World Business* 22; 19-29.

Farley, L. (1986) 'Going global: choices and challenges', *Journal of Business Strategy*, Winter: 67-70.

Hamel, G. and Prahalad, C.K., (1985) 'Do you really have a global strategy?' *Harvard Business Review* July-August: 139-48.

Hout, T., Porter, M.E., and Rudden, E. (1982) 'How global companies win out', *Harvard Business Review* Sept-Oct: 98-108.

Kogut, B. (1985) 'Designing global strategies: Profiting from operational flexibility', *Sloan Management Review*, Autumn: 27-38.

Kotler, P., Fahey, L., and Jatusripitak, S. (1985) *The New Competition*, Englewood Cliffs, NJ: Prentice-Hall, p. 174.

Levitt, T. (1983) 'The globalization of markets', *Harvard Business Review*, Sept-Oct: 92-102.

Ohmae, K. (1986) *Triad Power*, New York: Free Press.

Porter, M.E. (1986) 'Competition in global industries: A conceptual framework', in M.E. Porter (ed.) *Competition in Global Industries*, Boston: Harvard Business School Press.

Prahalad, C.K. and Doz, Y.L. (1987) *The Multinational Mission: Balancing Local Demands and Global Vision*, New York: The Free Press.

Quelch, J.A. and Hoff, E.J. (1986) 'Customizing global marketing', *Harvard Business Review*, May-June: 59-68.

Walters, P.G.P. (1986) 'International marketing policy: A discussion of the standardization construct and its relevance for corporate policy', *Journal of International Business Studies*, Summer: 55-69.

Yip, G.S. (1988) 'A framework for global competitive strategy: Industry globalization drivers and global strategy levers', *Georgetown University School of Business Administration*, working paper no. 88-01.

Yip, G.S. (1989) 'Global strategy: opportunities for competitive advantage', *Sloan Management Review*, Fall, forthcoming.

Yip, G.S., Loewe, P.M., and Yoshino, M.Y. (1988) 'How to take your company to the global market', *Columbia Journal of World Business*, Winter.

Yoshino, M.Y. (1986) 'Global competition in a salient industry: The case of civil aircraft', in M.E. Porter (ed.) *Competition in Global Industries*, Boston: Harvard Business School Press, pp. 517-38.

Chapter thirteen

Linking strategic change, competitive performance and human resource management: results of a UK empirical study

Chris Hendry, Andrew Pettigrew and Paul Sparrow

Introduction

This chapter reports on findings from a one-year study of twenty firms' involvements in training. This is part of a larger, continuing programme of research into corporate strategy change and human resource management (HRM). We begin by arguing that previous treatments of HRM, strategic change and competitive performance fail to deal with the processes linking these. Having outlined the character of the research programme, its objectives, and conduct, we briefly identify a series of changes in the outer context of firms and the strategic responses they have made, the changes accompanying these within firms, and the range of HRM responses they have initiated. We then take up the critical question of how transformations in training and development, and in HRM have actually occurred. We conclude that effective transformations in firms' training and people development result from the mobilization of the spatial and temporal context, and develop a series of models to show how this works. In so doing we return to the question of the linkages between strategic change, HRM, and competitive performance, and outline some implications for public policy.

Strategic change, human resource management, and competitive performance

The burgeoning of interest in Human Resource Management (HRM) in the 1980s owes much to the popularization of Porter's (1980) notion of competitive advantage, on the one hand, and, on the other, the idea of 'excellent companies' through the work of, among others, Peters and Waterman (1982), Ouchi (1981), and Levering *et al.* (1984). The idea that there are firms that are excellent in their corporate culture, and that the relevant characteristics can be discriminated and copied, has been expanded into an analysis of the management of human resources more generally and linked to the business strategy literature, in the belief that human resources are one means towards achieving competitive advantage (Porter, 1985; MacMillan and Schuler, 1985).

Nevertheless, this literature is as yet very imperfectly integrated, and gives two distinct connotations to Human Resource Management. While the 'corporate culture' literature adopts the language of 'competitive advantage', it makes only limited use of the analytical framework, and far from discriminating HRM strategies to meet different competitive conditions, it tends to portray a general set of characteristics as universally excellent. Its central concern is with the operation of a coherent value and behavioural set to sustain strategy. In practice, this favours adoption of 'progressive' employment policies, 'reflective of a coherent set of management attitudes and values [rather] than . . . of the economic environment in which that organisation operates' (Beer *et al.*, 1984).

By contrast, the strategy literature itself, in arguing the need for 'fit' between strategy, structure, and the human resource policies which channel behaviour and create organizational culture (Galbraith and Nathanson, 1978), has given rise to theories of 'strategic human resource management'. Their goal is 'to align the formal structure and the HR systems so that they drive the strategic objectives of the organisation' (Fombrun *et al.*, 1984), and various strategy models have been used to suggest appropriate HR policies to be followed. (For a fuller discussion of the different meanings attributable to HRM and the origin of these, see Hendry and Pettigrew (1986), Guest (1987), and Armstrong (1987).)

One feature of the literature is that it orders the relationships between strategic change, competitive performance, and HRM in different ways. The latter, for instance, is quite explicit in seeing people and HRM policies as a means towards achieving strategic objectives – matching people to strategy, not strategy to people – while assuming that 'fit' is the key determinant of performance. As Lengnick-Hall and Lengnick-Hall (1988: 456) put it:

> Rarely are human resources seen as a strategic capacity from which competitive choices should be derived. When human resources are used to determine strategic direction, the approach is uni-directional from human resource problems to strategic solutions, rather than interactive. Consequently, the potential contribution that human resources might make to the competitive position of the firm is unnecessarily limited.

All of these literatures are equally weak, however, in their treatment of the actual linkages between strategic change, competitive performance, and HRM policies. This includes, but goes beyond, the more familiar criticism concerning neglect of 'process' – that descriptions of the process of business strategy-making, for example, are over-rationalized (Pettigrew, 1985). It concerns the essentially linear treatment of HRM,

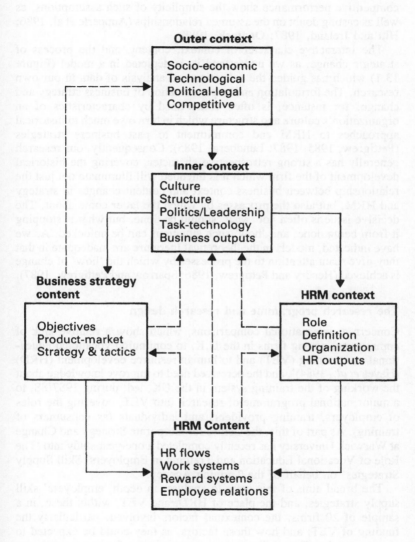

Figure 13.1 Model of strategic human resource management

business strategy change, and improvements in competitive performance, where what is needed is an appreciation of their interactivity. Attempts to test whether supposed excellence in HRM does equate with high competitive performance show the simplicity of such assumptions, as well as casting doubt on the assumed relationships (Aupperle et al, 1986; Hitt and Ireland, 1987; Ondrack, 1988).

The interactive character of context, content, and the process of strategic change, as we understand it, is depicted in a model (Figure 13.1) which has guided the collection and analysis of data in our own research. The formulation and implementation of business strategy and change, for instance, is often constrained by characteristics of an organization's culture and structure which in turn owe much to historical approaches to HRM and commitment to past business strategies (Pettigrew, 1985, 1987; Lundberg, 1985). Consequently, our research generally has a strong retrospective character, covering the historical development of the firm which it is intended will illuminate not just the relationship between business context and content changes in strategy and HRM, but also the processes by which the latter come about. The decisive issue is often not 'what' should be done, but what is stopping it from being done, and 'how' such situations can be unlocked. As we have indicated, models in the theoretical literature are inadequate in that they give scant attention to the processes by which the 'how' of change is achieved (Hendry and Pettigrew, 1986; Sparrow and Pettigrew, 1987).

The research programme and research design

Concern at international comparisons, which show a relative lack of commitment among firms in the U.K. to continuing vocational educational and training (VET) and to human resource development (HRD) (Hayes *et al.*, 1984)', and the perceived need to improve knowledge about the working of the training system in the UK, led, during 1987/88, to a major national programme of research into VET, covering the roles of employers, training providers, and individuals (as consumers of training). As part of this, the Centre for Corporate Strategy and Change at Warwick University has recently completed a one-year study into 'The Role of Vocational Education and Training in Employers' Skill Supply Strategies' on behalf of the Training Agency.

The broad aims of this were to analyse, in depth, employers' skill supply strategies, and the place of HRD, and VET, within these, in a sample of 20 firms; the contextual factors involved, particularly the funding of VET; and how those factors, as they could be expected to change, might affect skill supply strategies in the future. A particular area of interest, consequently, was in firms' processes of decision-making towards training. Ten of the firms in the sample were drawn from an existing study, and the other ten were added to balance the sample in various ways. Table 13.1 summarizes some aspects of these.

Table 13.1 The sample of twenty firms

	Number of employees	Ownership	Head office location	Main product or service
Small				
Small Engineering A	60	Independent	Rugby	Manufacturer of press tool punches and dies
Small Engineering B	28	Independent	Coventry	Manufacturer of press tools
Computer Services A	158	Independent	West of London	Business Systems and Software
Computer Services B	116	Part of UK Group	West Midlands	Business Systems and Software
Medium				
Manufacturer C*	300	Part of UK Group	North of England	Special Purpose Valves
Pharmaceutical Manufacturer	265	Part of US Group	Berkshire	Gelatine Capsules
Large				
Computer Supplier A*	2,650 (UK)	Part of US Group	West of London	Computer hardware, systems & software
Computer Supplier B*	21,000 (World wide)	UK Group	London	Computer hardware, systems & software
Computer Supplier C*	1,059 (UK)	Part of US Goup	London	Computer hardware, systems & software
Retail Banking A*	3,255	Part of UK Group	Scotland	Banking and financial services
Retail Banking B*	5,343	Part of UK Group	South Midlands	Credit card
Manufacturer A*	750	Part of UK Group	West Midlands	Safety glass
Manufacturer B*	1,789	Part of UK Group	West Midlands	Automotive Components
Public Sector A	9,000	Public	South of England	Water Authority
Public Sector B	75,000	Public	North of England	Health Authority
Retailer A*	5,305	Part of UK Group	West Midlands	Auto parts and bicycles
Retailer B*	31,600	UK Group	North of England	Fresh foods and provisions and non-food products
Hotel Group	3,900	Part of UK Group	Scotland	Hotel catering
TV Rental Firm	7,020	Part of UK Group	South Midlands	TV rental and Midlands retailing and Hi-fi
Road Transport Firm	1,500	Part of UK Group	North of England	Road Freight

*Denotes firms who are part of the contractor's other MSC project on 'Corporate Strategy Changes and Human Resource Management'.

The ten firms drawn from the existing project on 'Corporate Strategy Change and Human Resource Management' were studied very much more intensively than the others, with an average of 40 interviews and periods of 'real-time' observation. This meant that the patterns and conclusions of the study were strengthened by the depth and quality of historical and real-time data collected from these intensive cases. In the remaining ten firms an average of six interviews were completed, the majority of this work being carried out by Coopers & Lybrand Associates. These interviews included personnel directors, senior line managers, training managers, middle and supervisory management, and shop floor employees and shop stewards. In all cases, the interviews were supported by company documents and reports, and quantitative data on manpower, training activities and training expenditures.

In the analysis which follows (the findings from which are reported more fully in Pettigrew, Hendry, and Sparrow, 1989), Vocational Education and Training (VET) refers to processes and activities for acquiring knowledge and skills related to current or future work requirements, by formal, structured, or guided means. To all intents and purposes it is synonomous with the term 'training'. Human Resource Development (HRD) is activity which contributes to the development of people. It includes career moves and career development, appraisal and reviews, organization development and restructuring, and cultural change processes in the organization. Human Resource Management (HRM) includes recruitment, compensation, employee relations, work organization and job design, and managing the outflows of people. HRM is also inclusive of both VET and HRD, and involves managing the full range of people-related activities and processes in the organization.

The competitive context and firms' strategic responses

The clear pattern across the sample of 20 firms was of substantial change in their business environment and inner context. Most of the firms had been influenced not only by the post-1980 economic circumstances of the UK but also by consequential adjustments in the fortunes of their own and related industry sectors. The pattern in many firms was for a dramatic stiffening of the competitive environment since the late 1970s, often a loss of competitive advantage, and rapid changes in business strategy, structure and employment levels.

Eight of the twenty firms were making substantial losses at some point in the early 1980s. All to varying degrees have recovered. The multiple paths to regeneration have included reducing fixed costs, technological change, new product developments and significant divestments, internationalizing of activities, new channels of distribution, an emphasis on quality and improving image, and acquisitions for diversification. The period 1980–1988 has thus been an era of radical change.

The complexity of such externally inspired changes, frequently combining in their impacts on firms, created needs for new operating structures and systems, and new skills, knowledge and capability from staff at many organizational levels and in a variety of functions. Although the origins of HRM issues were diverse, they were nevertheless manifestly connectable to the business and technical changes in the outer context of the firms. On the other hand, why firms undertook HRM change, and certainly their ability to carry it through, also had much to do with the considerable degree of internal organization and cultural change occurring. Changes in leadership, major redundancy programmes, attempts to create a more performance and quality-oriented culture, or to create a culture receptive to a wide range of interrelated changes, and the balancing of technical cultures with more strategic management skills at the top and with people management skills, all contributed to the climate within which HRM changes were carried out and the operating situation of the HRM function itself. In the process there has been a considerable degree of decentralization of responsibility for HRM activities (although HRM strategy remained a central function), with many firms expending considerable effort to inculcate an ethos of line ownership of HRM problems (Purcell, 1985; Purcell and Gray, 1986; Evans and Cowling, 1985).

Human resource management issues

Such external and internal changes raised issues across the whole spectrum of HRM activity. Put simply, and generally, competitive pressures led to the perception of a business performance gap. Firms generally responded to this gap in two ways. First, by the development of their products and their market position. Second, by technical change within the organization. These responses were made singly or together and, in turn, led to perception of a skills performance gap. This in turn produced responses to tackle issues of skill supply, training and retraining, etc. Thus, business and technical change has been a significant driving force for HRM change. Figure 13.2 describes this basic process.

The HRM issues arising are complex, and highly interrelated and challenge the firm across short, medium, and long-term perspectives. Few of the issues can be tackled by pulling one human resource lever, be it training, recruitment, or compensation. The central issue of skill supply illustrates this.

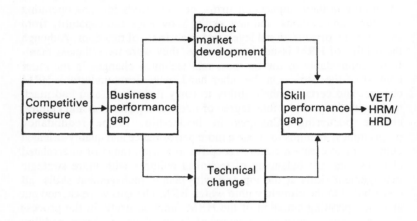

Figure 13.2 Business performance – VET/HRM/HRD linkage

Skill supply

The acquisition of new skills has become the underlying imperative, both in conditions of growth affecting many of these firms now, and in situations of change affecting those that had been through a trough and were beginning to strike out in new directions. The majority of firms had thus experienced a shift in skill requirements, as a result of the various product and business market changes outlined.

There was, however, a wide spectrum of behaviour in terms of whether firms had a strategy towards skill supply. Managing shrinkage of the business and employee numbers through the recession had been for many a matter simply of survival, and not conducive to 'strategic' behaviour – although within the constraints of LIFO arrangements and voluntary redundancy schemes firms may have sought (with limited effect in our firms) to retain their 'better' employees. However, those business environment changes now associated with internationalization, technological change, and moves into new business areas have forced many firms to begin to develop more explicit HRM strategies. These have changed the demand for skills, while the supply is affected by external labour market factors (especially acute in sectors like computing, and certain branches of engineering), and by internal factors (such as abrupt headcount changes during the recession creating missing cohorts of new recruits, and hence 'development gaps', and the inheritance of an unsuitable skill base for the new tasks in hand). Many firms consequently experience a 'skill gap' which is not amenable to simple solutions.

Thus, the evidence overwhelmingly shows that the strategies employed by firms to overcome this gap involve a number of components, including recruitment, more flexible pay, more flexible and varied employment contracts, training and development, and both the upgrading and downgrading of job skill levels. Some examples of how these have been applied show how they may stimulate wider consideration of HRM issues. (A fuller treatment of firms' strategies may be found in Pettigrew *et al.*, 1988).

A major tool has been the manipulation of recruitment criteria. Some firms raised recruitment standards to develop a more flexible skill base, while others (in quite diverse sectors) relaxed them to broaden the net and increase the volume of recruits. The effect of the former has often been to challenge other aspects of the HR system, such as career opportunities and training, management style, and employment conditions; while the effect of the latter has been to put pressure on training to fill the gap between required job skills and entry standards.

Difficulties associated with attracting and retaining people with new skills (skills now seen as central to the strategic drives of the firms) often triggered serious efforts to reduce attrition. Even in industries making high use of part time and cheaper labour, the need to create a more stable and informed workforce capable of providing a higher level of service (as in 'the Hotel Group') has led to efforts to reduce and control attrition, by enhancing job prospects.

Part-time employment has become more important in many firms, accounting for much of their growth in employment, while, in conjunction with this, firms in banking and retailing especially have moved to more flexible working time patterns. The use of freelances, temporary staff and sub-contracted labour was an important strategy for firms managed on headcount (as opposed to a paycosts basis), subject to seasonal fluctuations in business, or wishing to protect a core manpower profile from fluctuations in demand. On the other hand, a firm like 'Computer Services B' has pursued a deliberate policy to reduce its dependence on contract staff, both to cut costs and secure knowledge of its systems in-house. The alternative for them was to establish a graduate recruitment scheme with a two year programme of training and placement, both in-company and in other companies in the Group, and to ensure it provided the intrinsic and extrinsic satisfactions to retain them, once trained. This is a classic instance, therefore, of how recruitment policy implicates HRM generally.

Skill structures have been actively changed through combining job categories and tasks, in engineering especially, in order to reduce employee numbers and labour costs, and to increase flexibility. In computer supply and computer servicing firms, cross-functional integration of IT and customer relations skills (across sales, support, and systems engineering functions) has been critical to execute competitive strategies. These, in turn, involved formal retraining programmes to multi-skill individuals, or recruitment, or even simply an improvement in the management process across and within functions to avoid recruitment or training solutions.

Equally, there were several examples of redesigned product or process technology reducing the skill level of existing jobs or creating new, lower skilled jobs. Overall, however, it is difficult to determine a consistent pattern in the use of deskilling as a strategy to ease skill supply problems, and there is much debate, indeed, about whether particular changes in job requirements constitute 'deskilling' or 'upskilling' (Hendry, 1988; Wood, 1982).

Vocational education and training (VET)

VET is an important component of skill supply for the majority of firms. An important general finding is the increase in formal training activities that has occurred across firms in the sample within the last few years. This is confirmed by the wider survey undertaken by Deloitte/IFF for the Training Commission (1988) covering 1986 when compared with figures for 1984 (MSC/IFF Research, 1985). This gives the average of training days for all employees, across all establishment sizes, as 7 days, compared with an average for all adult employees, in establishments of more than 25 employees, of 5.3 days in 1984.

Levels of training are influenced by short- and long-term influences. Pressures to cut financial costs, large reductions in headcount, high levels of staff attrition and reorganizations tend to constrain immediate training levels. Over a longer period, however, training levels are more influenced by the organization of responsibilities for training, differential conditions of entry, and the nature of the training system. The ability to deliver training, however, has itself tended to suffer from recessionary cutbacks.

Entry into training is governed by a number of factors. Where entry to training of different kinds is limited by qualification level, the opportunity to train is clearly linked to recruitment practices. A result of banks' tiered recruitment strategies, for example, is that rising standards of entry level qualification applied to a few have increased the selectivity, or 'focus', in the training and development offered.

Initial training in the guise of apprenticeships generally has become less important, with lower skill content and shorter courses. On the other hand, although reactions to YTS varied, its advent often influenced other initial training schemes by helping to change managerial attitudes and showing managers that training could be a practical alternative to open market recruitment, at the same time as it has raised basic training standards for new recruits (as in 'Retail Banking A'). Similarly, the content of apprenticeships has been influenced by YTS, as in the 'Road Transport Firm'.

Fewer firms were involved in continued skill provision. In particular, management training in most firms did not operate in as structured a way as technical training, and levels of investment tended to be relatively low. The dissolution of traditional skills and job structures has caused 'top up' training to fall into some disrepute. On the other hand, retraining activities were much in evidence, being mainly project based and triggered by changes in product design, manufacturing processes, management systems, new services, or improvements in the quality of existing ones. Major changes of this kind, linked to a renewal of competitive edge, have been the principal engine for the increase in training activity observed.

Human resource development (HRD)

HRD as a linguistic concept and a basis of activity tends to be the prerogative of larger firms. Most firms do not have any formal or stated philosophy of HRD although many actually carry out activities that in practice serve a developmental purpose. Such activities tend to be confined to managerial staff.

Managing entry into the HRD system is an extremely important activity because the ability to attract and place the right calibre of employee crucially influences the ability to develop them. The way in which this entry is managed through graduate recruitment illustrates the wider applicability of HRM systems to training and development issues. Although the increase in graduate recruitment may simply be the result of their ready availability in a buyers' market, to do jobs where lower qualifications previously sufficed, the firms in the sample were firmly of the belief that it would enable them to sustain rising skill levels. However, relying on such an entry mechanism often raised expectations, creating pressures for firms to offer better employment conditions. Failure to provide these, as in the 'Road Transport Firm', simply led to graduate recruits leaving. One way to cope with such raised expectations is to operate 'tiered' recruitment streams, each with a separate set of HRM conditions and career expectations, as has become common in banking.

Appraisals have become more important for firms that need to assess performance and promotion readiness, link cultural and strategic changes to rewards, and identify training and development needs. The appraisal process therefore often represents a firm's first step into HRD activities.

HRD (through, for example, job rotation, mentoring, and appraisal) has necessarily to engage line managers to be effective. There is some evidence that line managers are being drawn into a more active role in HRD and becoming more aware of their responsibilities in this area. Part of this growing awareness is a recognition of the importance of recruitment to the ability to develop, which is therefore causing managers to question their recruitment practices, criteria and standards. Second, there is an awareness that recruitment of more highly educated employees (and not simply graduates) challenges the range of HRM provision and practices, and thus is forcing a wider perspective on line managers as they begin to address HRM questions for themselves and not regard them as issues just for the personnel department.

Creating transformations in VET, HRD, and HRM

Firms' behaviour towards VET, HRD, and HRM nevertheless varied, and the broad patterns of change and response outlined merely provide a resume of trends. Firms varied in their degree of concern for HRM issues, and in their level of activity, while concern and activity might (though not necessarily) also have a knock-on effect on either expenditure or delivery of VET.

The 20 firms in the sample covered a wide spectrum of such concern and activity. The key queston to be answered, therefore, was, 'why do some firms give more attention, and money, to VET and HRD activity, and how can this level be raised?' Or, put another way, what produces a sustained high level of VET and HRD effort, and how do organizations get to a point where training and development is in the 'bloodstream'? The answer to this question rests on an understanding of the interlinkages of context and processes with VET, HRD and HRM change.

First, it was clear that the patterns of change differed. Thus, it was possible to identify seven pathways to transformation, while the degree to which firms had successfully completed such transformation and were down these paths varied.

Second, in analysing processes of decision-making, the environment in which this was carried out, and actions firms took, it was apparent that there were certain features (or 'factors') which were conducive to high levels of training concern and activity, and, conversely, there were others which had a negative impact.

When these two modes of analysis – one of process, one of context – are combined, the depth and extent of VET and HRD changes can be understood through an explanatory frame which argues that effective change results from the mobilization of context (Pettigrew, 1985), and that what distinguishes firms is the richness of the context for VET and HRD that key actors can mobilize.

Pathways and levels of change in VET/HRD/HRM

Although changes in the outer and inner context of firms had provided the essential trigger and drive for VET, HRD, and HRM transformation, the 20 case firms had responded differently to external change and exhibited different levels of VET, HRD, and HRM change, so that no one simple or effective pattern of change was discernible. We identified seven and a large sample may reveal yet more. Figure 13.3 summarizes these.

The first of these, for example, is one in which changes in the business environment and in the strategy, structure, and other aspects of the internal environment of the firm have directly stimulated VET. As these have progressed, they have opened up change in a wider range of human resource activities. In the second, the pattern is essentially reversed, with a broader set of human resource initiatives being developed in response to a new buisness strategy, within which training has emerged as a key component. These two are the most common patterns.

The fourth is again common, where a firm has relied on just recruitment, for example, to supply its skills during its initial growth phase, and then realized the need to train to ensure its own internal sources and the need for career and management development to attract and retain professional staff. Sometimes, high volume VET activity can develop without having a wider impact, and the emergence of a broader sweep of human resource policies has had to await changes in the business environment and greater complexity in internal operations, at which point there has been parallel development of the two. This is the fifth pattern, characteristic of the two banking organizations. The sixth and seventh patterns are ones of only limited change, with basic training taking place in response to particular product or process innovations, or on an *ad hoc* basis, but without any knock-on or spill-over effects on other HRM activity.

Though the models lay out the general pathways to change, two qualifications need to be made. First, the pathways are iterative and not simply linear. There is a considerable amount of 'learning by doing', with changes in training feeding new HRM activities, and vice versa, and both these affecting the context in which they are conducted. The opportunities for reinforcement and modification of activities are illustrated in relation to the first of these in Figure 13.4.

Second, firms were not necessarily all the way down their particular track. Some had made more progress than others. It was thus evident that transformation in firms' VET, HRD, and HRM was a multi-level process, proceeding from concern to activity and to the commitment of adequate funding on a long-term agreed basis, as Figure 13.5 illustrates.

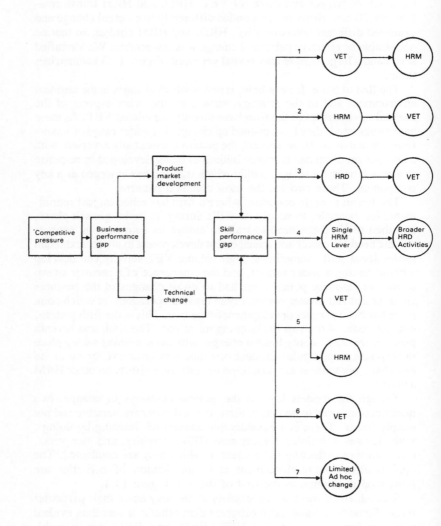

Figure 13.3 The Warwick model of change in VET, HRD, and HRM

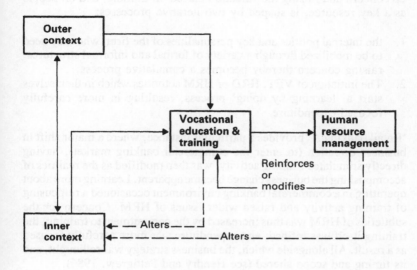

Figure 13.4 VET activities leading to a change in HRM

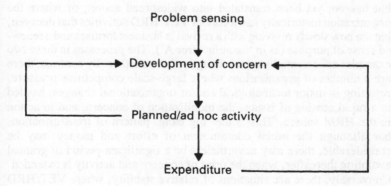

Figure 13.5 Levels of VET/HRD/HRM transformation

Again, these processes are not necessarily linear and direct. Building up concern and raising the valuation placed on training, and on people as a key resource, is shaped by two iterative processes:

1. the internal politics and key personalities of the firm, who may need to be mobilized through a variety of formal and informal structures: raising concern thereby becomes a cumulative process:
2. The initiation of VET, HRD or HRM activities which in themselves start a 'learning by doing' process, resulting in more carefully focused expenditure.

'Retail banking A' provides a particular instance, where a major shift in business direction (to enter the commercial banking market), having directly stimulated training activity, was then modified as the realities of accomplishing the business change became apparent. Learning more about operating in a commercial banking environment occasioned a refocusing of training activity and raised wider issues of HRM. Concern for the subtleties of HRM was thus increased by the commitment to training; the training itself was refined; and expenditure was more carefully focused as a result. All alongside which, the business strategy was rethought, and its timing and scope altered (see Hendry and Pettigrew, 1986).

The sample provided instances of six varying levels of transformation, illustrating how processes of transformation are not linear, nor take the form of a single strategic response at one point in time, but how, like business strategy, they are emergent over time. These six levels include where problems are sensed and concern about training has been raised, but has not yet been translated into widespread action; or where the organization historically had a core of VET/HRD activities that decayed, but are now slowly reviving with a revival in business fortunes and a renewed sense of purpose (as in 'manufacturer A'). The processes in these two examples are essentially mirror images of one another. By contrast, there are a number of organizations where large-scale competitive pressure, resulting in major technological and/or organizational changes, has led to a rapid sensing of issues, the mobilization of concern, and to action in the HRM sphere. This is the 'big bang' pattern of transformation, but although the initial commitment of effort and money may be considerable, there may nevertheless be a significant period of gradual evolution thereafter, when the orbit of concern and activity is extended. Conversely, there are situations of relative stability, where VET/HRD levels are fixed at medium-to-low levels because there is little actual change in the outer context; or there is change that is not perceived or understood, and therefore as yet little response. The small specialist engineering firms enjoying secure product markets illustrate this pattern.

Positive and negative factors driving, stabilizing, and inhibiting VET and HRD

The second mode of analysis was to summarize those features in firms' environments, internal and external, which were conducive to high levels of training concern and activity, and, conversely, those which had a negative impact.

Sampling the 20 cases, it was apparent that high concern/activity in VET and HRD was the result of four sets of positive factors being all present which variously drove and stabilized training activity. These fell into four categories: business strategic; the external/internal labour market; internal factors, training systems, philosophy and management organization; and external training stimuli and support, including funding. By the same token, decay or inertia in training activity was accompanied by decline in any or a number of these forces ('contra-indicators'), along with additional, specifically negative forces.

The distinction between 'driving' and 'stabilizing' forces, is an important one for understanding firms' inclination and capacity for generating training activity. While the major initial trigger (or 'necessary' condition) for training is 'technical change' or 'product-market developments', leading to recognition of a 'skill gap', neither is a 'sufficient' condition, and the other factors need to be equally present to achieve effective sustainable activity in training. Thus, the propensity to train was enhanced where a sufficient combination of these factors occurred. Cursory analysis of the sample shows that:

- those firms most highly rated in terms of levels of concern/activity in training have a considerable variety of positive factors in all four areas;
- those in the middle reaches have significant gaps in one or more of the four areas, with contra-indicators and additional negative factors, such that they serve to cancel the positive forces for training that do exist;
- those most negatively rated have few positive factors of any kind, but, rather, contra-indicators in these areas as well as additional negative factors.

Figure 13.6 summarizes the factors driving, stabilizing, and inhibiting training activity. These have been described in detail elsewhere (Pettigrew, Hendry, and Sparrow, 1989, 1988; Hendry *et al.*, 1988), and there is not space to do so here. As an illustration, though, of the kind of effect we have in mind, the impact of technological or product-market changes is greatest where these are so integrated or pervasive that they affect total system requirements and attendant skills. Thus, a manufacturing system, like that introduced at 'manufacturer B', which automates

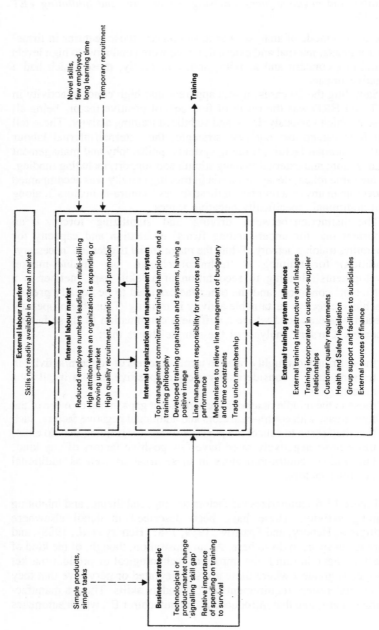

External labour market

Skills not readily available in external market

Internal labour market

Reduced employee numbers leading to multi-skilling

High attrition when an organization is expanding or moving up-market

High quality recruitment, retention, and promotion

Internal organization and management system

Top management commitment, training champions, and a training philosophy

Developed training organization and systems, having a positive image

Line management responsibility for resources and performance

Mechanisms to relieve line management of budgetary and time constraints

Trade union membership

External training system influences

External training infrastructure and linkages

Training incorporated in customer-supplier relationships

Customer quality requirements

Health and Safety legislation

Group support and facilities to subsidiaries

External sources of finance

Business strategic

Technological or product-market change signalling 'skill gap'

Relative importance of spending on training to survival

Novel skills, long learning time

Temporary recruitment

Training

Simple products, simple tasks

Figure 13.6 The interaction of positive and negative factors on VET

material transfer processes, radically changes the front-line skills of production workers and this has knock-on effects on maintenance staff, production management, and production engineers (Hendry and Pettigrew, 1988). The task and skill implications are overwhelming and demand comprehensive training solutions. On the other hand, a business which produces a small number of simple, standardized products/ services, in which simple tasks with a short learning time predominate, is likely at best to engage in limited 'maintenance (or 'top up') training' only.

Similarly, three features of the internal labour market of the firm are favourable to training. Reducing the numbers of employees to improve productivity may often lead to an expansion in the tasks and skills demanded of individuals – requiring 'composite skills' in production operatives, and 'multi-' and 'cross-skilling' in maintenance staff. These have to be added on in some systematic way. Second, when an organization is experiencing high levels of attrition in the course of expanding or moving upmarket, it may discover that a positive approach to training and development is necessary to recruit high quality staff. And third, a tradition of high quality recruitment, retention, and promotion, makes training in higher level skills a viable option for a firm undergoing or contemplating change.

Figure 13.7 similarly identifies the factors that specifically influence attention to HRD. Attention to HRD mostly only follows high concern/ activity in VET, though there is not a necessary causal relationship. Previous development of VET leads on to HRD more particularly where it generates new forces in the internal labour market of the firm. VET can be undertaken for a variety of motives, which may be purely instrumental, and therefore not in itself signify a training 'culture'.

On the other hand, attention to HRD is necessary to cement attention to VET, because it is only when HRD is addressed that thinking about, and devotion of resources to, training and development is embedded in a wide-ranging and inclusive approach to HRM. (To that extent, HRD and HRM are synonymous.) VET alone, for most firms, represents a tap which can be too readily turned on and off. Thus, an essential feature of the 'pathways to transformation' models is that both a sustained commitment to training and effective training activities are nourished by a broad approach to HRM.

Again, the influences on HRD activity are detailed elsewhere, and cannot be here. A critical factor, however, is where business strategy increases the complexity of the internal and external environment to be managed. This frequently leads to redefinition of the management task, and is often accompanied by structural organizational change. This may well then produce a recognition that management resources are stretched (i.e. that there is a visible 'people performance gap'), and may also extend to recognizing a need for change in role and

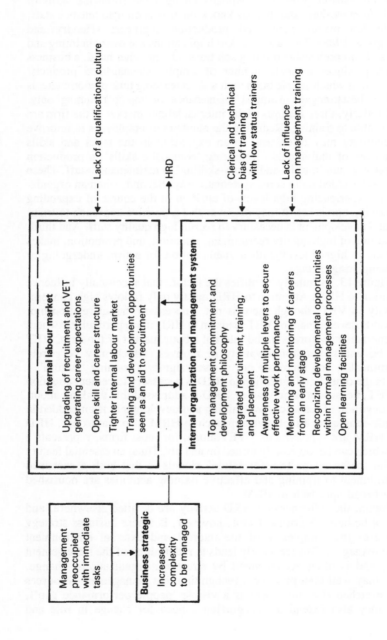

Figure 13.7 The interaction of positive and negative factors on HRD

attitudes among staff at large (thus fostering 'attitude change' programmes).

The inference from this analysis is that effective change (towards high levels of VET and HRD) results from the mobilization (and where appropriate, neutralization) of such factors, as critical contextual variables. What, therefore, distinguishes firms is the richness of the context for VET and HRD that key actors can mobilize. Thus, there are receptive and non-receptive contexts. Such contexts develop over time as positive forces are mobilized and created – the evidence of training successes and business relevance, for example, having a cumulative impact on concern, while training initiatives set up 'learning by doing' processes. There are thus two dimensions to context, and effective change can be said to result from the mobilization of the spatial and temporal context. The result is patterns of change ('pathways') which are the product of a firm's particular historical context (pressures and opportunities) which training champions have been able to mobilize and intensify to raise the levels of awareness and action, to deal with skill performance gaps. A similar process is presumed to operate in the recognition and response to a business performance gap. Case examples of these processes in operation can be found in Hendry and Pettigrew (1987, 1988), and Sparrow and Pettigrew (1988).

Summary and conclusion

There are a number of approaches to persuading employers to train and develop their staff more. The first approach argues that there is a direct link between increased training activity and business performance. This is a key platform of the Training Agency, and was given force by the MSC/IFF (1985) survey. However, the assumed linkage is based on cross-sectional data from which it is hard to impute causal linkages. Indeed, some argue that the relationship is the other way round, with increased business performance coming first followed by increased training activity (Figure 13.8)

The interpretation put on the more recent Deloitte/IFF survey for the Training Agency (1988), however, is more ambiguous and could readily fit with a number of 'factors' identified as important driving forces in our own study: 'there is clear evidence that those establishments which are growing fastest, be it in output, profit, investment or people, tend to be the establishments providing higher levels of training.' (1988: 7).

Firms' own approaches to evaluating the benefits of training do not lend credibility to a belief in a simple, linear relationship. The basic systems to support evaluation are often deficient, with firms excusing the lack of information on the grounds that the collection of data is costly and resources are best devoted to front-end benefits. Cost-benefit

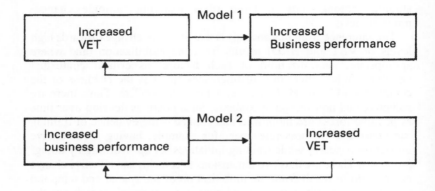

Figure 13.8 VET – business performance linkages

analysis is hardly ever attempted. Even so, despite information being inadequate, it is not clear that this affects the amount or direction of VET effort. A positive climate and commitment to training often relies, rather, on an act of faith among top managers (although such 'faith' can still be a highly rational one, based on a view that skills are a vital source of competitive advantage).

Evaluation is notoriously difficult, and the criteria that can be successfully applied weaken the further one gets from the training event, as the number of variables intervening between training and business performance increase. While both 'strong' and 'weak' criteria are employed in evaluation, our research shows that those firms which have the most positive attitudes and carry out the most training employ 'soft' criteria relating to broad human resource goals (to do with recruitment and retention, career management, etc.), which are 'intermediate to business goals, and they tend to be sceptical about 'hard' cost/benefit evaluation related to bottom-line outcomes. Thus, 'hard' criteria employed by firms in the sample include district sales performance and performance speeds after training (e.g. keyboard), the ability to earn maximum bonus on piece rates, and exam pass rates; while 'soft' criteria include such objectives as reduced turnover, promotability after training, improved communications between departments, improved ability to recruit, and maintaining balance in the career system.

To summarize, therefore, our argument concerning the linkages between strategic change, business performance, and human resource management:

1. Training is a business-related decision. It is changes in competitive pressure and the business performance gap revealed by that pressure that provide the trigger, or 'necessary conditions' for people-related changes.
2. Training decisions are made in the light of immediate requirements, and also what is seen as being possible and do-able. That is to say, training decisions are a response to specifics. However, despite being made in this time-frame, the decisions have a cumulative impact, much like business decisions.
3. The processes involved in the sensing of issues and the mobilization of concern about skill performance gaps are of critical importance. These processes are not linear, but iterative by nature, and involve a substantial degree of learning by doing. They are subject to a range of influences, to imperfect information, and to 'soft' criteria. While the process is not a tidy, rational one in terms of costs and benefits of alternative approaches being clearly weighed, nor is the process simply idiosyncratic. Parts of the whole process are subject to established methodologies (such as 'training needs analysis' in relation to investments in new technology). But equally, these become refined through 'learning by doing'.
4. There are extremely diverse and complex contexts, content areas, and pathways to change in VET, HRD and HRM. These are also likely to be shaped by a highly situational collection of factors and processes. This suggests extreme caution in the use of universalistic or programmatic solutions to effect VET, HRD and HRM change.
5. Although the necessary condition for change is likely to be environmental pressure and associated business responses, the sufficient conditions involve the gathering together of a critical mass of positive or supporting factors. These factors have been broadly categorized as business strategic; labour market (internal and external); internal factors, training systems, philosophy and management organization; and external training stimuli and support. The latter set of factors are not important in driving change in HRD.
6. VET is more sustainable when framed within broader HRD and HRM processes. Problems of skill supply are therefore usually best conceptualized using the language of HRD and HRM, since this implies the use of a multiple set of levers. Effecting change in VET and HRD involves thinking in broad HRM terms and creating a wide set of pressure points for change. If activities are driven through this wide set of pressure points, they can produce positive spirals of activity which may then be stabilized.

Consequently, for those engaged in managing these complex processes there is a need for competences across a wide range of HRM specialisms, along with the capability to link business and technical changes to HRM considerations, and the necessary process skills to develop activities in specific situational contexts. If the character of decision-making about VET/HRD/HRM is situation-specific, reactive, often short term, but also cumulative, then interventions by public agencies have to include a high level, close and continuing relationship between the interventionist and the client. In such circumstances, the blanket use of grants and financial incentives is likely to be wasteful. On the other hand, mobilizing other (external) sources of pressure, such as influencing the customer–supplier relationship, safety legislation, and getting to external consultants engaged in strategic and technological planning activities, represents a powerful policy tool.

In addition to further research seeking to validate the factors, levels, and pathways to transformation of VET and HRD, analysis of firms by business sector, to establish whether sectors are strong or weak in any particular constellations of factors, would be of considerable value for the focusing of policy on firms.

References

Armstrong, M. (1987) Human resource management: a case of the Emperor's new clothes? *Personnel Management* 19 (8); 30–5.

Aupperle, K., Acar, W., and Booth, D. (1986) How excellent are the excellent companies? *Journal of Management*, Winter:

Beer, M., Spector, B., Lawrence, P.R. Mills, Q.N., and Walton, R.E. (1984) *Managing Human Assets*, New York: Free Press.

Beer, M. and Spector, B. (1985) Corporatewide transformations in human resource management, in R.E. Walton and P.R. Lawrence (eds) *HRM Trends and Challenges*, Boston, Mass.: Harvard Business School, pp. 219–53.

Evans, E. and Cowling, A. (1985) Personnel's part in organisational restructuring, *Personnel Management* 17 (1): 14–17.

Fombrun, C., Tichy, N.M., and Devanna, M.A. (1984) *Strategic Human Resource Management*, New York: John Wiley.

Galbraith, J.R. and Nathanson, D.A. (1978) *Strategy Implementation: The Role of Structure and Process*, St Paul: West Publishing.

Guest, D. (1987) Human resource management and industrial relations, *Journal of Management Studies* 24 (5); 503–21.

Hayes, C., Anderson, A., and Fonda, A. (1984) *Competence and Competition: Training and Education in the Federal Republic of Germany, the United States and Japan*, London: NEDO/MSC.

Hendry, C. (1988) New technology . . . new careers, *6th Annual Aston/UMIST Conference on the Organisation and Control of the Labour Process, Birmingham*, 23–25 March.

Hendry, C. and Pettigrew, A.M. (1986) The practice of strategic human resource management, *Personnel Review* 15 (5); 3–8.

Hendry, C. and Pettigrew, A.M. (1987) Banking on HRM to respond to change, *Personnel Management* 19 (11): 29–32.

Hendry, C. and Pettigrew, A.M. (1988) Multiskilling in the round, *Personnel Management* 20 (4): 36–43.

Hendry, C., Pettigrew, A., and Sparrow, P. (1988) Changing patterns of human resource management, *Personnel Management* 20 (11): 37–41.

Hitt, M. and Ireland, D. (1987) Peters and Waterman revisited: the unending quest for excellence, *Academy of Management Executive* May: 91–7.

Lengnick-Hall, C.A. and Lengnick-Hall, M.L. (1988) Strategic human resources management: a review of the literature and a proposed typology, *Academy of Management Review* 13 (3): 454–70.

Levering, R., Mokowitz, M., and Katz, M. (1984) *The 100 Best Companies to Work For*, New York: Warner.

Lundberg, C.C. (1985) Toward a contextual model of human resource strategy: lessons from the Reynolds Corporation, *Human Resource Management* 24 (1): 91–112.

MacMillan, I.C. and Schuler, R.S. (1985) Gaining a competitive edge through human resources, *Personnel* 62 (4): 24–9.

MSC/IFF Research (1985) *The Adult Training Survey*, London: IFF Research Ltd.

Ondrack, D. (1988) An assessment of the relationship between human resource management and the financial performance of the firm, *EIASM 3rd Workshop on Strategic Human Resource Management, Stuttgart*, 24–25 March.

Ouchi, W. (1981) *Theory Z*, Reading, Mass.: Addison-Wesley.

Peters, T. and Waterman, R. (1982) *In Search of Excellence*, London: Harper and Row.

Pettigrew, A.M. (1985) *The Awakening Giant: Continuity and Change in ICI*, Oxford: Basil Blackwell.

Pettigrew, A.M. (1987) Context and action in the transformation of the firm. *Journal of Management Studies* 24 (6): 649–70.

Pettigrew, A.M., Hendry, C., and Sparrow, P.R. (1989) *Training in Britain: Employers' Perspectives on Human Resources*, London: HMSO.

Pettigrew, A., Sparrow, P., and Hendry, C. (1988) Getting training into the bloodstream, *Personnel Management* 20 (12):

Porter, M.E. (1980) *Competitive Strategy*, New York: Free Press.

Porter, M.E. (1985) *Competitive Advantage*, New York: Free Press.

Purcell, J. (1985) Is anybody listening to the Corporate Personnel Department? *Personnel Management* 17 (9): 28–31.

Purcell, J. and Gray, A. (1986) Corporate personnel departments and the management of industrial relations: two case studies in ambiguity, *Journal of Management Studies* 23 (2): 205–23.

Sparrow, P.R. and Pettigrew, A.M. (1987) Britain's training problems: the search for a strategic human resources management approach, *Human Resources Management* 26 (1): 109–27.

Sparrow, P.R. and Pettigrew, A.M. (1988) How Halfords put its HRM into top gear, *Personnel Management* 20 (6): 30–4.

Training Commission/Deloitte (1988) *The Funding of Vocational Education and Training: Some Early Research Findings*, Background Note 2, Sheffield: Training Commission.

Wood, S. (1982) *The Degradation of Work?* London: Hutchinson.

Chapter fourteen

The motivation, satisfaction and company goals of business proprietors

Stanley Cromie and Simon Ayling

In recent years many researchers have commented on the motives that lie behind the efforts of individuals to create their own business enterprises (Stanworth and Curran, 1973; Cross, 1981; Storey, 1982; Cromie, 1987) and Cromie and Johns (1983) have reported that the need for achievement and the locus of control scores of new business proprietors are significantly higher than those of established owners. However, fewer writers have reported on the satisfaction that entrepreneurs obtain when their business is up and running.

Motivation and satisfaction are related concepts, the former referring to why individuals expend energy in accomplishing goals, Mitchell (1979), the latter to a state of contentment Du Brin (1984), but, there is little in the entrepreneurial literature which examines the association between them. Because many entrepreneurs create their ventures in the expectation of increasing the level of their job satisfaction it is important that we check on how the reality of business ownership matches their expectations.

Motivation theory indicates that much behaviour is goal directed in pursuit of ends which satisfy needs. Therefore, in the course of a study of motives, and the extent to which they are satisfied, we will gain some insight into individual goals. Since the individuals in this study are in charge of small organizations it is plausible that individual and organizational goals are similar. We feel therefore, that we should explore the objectives or goals of our samples' business enterprises and compare these organizational goals with their personal motives.

We feel that there may be an association between the motivations, satisfactions and business goals of business proprietors and in this study we propose, therefore, to focus on the owners of young business ventures and report on: (a) their motives at the time of the launch of their businesses; (b) their NAch and locus of control scores at the initiation of their businesses compared with their corresponding scores four years later; (c) the satisfaction that they derive from running their enterprises; (d) the goals that they seek for their businesses and (e) the association between the variables.

221

Method

The sample

We want to compare motives at two points in time and to compare motives expressed before the launch of firms with satisfactions gained and we are able to do this because this study builds on one conducted around four years ago. In the original enquiry 69 male and female owner/managers were interviewed at the time of the launch of their enterprises to explore their motives for founding and the extent of their preparation for the task of running an enterprise. Of the original sample 20 have gone out of business and 49 are still trading although some of the latter are in a weak economic position. In spite of numerous telephone calls we were unable to conduct interviews with four of the 'survivors' which left us with 45 respondents.

We added 23 new enterprises, which match our original sample in terms of ownership structure, gender, business area and age of the business, to our 45 'survivors' to obtain a total sample of 68 (34 male and 34 female firms). Of the 68 firms 33 are predominantly service organizations and 35 are primarily engaged in manufacturing. Quite a range of services are proferred by both genders: 17 firms provide industrial services and 16 offer consumer services. Whereas the men produce a wide range of manufactured goods, the women make a narrower range (12 make clothes, two soft furnishings and three produce food products). The firms are small – mean employment is 4.8 – and the turnover ranges from £4,000 to £46 million (a wholesale business) with a mean of £50,000. While the majority of firms are located in the Greater Belfast area a minority are scattered throughout small towns in Ulster.

Research questions and approach

We mentioned above that 45 of our current respondents are 'survivors' from the 69 people who were the subject of a previous investigation. For these 45 individuals we have a record of their expressed motives for launching their enterprises together with their scores on Rotter's (1966) Locus of Control scale (maximum = 23, minimum = 0, higher score indicates greater internal locus) and Lynn's (1969) Achievement Motivation scale (maximum score = 8, minimum = 0). In the current study respondents once again completed Rotter's and Lynn's scales and this allows us to report on the difference between the scores recorded by each individual.

To assess their level of satisfacton, and their business goals respondents were asked the following questions during tape-recorded interviews. (a) What satisfaction do you get from running your own business? (b) Could you tell me something about your business objectives? What do you see as the goals, the purpose or the mission of this business? Since we wanted to record the sample's responses to the open-ended questions without undue influence, the interviews were non-directive and tape recorded and the forced choice questions were asked at the end of the interview.

When the interviews were completed the tape recordings were examined thoroughly to identify key words and phrases in the responses to the open-ended questions. Recurring themes were noted and the researchers created a number of response categories for the principal question. Once the categories had been created the responses of the 68 respondents were allocated to the appropriate classifications by two researchers who had frequent discussions to iron out points of disagreement.

Results and discussion

Change in motives over time

Let us deal first with Cromie and Johns's (1983) finding that entrepreneurial predisposition, as indicated by scores on Lynn's NAch scale and Rotter's locus of control, decreases as business proprietors establish themselves. For our 45 survivors we have their individual scores for then and now and are able to compute a 't' statistic for paired samples. In the case of NAch the difference between the means is not statistically significant ($t = 0.73$; df = 45, two-tail probability = 0.469) and the same holds for locus of control ($t = -1.29$, df = 45; two-tail probability = 0.204). Clearly, there has been no significant reduction in the scores on these scales and this casts some doubt on Cromie and Johns' suggestion. It could well be that some extraneous difference between the independent samples, other than the age of their businesses, contributed to the different scores.

Association between motives and satisfactions

Let us now report on the linkage between motivation and satisfaction. In the original study the sample were asked why they wanted to create a business and their principal expressed motives, in descending order of importance, were: autonomy, achievement, job dissatisfaction, money, career dissatisfaction, child-rearing, offer employment to others and the provision of an outlet for skills. Child rearing means that through proprietorship women can meet, simultaneously, their child rearing and career needs. The original study had 35 male and 34 female respondents but the only motives which revealed statistically significant differences between the genders were: money, career dissatisfaction and child-rearing.

It has been mentioned that motivation and satisfaction may be related notions. Table 14.1 presents the data on the satisfaction that the current sample are receiving. Clearly the major satisfactions revolve around the issues of autonomy and control over one's life; a sense of achievement; satisfaction derived from the job of running one's own business and the monetary rewards on offer. Significantly, however, 12 per cent of the sample felt that there was no satisfaction associated with the job of business proprietor.

Table 14.1 Satisfaction reported by business proprietors from running their businesses

Factor	Total frequency	Men	Women
Autonomy	44	23	21
Achievement	34	9	25
Job satisfaction	28	12	16
Money	18	12	6
None	8	6	2
Creativity	7	4	3
Offer employment	4	2	2
Inheritance	1	1	0
Work from home	1	0	1
Others	11	7	4
Total	156	76	80

When we look at the motives for business founding alongside the satisfaction that business proprietorship brings there is a strong correspondence between the two. Autonomy, achievement, job satisfaction, money, offer employment and inheritance are found in both; child-rearing links strongly with working from home while outlet for skills may match the creativity category. In view of the fact that some of the original motives (e.g. career dissatisfaction) do not lead directly to a state of contentment the association between the expressed motives for founding and the expressed satisfaction associated with proprietorship are remarkably alike. The motives which drive aspiring entrepreneurs seem to be capable of generating satisfaction in practice.

The reported satisfactions of the sample

Having commented on the link between motives and satisfactions let us now concentrate on the expressed satisfaction of our 68 respondents. As Table 14.1 indicates the most gratifying aspect of ownership is autonomy. The sample used the following words and phrases in expressing satisfaction: 'I enjoy the freedom'; 'I am master of my own destiny'; 'It is important for me to be in control'; 'I do-what I like when I like'. Running one's own concern does allow the individual to make his or her own decisions and choose a suitable posture and direction for the business. Autonomy is an important source of satisfaction to the men and women in our sample and this finding is in keeping with previous investigations which indicate that entrepreneurs have a high internal locus of control over events (Cromie and Johns, 1983; Welsch and Young, 1984).

Another major source of satisfaction is the sense of achievement that business proprietors feel when they put a venture together and run it successfully. This sense of achievement is felt particularly strongly by the women in our study. Jean Luckhurst expresses this attraction powerfully when she says '. . . the major attraction is self esteem . . . the ah . . . carrying a job through from beginning to end . . . ah . . . I suppose putting my standard on things. I had four children and so all I felt I was good for was being a mum and you don't always get a lot of appreciation for this.'

Table 14.1 shows that nine men and 25 women mentioned achievement as a source of satisfaction. To discover if these differences are statistically significant we followed Oppenheim's (1966) recommendation and computed a Chi-squared statistic using a 2×2 contingency table which compares the responses on achievement with the sum of all the other frequencies. The difference is significant (χ^2 value $= 8.6$, df $= 1$, $P < 0.03$). The greater sense of achievement on the part of women may well reflect the kind of employment difficulties reported by Jean Luckhurst: if women see little prospects of developing conventional careers it is not surprising that successful business ownership is regarded by them as a fine achievement.

Job satisfaction is reported as a source of gratification by more than 40 per cent of the sample. Many of the original respondents did not have enjoyable pre-entrepreneurial jobs and they were hoping for more satisfying work. This expectation was realized for a number of the sample and important contributory factors are the variety and pace of the work together with a feeling that if they put a lot of work into the business they will get a lot out of it.

Table 14.1 reveals that although more women than men report this as a source of satisfaction the differences between the genders is not statistically significant.

While this line of work can lead to job satisfaction there are those who get little or no pleasure from running their firms. Our respondents work long hours (mean = 50.9) and some had to really struggle to make a success of their ventures. The great majority were poorly prepared for the job of running their enterprises, and several made serious mistakes in the post launch years. Things got really bad for some and 12 per cent of respondents reported that they gained no real satisfaction from owning a firm: the exertion was too severe.

Developing a small firm is not an easy job and for some the stress becomes too much. Table 14.1 discloses that more, but not significantly more, men than women fall into this category. However, this may well arise because all of the men must make an economic success of their ventures whereas some of the women are running highly marginal businesses which merely supplement their spouse's earnings.

This lack of satisfaction may well tie in with the fact that only one-quarter of the total sample and 30 per cent of the men are satisfied with the money that the business brings in. We did try to obtain data on the profit that each firm was earning but we abandoned this because the information was not forthcoming. However, based on figures for turn-over, number of employees and our general knowledge about the businesses in the survey, we believe that few of our firms are currently making a lot of money and we are not surprised that so few individuals express satisfaction with their earnings. As we shall see, when organiza-tional goals are discussed below, many of the proprietors aspire to grow and earn more money but these goals are not being fully attained just now. Given the stage of development of our firms this desire to grow and prosper together with a general dissatisfaction with earnings is hardly surprising.

The remaining frequencies on satisfaction are small and need not detain us here.

We can conclude this section by arguing that there is a fair degree of correspondence between the motives (goals) which the sample aspired to approximately four years ago and the satisfaction resulting from the attainment of these goals. Turning to the expressed satisfactions there is only one area, achievement, where men and women differ statistically. We have offered an explanation for this specific difference but in general we should hardly be too surprised at the lack of dichotomy. After all both genders are performing the same job and it is only to be expected that the rewards and difficulties are similar.

Business goals

There are some difficulties associated with analysing organizational goals but we suspect that in small young firms organizational goals will emerge as an extension of the goals of the individual owner manager and he will communicate them directly to his staff. Goals reflect the general direction which the owner wants to take and he will usually ensure that his will prevails in these matters.

What exactly do our sample aspire to; what do they want for their organizations? We analysed the tape-recorded responses to the open-ended questions on the objectives of the businesses in the manner discussed above and classified statements into eleven major categories. They are presented in Table 14.2.

Table 14.2 The organizational goals of the sample

		Frequencies	
Goal	All	Men	Women
Profit	29	15	14
Grow, export, diversify	25	12	13
Earn a living	22	12	10
Job satisfaction	21	8	13
Reputation, quality	20	10	10
Offer employment	14	7	7
Product goals	12	4	8
Security, survival	9	6	3
Sell the business	8	6	2
Consolidate	2	1	1
Miscellaneous personal	16	8	8
Total	178	79	79

For comparative purposes let us present the categories of goals proposed by Perrow (1971). He argues that organizations have five different types of goals: (1) societal goals which refer to the major sectors of society towards which the organization's energies are directed; (2) output goals which define which business the organization is in; (3) system goals which depict how the organization will proceed to manage its systems, e.g. whether it will pursue growth or cost reduction as a means of running the system; (4) product goals which pertain to the characteristics of the goods and services on offer, e.g. whether to aim for high volume low price or high quality products; and (5) derived goals which refer to the choices which running an enterprise affords to its owners and other goal setters.

Table 14.2 shows that no societal or output goals are mentioned but that system goals, e.g. profit, growth, security, offer employment, consolidate, and product goals, e.g. quality, and specific product goals, are much in evidence. Some derived goals, e.g. sell the business, are represented alongside personal goals, e.g. job satisfaction and miscellaneous personal goals. The fact that 31 per cent of our sample mention job satisfaction as a business goal and that several of the business goals coincide with the satisfactions and motives discussed above, indicates that there is some association between personal motives/satisfactions and business goals. However, before we discuss any association between these variables let us examine the expressed business goals in some depth.

The most prominent business goal is making money. More than 40 per cent of men and women said that a major objective of the business was to generate profit. Respondents were classified in this category only if they emphasized money or income as a goal: individuals who talked of 'earning a decent wage', 'getting enough money to get by', or 'making a reasonable living' were not. Those who were included in the profit category used phrases like: 'The business is there to make lots of money', 'I am seldom satisfied with the profit we make', 'we aim to achieve a return on investment in excess of 20 per cent' and 'making money is very important to me'. In the entrepreneurial literature money is often depicted as the primary motivation for entrepreneurial behaviour and while money was not the primary motivator of our sample when they launched their enterprises the attachment to money as the major business goal offers some support for those who argue that economic issues dominate business decision-making.

While profit and making money is an important goal for our sample we must remember that this is an aspiration. Our data above on satisfaction reveal that only a quarter of respondents report that their earnings are a source of satisfaction. We might also note that the aspiration of making money is shared equally between the genders.

The second most important objective is to grow. Those people who mentioned growth directly were placed into this category as were those who wanted to export and diversify. In all 37 per cent expressed a desire to grow. Since our firms are young and starting from a small base it is not surprising that a number were keen to expand although a certain proportion said explicitly that they were content with their current situation and thought that growth would bring problems with employing labour etc.

One female proprietor's company is growth oriented. She wants 'to build up a top business advisory agency with branches throughout the UK. I want an agency with the full range of services and I want to move into management consultancy.' She is clearly keen to grow but it is interesting to note that she wants to consolidate her existing business before developing further. Later in her interview she talked of growing in spurts with consolidation phases between the growth thrusts. This is precisely the manner in which Mintzberg and Waters (1982) argue that entrepreneurial firms grow. Some other owners argued that while they wanted to grow they did not want unlimited growth because they saw difficulties in the way.

228

Around one-third of the sample see the business as a means of earning a living. What differentiates them from the profit seekers is their limited money-making aspirations. Typical phrases used by these persons are 'I want to make a decent living from the firm', 'I want reasonable earnings until I retire', 'I don't want to kill myself – I just want a reasonable wage', 'I want enough money to let me do what I want – but I don't really want a fortune'. Money is not unimportant but, the effort required to earn a lot of money discourages some while others are quite contented with their lot.

Around one-fifth of respondents mentioned job satisfaction as a business goal. Strictly speaking this is not a business goal, but it illustrates the difficulty of separating personal from business goals. In a sense this is a derived business goal: having the business allows some owner managers to enjoy their work. Since previous research on this sample revealed that many were unhappy in their pre-entrepreneurial jobs the pleasure of doing work that they like may be an important derived goal of business proprietorship. Individuals in this category used the following phrases to make their points: 'The business provides me with an opportunity to have an enjoyable job and a successful, secure life', 'owning this firm allows me to use my talents', 'this business gives me job satisfaction'.

Almost one-third of respondents regarded quality and reputation as the key goal for their organizations. A number talked of wanting their own logo, of wanting to see their products displayed in shops and of producing instantly recognizable items. Others talked of being leaders in their field, of making a quality product or providing an excellent service. In some cases quality was seen as a means to an end – as the best way to get customers to buy products – but in other cases quality was more of an end in itself.

A lady who manufactures clothes, expressed her commitment to quality succinctly. She said '. . . I would love to have my own label . . . that's the idea of going into large-scale manufacturing. I would also like my own shop to display my products. I feel that that would show that I had arrived'. Reputation, recognition and quality are important goals for quite a proportion of our sample. These goals combine some personal aspirations such as self esteem and recognition with a business system goal.

We saw above that a few people, when they started their enterprises, were motivated to offer employment to others and Table 14.2 shows that one-fifth of the sample retain this aspiration. In a province like Ulster, with an unemployment rate in excess of 20 per cent, it is not unnatural that a desire to alleviate the situation should be important to our proprietors, but it is worth mentioning that this was a secondary goal for most respondents.

Twelve participants made mention of product goals. Before proceeding, let us think back for a moment to what Perrow (1971) said about product goals. He argued that they referred to product characteristics, that is, to the nature of the product or service supplied to consumers. Turning to our sample, a nursing home owner talked of '. . . providing a decent environment for the elderly to enjoy the remainder of their lives', a landscape designer talked of 'only accepting contracts which will enhance the quality of the environment', a manufacturer of childrens clothing talked of '. . . aiming for the top end of the market because I can't compete with the high volume mass-produced goods', while an insurance broker revealed that he 'focuses on the investment side of the business because the big companies have been handling general life policies for years and years'. These product goals are statements about the kind of business or the niche in the market that the proprietor is pursuing. In some cases these statements reflect market assessments but, in others product goals are statements of basic beliefs or values. One clothing manufacturer wanted to 'improve the fashion consciousness of people in Derry', while a woman who offers an electrolysis service refused to get into the beauty business because 'there are people around with real problems . . . and not just the worry of removing a few wrinkles from their face'. The latter could have made far more money from the beauty side of electrolysis but it just wasn't her scene.

The remaining goals of security and survival along with the desire to sell the business have relatively small frequencies and need not detain us.

Finally, there was quite a range of personal goals. The fact that these were expressed in response to a question on business goals points to the difficulty some small business owners experience in separating the person from the business. Statements relating to these personal goals include the following:' the business allows me to achieve something in my own right', 'the firm is there to allow me to have an enjoyable, successful, secure life', 'it allows me to use my talents', 'it is an outlet for my creativity', 'through the business I can meet my family and work needs in an environment that I like', 'running this firm allows me to live in Fermanagh and preserve an older way of life'. Their businesses were the vehicles which allowed these persons to enjoy their lives, or use their skills and it seems appropriate to talk of these personal goals as derived goals. The income created by these enterprises gave a number of owners the possibility of behaving in ways that they found to be agreeable.

Associations between expressed motives, satisafaction and business goals

To date we have presented some data on NAch and locus of control scores before and after the business launch, the expressed motivation of business founders prior to launching their enterprises, the satisfaction gained as a result of running their enterprises and their expressed business goals. We did say that motives and satisfaction are related topics and that it may be difficult to distinguish between personal goals and business goals. This begs the question of whether there is any association between motivators, satisfiers and business goals. We have noted already that there is quite a strong link between motivation and satisfaction but, overall there is not much direct correspondence between these two variables and expressed business goals. In spite of this we feel that a few of the variables are reported as motivators, satisfiers and goals. For example, job satisfaction, money and offer employment are reported in all three situations and we can envisage a link between outlet for skills, creativity and reputation and between achievement and business growth. We can say, therefore, that there are some areas where there is a very strong link between motivation, satisfaction and business goals, some with indirect links and many with no links. The latter occurs in those areas where respondents expressed strong business oriented goals such as product goals, consolidating or selling the business.

Conclusions

In this study we report on the important links between motivation and satisfaction on the one hand, and between these variables and expressed business goals. We see that there is considerable congruence between motives and satisfaction but not a great deal of association between satisfaction achieved and business goals. The latter should not surprise us unduly. Satisfaction derives from actual experience whilst goals are aspirations and in the turbulent world of business formation and functioning there are many gaps between expectations and reality.

Expectation versus reality may account for the difference between satisfaction and business goals. Motives expressed at the time of founding are personal aspirations which might be expected to link with business aspirations but, with the exception of job satisfaction, making money and to a lesser extent offering employment, there is no strong link between these variables. We are forced to conclude that business proprietors seem to have distinct personal aspirations when launching their firms which do not correspond with business objectives. In spite of the fact that the owner manager is the principal actor in the goal formation process in his firm it seems that individual and organizational aspirations are somewhat separate. Of course, these differences could also be the product of experience. What the person wants on launching a business and what he or she wants four years on will be influenced by events in the intervening years.

Note

This research was supported by grant F00232409 from the Economic and Social Research Council.

References

Cromie, S. (1987) The aptitudes of aspiring male and female entrepreneurs. in K. O'Neill *et al.* (eds) *Small Business Development*, Aldershot: Gower.

Cromie, S. and Johns, S. (1983) 'Irish entrepreneurs: some personal characteristics', *Journal of Organisational Behaviour* 4: 317–324.

Cross, M. (1981) *New Firms and Regional Economic Development*. Farnborough: Gower.

Du Brin, A.A. (1984) *Foundations of Organisational Behaviour*, Englewood Cliffs, NJ: Prentice Hall.

Lynn, R. (1969) 'An achievement motivation questionnaire', *British Journal of Psychology* 60: 529–34.

Mintzberg, H. and Waters, J.A. (1982) 'Tracking strategy in an entrepreneurial firm', *Academy of Management Journal* 25: 465–99.

Mitchell, T. (1979) 'Organisational behaviour', *Annual Review of Psychology* 30: 243–81.

Oppenheim, A.N. (1966) *Questionnaire Design and Attitude Measurement*, London: Heinemann.

Perrow, C. (1971) *Organisational Analysis*, London: Tavistock.

Rotter, J.B. (1966) 'Generalised expectancies for internal versus external control of reinforcement', *Psychological Monographs* 80: no. 609.

Stanworth, J. and Curran, J. (1973) *Management Motivation in the Smaller Business*, London: Gower.

Storey, D. (1982) *Entrepreneurship and the New Firm*, London: Croom Helm.

Welsch, H. and Young, E. (1984) 'Male and female entrepreneurial characteristics and behaviours: a profile of similarities and differences', *International Small Business Journal* 2: 11–20.

Chapter fifteen

The roles of accounting in organizational maintenance and change: insights from a case-study[1]

Brendan McSweeney

UK investment in accounting continues to expand in the public and private sectors. Much of that expansion is described, promoted, and understood in the name of accounting's assumed capacity to improve or reform organizations. However, in contrast with a vast literature expounding techniques, the actual roles of accounting in organizational processes and their outcomes remain largely neglected, and hence inadequately understood.

A 'decision-making' focus has meant that issues of implementation are neglected (as they are in many other organizational disciplines). The dominant epistemological, and power, assumptions made about accounting practice both within the academic discipline of accounting, and other disciplines reinforces the neglect[2] of studying accounting in action — in situated interactions (other than at the level of individuals). Accounting is widely understood as simply constituted by reflecting or illuminating a separate reality which it does not create or change (save in the narrow sense as an input to decision-making). The discipline's role is essentially seen as developing ever more 'accurate' techniques.

However, there is a growing ackowledgement within the discipline that it is our knowledge of accounting in action not the topic that is trivial, hence, the increase in calls for studies of accounting in the contexts in which it is actually used (Hopwood, 1983; Kaplan, 1984). To date, there have been few such studies. The constraints are principally twofold. First, there are theoretical limitations. The development and acquisition (from other organizational disciplines, and elsewhere) of adequate and appropriate theories and methods is difficult and sluggish — inevitable in what is yet a nascent discipline, or sub-discipline. Second, there are observational or immersion constraints. Longitudinal studies of accounting in real-time have been few. Yet, without direct participation, analysis is restricted to ungrounded theory or descriptions based on documentation and interviewing about past events, with all the attendant problems of interviewee bias, retrospective construction and so forth. These limitations are especially intense for accounting where ex post analysis inevitably

233

over-emphasizes the reflective role of accounting to the neglect of its constitutive. It is only when determinant theories of organizational life are abandoned, and when organizational life is conceived not simply as inevitably, and exclusively, the outcome of contextual forces, or alternatively internal decision-taking that an additional agenda of accounting research questions is opened up. What role does accounting play in pluralist organizations; in discourses; in interpretations; in influencing contexts; in concepts of time; in understanding, and indeed creating the past, the present and in imagining the future. How does it intermingle with other organizational influences? What realities or meanings are the bases of accounting and how and to what extent are they an effect of accounting? What role does accounting play in power/knowledge relations (that is, the connection between ways of distinguishing between true and false and how we govern and are governed)?

The case study discussed below is a glimpse at just some of these issues which were observed in real-time. Principally the case addresses the question of the roles of accounting in the achievement of aligned action (ultimately agreement to make significant strategic[3] change) in an organization in the absence of shared meaning, or the exercise of coercive authority (Stokes and Hewitt, 1978; Weick, 1979). We shall see accounting being used to create belief in a crisis and to structure responses. In doing so we describe some important characteristics of accounting in action. The organizational setting was a large private sector manufacturing company: Premium Products[4]. During two periods (July 1986 to February 1987 and July 1987 to November 1987), despite initial opposition from a strongly organized workforce, strategic changes were implemented, albeit not identical to top-management's[5] original formulation. The changes proposed in the first period were alterations to working methods and practices. Those in the second period were much more extensive and opposed even more vigourously by the workforce's representatives. The proposed changes in the second period included a reduction of the workforce by 700 (about a quarter of the total), the remainder to work a week-on and a week-off, and further changes in working practices and methods. In the transition, in both periods, from opposition to acceptance, accounting was central.

The first change period

In July 1986 Premium's management wrote to the workforce's sole negotiating representatives the Joint Negotiating Committee (JNC) stating that it had prepared a 'Strategic Manufacturing Plan' to improve quality and reduce costs. During the following six months management–JNC negotiations took the usual form (bargaining) and despite many and lengthy discussions and attempts to persuade the JNC to agree to abandon the 'malpractices' no agreement was reached. The only role for accounting data during these negotiations was as part of an introductory explanation for the origins and urgency of management's proposed changes. At most the accounting information (principally cost and revenue forecasts) were treated as background information to which the JNC paid little, if any, attention. Nor did management try to focus joint discussion on the accounting data. It had completed its analysis and was anxious to have the changes it desired accepted. It concentrated on the specifics of changes although regularly justifying them as necessary responses to a continuing decline in the company's performance. For the JNC assertions about the future prospects of the company and explanations about the importance for that future of change seemed vague in comparison with the immediacy of the changes sought. The proposed changes meant reduction or elimination of benefits some of which the workforce did not want to abandon and others for which they wanted payment of a size management were unwilling to pay.

During the six months in which no changes were agreed sales volume continued to decline. At the beginning of 1987, for reasons not explored here, the focus of the discussions/negotiations changed: from the specifics of the changes sought to the specifics of the 'necessity' for change. Changes were no longer sought in the name of improved efficiency; the elimination of 'out-dated' practices or improved competitive position. Rather they were justified via accounting data as urgently required to avoid losses and consequentially redundancies. Management made the projected profit and loss accounts (for 1987; '88, '89, '90) the centre of attention. These forecasts emphasized committed cost increases (significantly higher than anticipated rates of inflation) and the impact on sales revenues (in pounds) of a decreasingly favourable US dollar exchange rate at which dollar sales would be converted. What was different was not so much an increase in the amount of accounting data management gave the JNC, but the emphasis they placed on it. It had moved from background justification to centre stage. The focus on Premium's no-change trajectory and likely future financial position via accounting data was the initiative of management but it also required the willingness of the JNC to accept that agenda, that focus of analysis. For the first time the joint discussion was primarily about 'evidence' that the firm might no longer be, as distinct from willing, to give or have extracted from it the benefits the workforce had previously obtained. The assumptions and actions of pluralism moved (even if only temporarily) to a unitary level.

The evidence of impending danger was the accounting data with its capacity to make a possible future real in the sense that an apparently possible precise financial future could become part of present discourses. The projected profit and loss accounts envisaged a future state towards which Premium was (management claimed) heading if its current trajectory was not changed. That state, if real, was one in which workforce benefits would be diminished more so than in the changed state.

The JNC could have chosen to disregard the accounting data and continue opposing the proposed changes. However, they chose not to do so because a future forecast in projected profit and loss accounts was potentially detrimental to them. To assume that management were trying to deceive them, or were mistaken, was an uncertainty upon which they were not willing to gamble through unanalysed rejection. But neither were they willing to accept management's claims without an evaluation. To assist them they hired an accounting academic (Mitchell) to consider management's case. This analysis was encouraged by management who offered full access to all Premium's accounting data. Over about a six week period he alone with the JNC, with the JNC and all shop stewards, and with the JNC and management interrogated and discussed the accounting data. The central emphasis was on the assumed trends and inter-relationships (past, present and prospective) between costs; revenues, and the declining US dollar/pound exchange rates. The JNC and the wider trade union became familiar with an income and expenditure model portraying the firm as it was and more importantly as it might become. Limited, partial, as the accounting model might be it nevertheless appeared to have some empirical grounding: for example the JNC were aware of the size of their three-year wage agreement in a labour-intensive industry; they could see that stocks were increasing as production continued to exceed sales; they recognized that quality had disimproved. The JNC immersed in the production process were now considering their benefits also as costs. Their attentiveness to the accounting model was because of the future it predicted or through which it was predicted. Its credibility was not only its acceptance by someone they trusted but also due to the model's explanatory power through its integration of their fragmented experiences. They did not merely accept but were changed. Exploration of, and increasing acquaintance with the accounting model's integrating representations opened up and enhanced its apparent power to predict an imminent future in which, without change, the resources and benefits received through the company would diminish. Mitchell's report, whilst expressing some doubt about the optimism of medium-term sales volume growth judged the future focused on, and quantified in, the projected profit and loss accounts to the most probable outcome. Aligned action between the JNC and management emerged from the described process — a commitment from the JNC and the wider trade union to accept the work practice and method changes. The change can be explained solely on the basis of acceptance of an organizational crisis[6] made part of their present through accounting. Concepts such as shared meanings or cultures are unnecessary (in this context). Accounting was central in changing the JNC's and the wider trade union's beliefs about the present and future prospects for Premium.

The second change period

In the next few months many production and other changes were agreed between management and the JNC. However, the upturn in volume sales predicted by management did not emerge, but instead continued to decline. By June 1987 sales in the first half of the year were down by 18 per cent on 1986. At the end of that month management stunned the workforce by announcing that as a result of further deteriorations in Premium's financial prospects, dramatic action was required. That proposed action was mainly a reduction in the workforce by one-quarter through voluntary redundancies and further working method and practice changes.

As in the first period management could not, or chose not, to use coercive power to impose changes. JNC opposition to the proposals was intense. Rejection was not a negotiating posture intended to reduce management's demands or improve the redundancy payments. Trade union policy was no redundancies and the JNC's commitment was to a continuity of each job which it saw as distinct from its current holder who it argued had no property rights in a job and was not, therefore theirs to sell for a redundancy payment. Neither management, nor the JNC, knew how many would apply for redundancy. But all JNC members believed that if it could argue that a crisis did not exist, or if it could identify adequate non-workforce reducing alternatives it could credibly (within Premium and for the national media which was extensively covering events) prevent or certainly reduce substantially the number of redundancies. Management's claim of crisis had suspended an essential condition of the JNC's bargaining power — a belief by the workforce that negotiation demands would not eliminate the joint entity: Premium. The JNC needed to evalutate the credibility of management's crisis claim. As in the first period, management offered full access to all data and the JNC again hired Mitchell as a consultant. At a meeting of the entire workforce the JNC's analytical approach was unanimously approved and it was agreed that no individual would seek details of the redundancy scheme until after completion of the JNC's study. Management were anxious to release details of the redundancy scheme but agreed to the JNC's demand for postponement. To have refused would have diminished the credibility of the crisis claim in the eyes of the JNC and the workforce generally.

In the JNC's discussions with management some of the influences of the earlier change period were evident. The veracity of the historic and current data (such as declining sales volumes and rising costs) were now accepted and the JNC were now both able and willing to view and discuss Premium, present and future, within an albeit broad, accounting model. The issue was no longer were management being untruthful but rather were their forecasts mistaken. If not, did the accounting projections mean that management's solutions were necessary for continuity of Premium, and if so, could non-workforce reducing alternatives be found. In the first change phase the JNC had little incentive or opportunity to consider the product market, and the sales revenue forecasts specifically. Whilst during that period sales volume had continued to fall management had regarded this as merely a temporary response to price increases and the forecasts presented to the JNC during the first change period assumed an upturn in demand. The identified pressures for change were then rising costs and revenue loss from a weakening dollar but not a forecast continuation of volume declines also. But now in July 1987 management, in addition to rising costs and increasingly unfavourable exchange rate, were presenting a different product demand context. Volume sales were expected to continue to decline throughout that year and into 1988. For 1989 and 1990 very limited sales volume growth and very small price increases were assumed. Both the product and financial markets were portrayed as unalterable and workforce size and practices (and therefore costs) were identified by management as significant contributors to the 'crisis' and the only area in which effective change was possible. The accuracy of management's revenue forecasts and the efficacy of its marketing were now issues the JNC wanted examined. They acknowledged that volume sales were declining, that the US dollar was weakening, and costs were rising but they hoped that an analysis would judge the sales revenue forecasts too pessimistic, or alternatively would identify weaknesses in Premium's marketing which would lead to substantial increases in sales. Perhaps the revenue forceasts were not inevitable but alterable. This analysis was undertaken by a marketing and strategic management academic (Devoy) whom Mitchell recommended to the JNC. Devoy's terms of reference were 'to form an independent judgement of the reasonablesness of the revenue forecasts'. The accounting data, though the focus of attention of the JNC, had little analytical value for him — it was (or at least the revenue forecasts in the profit and loss accounts) the object of analysis not the means. Devoy's report was completed in late July 1987. It criticized some past marketing weaknesses but stated that these had been attended to. Whilst it recommended some changes which might result in longer-term improvements it broadly approved of management's revenue forecasts – arguing indeed that the 1988 forecasts were possibly over-optimistic. The JNC had hoped for salvation from a report which might argue either that Premium's prospects did not necessitate significant change from the workforce (especially a reduction) or is substantial change was required it could be achieved by alterations in Premium's marketing. Their hopes were not fulfilled.

The revenue side of the projected profit and loss accounts appeared to be unshakable and the JNC's attention now turned to the cost side. With growing desperation they asked Mitchell to analyse that data (current and projected), not as he had done before to judge its veracity (which they had since the first change period accepted) but rather this time to identify non-workforce reducing cost reductions. Mitchell was not encouraging about this, pointing out that a very high proportion of Premium's costs were fixed and a very significant amount of these were labour and labour-related costs. The latter category were 79 per cent of total costs (and materials 14 per cent). In its search for alternatives to workforce reductions the JNC now, for the first time, considered the possibility of a reduction in wage rates. It asked Mitchell to identify costs reductions made up of a mix of wage reductions and other cost-reducing proposals which would be an adequate response to the crisis they accepted existed whilst maintaining the full workforce. Mitchell calculated the impact of a range of wage-reduction alternatives. However, in a meeting with the JNC, Premium's Chairman rejected the proposals arguing that whilst such a reduction would achieve 'some of the required cost reductions in the short-term', the JNC would, he stated, soon renegotiate wages (and therefore costs) back up to their original level. A wage cut as a full, or partial, alternative to management's original proposals would only have been feasible (assuming workforce acceptance) if management had agreed to it.

Every 'escape route' so far sought by the JNC had been unsuccessful. A possible response to the progressive reduction of options might have been to argue with management that a smaller reduction in the workforce combined with work practice changes would be adequate. The JNC knew that regardless of what position it adopted some, although unknown number, of the workforce would apply for redundancy. A negotiating position open to it was to restrict that number to an amount to say, 300, rather than the 700 sought by Management. Mitchell told the JNC that such a reduction might be adequate. However, the JNC were still committed to a no redundancy policy. Mitchell believed this position to be unfeasible, nevertheless he suggested that the JNC obtain a second analysis of the accounting data.

On his recommendation the JNC asked another accounting academic (Condon) to 'examine management's plans and to access in the light of the company's financial position and its prospective financial performance, whether there are feasible alternatives to management's proposals.' This involvement was Condon's first contact with Premium. He had not participated in the first change period's analysis nor with the development of Devoy's report. Unlike the JNC (and Mitchell and Devoy) which accepted that the maintenance of Premium as a source of resources for the workforce required significant action, Condon re-opened the examination not only of costs but also revenue projections. The standard of proof he used to judge management's analysis was 'certainty'. Management should prove its 'case beyond all reasonable doubt'. The gravity of the changes for the workforce meant, he argued, that the evidence of its necessity should be undoubted. By contrast, both Mitchell and Devoy (independently) had used a standard of proof similar to that used in civil, not criminal, cases: 'on the balance of probabilities' (Eggleston, 1983). During August and early September Condon obtained an extensive range of information from Premium's management. As in the first change period most of this information was also given to the JNC. Management had agreed to postpone release of the redundancy terms until 14 September prior to which it would meet the JNC to consider if 'its alternative cost cutting plan was practicable and acceptable to the company'. By early September the JNC were under increasing pressure from management and the workforce to outline its alternative proposals.

A three-day meeting was arranged with the three consultants and the JNC early in the second week of September. Devoy's report was first discussed. He reaffirmed that he had not identified any short-term marketing panaceas and that the revenue forecasts were broadly the most accurate assumptions that could be made. Condon's report which had just been completed was next considered. Its conclusions were unexpected and jolting. Condon argued that Management's case was 'not sufficiently proved'. Based 'on the facts and arguments that Management have provided their case is not proven beyond reasonable doubt'. His recommendation was to be agnostic, to seek more information. His report was the first non-acceptance of a crisis and challenged the JNC's acquired belief in Premium's crisis.

What characterized Condon's report? Condon did not significantly question the accuracy of Premium's cost projections nor the appropriateness of the accounting techniques used. Two characteristics of Premium, and management's projections, limited the scope for such criticism's. First, a very high proportion of costs were labour or labour related which, with no redundancies, would continue to increase in a verifiable manner as there was a three year wage agreement which still had almost two years to run. Second, the financial projections were for the entire (or most of) entity and not the alleged costs of a part (a division; subsidiary; section; product or service) which is most common when non-liquidating reorganizations are proposed. Estimations of the costs (past or projected) of a sub-part or activity of a complete financial entity necessitates and permits the use of a wide range of arbitrary cost allocations. This was not the case with Premium's projections. Condon's main criticism was of management's revenue forecasts (which Devoy had previously approved). How was accounting data used to criticize management's revenue projections? Condon married management's figures with some macro-economic forecasts for the US economy. He accepted that because of forward currency contracts Premium were committed to rates which would reduce revenue by the amounts forecast by management but the key question he said was: 'are Premium locked into the US dollar prices or can they be raised' (without loss of sales volume) 'to compensate for the assumed foreign currency conversion losses?' Drawing on a forecast of general inflation for the US, Condon argued that if total revenue forecasts were increased by the same amount each year 'almost all the assumed foreign currency losses in management's forecasts would be avoided.' Supporting his assertion that this was at least plausible Condon drew on evidence that in 1986 US consumer expenditure had 'stalled' but was estimated to rise in both 1987 and 1988 and management 'should be asked to state what general economic factors they believe influence sales and how these are expected to change in the medium and long-term.' In his analysis he was assuming that Premium could be a cork 'in an economic sea',[7] that is the demand for its products could be entirely or at least predominantly, determined by broad 'macro' forces, specifically general levels of consumer expenditure and general rates of inflation. His lengthy report contained other criticisms, but the possibility of increasing revenue to a level adequate to avoid work-force reductions based on applying general economic forecasts to the projected revenues was the primary argument. Consistent with his proof criterion Condon did not argue that changes (including workforce reductions) were unnecessary or excessive, but rather that management's case was 'not sufficiently proven'.

In a bargaining context (not the then analytical context) where it is implicitly assumed that benefit increases or prevention of their reduction will not be self-damaging, any adversarially useful analysis would have been welcomed by the JNC. At the early part of the second change phase (in July) before Devoy's report; before the impending deadline; before the deep acceptance within the JNC of the existence of a crisis, a report using Condon's approach and proof criterion (even the same report, the same analysis of the accounting data) would have been judged differently. But now, six days before management's deadline the context was different. Where once questions or doubts were sufficient the pressure was now for answers.

Was there a crisis or not? The JNC had sought expert advice anticipating unanimity. Instead they got disagreement. The JNC began to divide into those who retained their belief that crisis existed and a minority who had either suspended judgement or believed none existed. Eventually, it was agreed to submit Condon's report to management requesting a 'satisfactory' response. Management initially refused to accept it arguing that it was not an alternative plan. Meanwhile workforce representatives spent a day studying Devoy, Condon and Mitchell's reports. The latter was a summary of his views given during the three day meeting which briefly was that there is a crisis but the changes need not be as extensive as management said it needed. At a full workforce meeting the JNC was criticized for neither having developed a non-workforce reducing plan or alternatively having been satisfied, and be able to satisfy the workforce, that no crisis existed. A proposal from some JNC members that release of the redundancy terms should be delayed until a reply to Condon's report was received was opposed by other JNC members and was defeated by a workforce vote.

Shortly after the redundancy terms were released. But the reorganization plans still had to be implemented. The attitudes and involvement of the JNC and the wider trade union would influence the speed and scale of change. Some members of the JNC believed that in Condon's report they still had the capacity to demonstrate to the workforce that crisis had not been adequately proven. Management's refusal to reply to the report gave credence to that view. After it became aware of this, management issued its reply. The JNC did not try to evaluate that response in detail. They understood parts of it but the meaning and implications of some of the responses would not have been readily understood. What was clear, however, to them was that management had been able to give a lengthy and apparently authoritative reply. Whilst not being able fully to judge the comparative 'accuracy' of management's response (or Condon's original report) it was clear that the arguments could go on for a long time, if not indefinitely. Premium's management had used the assertive power of accounting (its apparent hardness) in its initial claims about the company's future. Now under criticism it relied on accounting's defensive power (its softness, i.e. its many underlying assumptions). An accounting forecast is not an 'autonomous text', or a crystallization of a to be reality. It is an image of the future that may or may not ever be. It is the skeletal and apparently emphatic conclusion of many, and usually implicit, hopes, beliefs, prejudices, assumptions about an entity's possible financial future, ultimately the result of yet to occur, perhaps not yet even conceived, influences. Skepticism, such as Condon's using accounting data and some macro-economic forecasts was easy, but so too was defence. Accounting data does not have an epistemological status which permits its truth or falsity to be determined by examination of the data in-itself. The thick layers of assumptions upon which accounting projections rest were both the strength and weakness of Condon's use of the accounting data to criticize management's reorganization proposals. On the one hand it allowed him to argue that management had not sufficiently proved its case, but on the other hand it prevented him from stating whether he believed a crisis existed or not. This allowed management with a more intimate acquaintance to respond to his assumptions from an apparently more knowledgeable position. Both implicit and explicit in mangement's response to Condon was 'we know best'. The ultimate source of their beliefs about what happened and was likely to happen were 'our marketing men in the USA. These are the men in the field who are experts and who have performed a marketing miracle over the years. Against this evidence it would be irresponsible to gamble on an academic theory[8]'.

Futures may sometimes, or often, be uncertain but management had (and had to) make judgements/forecasts. Condon wanted to know more about their genesis. From what paths, what patterns, what webs, what models simple or complex had management's forecasts emerged (or been retrospectively understood or justified)? No matter how much, or how little access there might have been to the background assumptions of management's revenue forecasts they could not be evaluated by accounting. This was fundamental in the knowledge/power weakness of Condon's report in the context in which it was used. Management's apparently thicker knowledge of Premium's markets enabled it to counter the inevitably thinner assumptions upon which Condon's forecasts were built and through that, and more widely to appear to know not only more detail but appear more foresightful. The JNC had thought that analysis of management's projected profit and loss accounts would reveal the 'truth'. Instead, it led them into what seemed like a swamp of uncertainty, indefiniteness, disagreement, a potentially never-ending clash of views. It was a contest in which the insiders had the advantage. In the battle of assumptions accounting was a weak weapon for outsiders. Accounting had the appearance of precision but turned out to be a Gordian knot of assumptions.

On 23 September Condon replied to mangement's reply, but the JNC and the workforce were no longer listening. A workforce meeting had already instructed the JNC to get involved in the reorganization programme (excluding the week-on-week-off) which management withdrew. Improvements were agreed to the redundancy payments. Ultimately about 1,000 employers accepted the terms. Management experienced 'remarkable' willingness to change work practices.[9,10]

The roles of accounting in two periods of significant change in a large manufacturing company have been explored here. Judgements were not made about the 'accuracy' (in the sense, say, of predictive correctness) nor the 'rigour' (in the sense, say, of normative guidelines in textbooks, or elsewhere) of management's or the accounting or marketing consultant's analysis as such concepts or criteria are not relevant or meaningful in this processual study of accounting in action. Analysis has been inter-mingled with the portrayal of the process through time. Below, some propositions about both accounting in the interplay of power/knowledge relations and about the properties of 'accounting-as-such' that emerge from the study are set out. These may be insightful, enriched, or rejected in further studies of accounting in situated interactions in organizational change.

1. Neither coercive authority or shared culture were required for change through aligned action between management and the workforce, but rather a minimal agreement of the existence of a 'crisis'. Accounting created imaginal experiences, making a possible future present, and belief in a 'crisis' possible (Weick, 1979; Donnellon *et al.*, 1986).
2. The definitions of crisis and the content of possible changes were mutually reinforced through accounting.
3. Accounting's role in the changing power relationship in Premium was not to act directly on the JNC or the workforce (or facilitate or direct such actions) but to structure their possible fields of action (Foucault, 1982).
4. Accounting enabled greater general control of the workforce without an increase in detailed control (the latter may also be intensified through accounting, but was not in this context) (Edwards, 1986; McSweeney, 1988).
5. The JNC's limited familiarity with accounting's calculative technology did not diminish its role in Premium's power/knowledge relations.
6. Accounting had a relative autonomy in the sense that it has a system of categories specific to it, but these only had meaning in contexts of action.
7. The meaning of accounting was not a reflection of some underlying reality nor was it reified meaning contained either in texts (written accounts) or words (spoken about accounts). Rather, it inhered in the relationship between reader and text, listener and speech. The accounting–organizational action relationship was an irreducible dynamic synergy. Accounting (as calculative technology) did not change in the two change periods, but accounting as meaning in situated interactions did (Honeck and Hoffman, 1980).
8. Accounting was interlinked with other organizational languages and practices and their influences co-dependent.

Notes

1. The comments of Anthony Hopwood, Keith Hoskin, Andrew Pettigrew, Robin Wensley, and participants at the 2nd Annual Conference of the British Academy of Management (Cardiff Business School) on an earlier version are gratefully acknowledged.
2. The neglect is not total, there are a number (albeit very few) studies of accounting in action.
3. Large-scale and not easily reversed.
3. Premium Products is a listed company which continues to operate. For reasons of confidentiality its name has been changed here. All data in the remainder of this note refers to the position in mid-July 1988. Size: turnover approximately £80 million; employees 3,000 (about half 'skilled'). *Product*: hand-made consumer product; top-end of its market. Costs: 79 per cent labour, or labour related; average wage £14,000 (gross); some skilled workers earning in excess of £40,000 (gross); three year wage agreement well in excess of anticipated inflation rates. *Context changes*: sales volume declining since mid-1985; substantial price increases in main markets about the same time; competitor's costs declining and quality improving (cheaper sourcing of partly completed products and machine-made products increasingly more similar in appearance to hand-made). *Main Market*: directly, and indirectly, in excess of 80 per cent of sales were in US dollars; dollar exchange rate declining and forecast to continue doing so; main US distribution channels under some threat.
5. The Managing Director; the General Manager-Operations (who was an accountant and effectively a director of finance also), the General Manager-Personnel. Subsequently referred to as 'management'.
6. Two characteristics of crisis definition: (a) threat: mutual benefits (possibly all) threatened. (b) time: time within which to take remedial action limited — otherwise would be made in much less favourable circumstances.
7. Quoted in Pettigrew (1985).
8. From management's reply to Condon's report.
9. From an interview with the General Manager-Operations.
10. In February 1988 Premium's Chairman reported to shareholders that 'sales in the US were much improved in the second half of 1987 but sales potential was hampered by delivery difficulties arising from the production restructing programme. These difficulties affected all markets and consequently it was not possible to take advantage of a generally stronger demand.'

References

Donnellon, A., Gray, B., and Bougon, M.G. (1986) 'Communication, meaning and organized action', *Administrative Science Quarterly* 31: 43–55.

Edwards, P.K. (1986) *Conflict At Work*, Oxford: Basil Blackwell.

Eggleston, R. (1983) *Evidence, Proof and Probability*, 2nd edn, London: Weidenfeld & Nicolson.

Foucault, M. (1982) 'The subject and power', *Critical Inquiry* 8.

Honeck, R.P. and Hoffman, R.R. (1980) *Cognitive & Figurative Language*,

Hillsdale, NJ: Lawrence Erlbaum.

Hopwood, A.G. (1983) 'On trying to study accounting in the contexts in which it operates', *Accounting Organizations and Society* 8: 287–305.

Kaplan, R.S. (1984) 'The evolution of management accounting', *The Accounting Review* LIX: 390–417.

McSweeney, B. (1988) 'Accounting for the audit commission', *The Political Quarterly* 59: 28–43.

Pettigrew, A. (1985) *The Awakening Giant: Continuity and Change in ICI*, Oxford: Basil Blackwell.

Stokes, R. and Hewitt, J.P. (1976) 'Aligning actions', *American Sociological Review* 41: 838–49.

Weick, E. (1979) *The Social Psychology of Organizing*, 2nd edn, Reading, MA: Addison-Wesley.

Chapter sixteen

Two modes of organization

Robert Cooper and Stephen Fox

This chapter addresses the problematic status and nature of the concept of 'organization'. Specifically, we wish to argue that the concept of organization, although one of the most pervasive processes in modern life, is also one of the least understood, despite the industry applied to it by organizational studies. The reason for this, we suggest, is our urge to see organization as a 'natural' feature of the world — hence we privilege organizational correlates such as unity, identity, permanence, foundation, structure, etc., over 'anti-organization' processes such as dissonance, disparity, change, etc.

In his book on 'organizational images', Morgan (1986: Chapter 8) deals with the same issue when he views organization from the perspective of flux and transformation. Quoting the ancient Greek philosopher Heraclitus, Morgan notes that the world is in a constant state of flux: 'Everything flows and nothing abides; everything gives way and nothing is fixed'. This leads Morgan to express the problem of organization as a derivative of flux and change, which now become the fundamental level for understanding organized activity. The argument is further elaborated in terms of two interrelated ideas from modern physics: the implicate and explicate orders. The implicate order is the 'raw material' of flux and change, marked not only by continuous movement but also by an intrinsic undividedness or wholeness in which forms participate in each other. The explicate order derives from the implicate order which it 'lays out' in rational, cause-effect terms. Two points are worth emphasizing here: (1) the explicate order is the mode by which we normally understand the world of formal organization, but (2) the implicate order is the 'source' of the explicate. This leads us, therefore, to suggest an approach to organizational analysis based on the interdependence of two such forms of order which we shall call the nomadic mode (characterised by flux, change and contradiction) and the control mode (characterized by rationality, coherence and identity). Basic to our argument is that 'nomadism' is the privileged mode and that the control mode of organization can only be properly analysed and understood as a construction out of the nomadic mode (see Bohm, 1980, for a similar argument).

The control mode of organization

In a comprehensive survey of the organizational literature, Whitley (1977) has identified three approaches to the problem of organizational control: control (1) by cybernetic system; (2) by power; and (3) by authority. In the cybernetic approach, the problem of control is the 'problem of coping with external disorder' through feedback mechanisms. The representatives of this approach use analogies from engineering and biology. In the 'power' approach, control is effected through the use of inducements and incentives applied mainly at the level of the individual. The representatives of this approach use metaphors from utilitarianism and Hobbesian political psychology where disorder is expressed as a 'war of all against all'. In the 'authority' approach, ideas of control 'rely more on group consent and institutionalized values'. Proponents of this view tend to use 'organicist' metaphors in which people somehow naturally gravitate to a common standard of shared values. Whitley's criticisms of the three approaches to control are based on the argument that organizations cannot be viewed in isolation from other societal agencies and institutions; in fact, organizational control is legitimated by the wider system of dominant values and social institutions. Without elaborating Whitley's criticisms further, what is of significance for us here is the fact that not only do the various representatives of the three schools write about organizational control but control is also exercised in their own presentations. In other words, control is both realized through and communicated in writing. The same idea is caught by Giddens when he argues that writing and administrative power go hand in hand: administration/management is always 'textually mediated organization' Giddens, 1985: 179): '. . . . writing became connected to the categorizing and discovery of knowledge in a systematic fashion' (p. 43). As an example of 'textually mediated organization', Giddens quotes the time-table, which he describes as 'one of the most significant of modern organizations' (p. 174). . . 'Thus, rather than the steam train, it is Bradshaw's directory . . . that epitomizes modern transportation' (p. 175).

The organizational theorists surveyed by Whitley study organization in order to reveal the programmes or protocols which constitute the process of organizational management. At the same time they organize their own arguments in terms similar to those protocols, so that, for example, the 'writing' of the cybernetic programme insinuates itself into the 'writing' of the behavioural science protocol. We will return to this issue later since at this point in the argument we are more interested in developing the idea of 'writing' as a form of organizational control.

Writing, control and disorder

We now wish to illustrate in some detail the complex relationship between writing and control. At this point we also wish to emphasize the important idea that writing is not merely a vehicle for communication – this widespread belief blinds us to the more fundamental function of writing which is to create order out of disorder, form out of formlessness. In other words, writing returns us to the control/nomadic problematic with which we began. To illustrate the writing/control interaction, we draw upon the research of Latour and Woolgar (1979) on the 'construction of scientific facts' in a biochemical research laboratory. Latour and Woolgar develop a materialist approach to the production of scientific knowledge; their approach is therefore fundamentally different from traditional organizational-management research on scientific laboratories which looks at the effect of such factors as leadership style or group composition on research performance. The basic question asked by Latour and Woolgar – how are scientific products organized? – is answered: by means of writing or, more specifically, what they call 'inscription devices'.

Much of the apparatus in the laboratory functions as 'inscription devices' which can transform a material substance – a chemical, rats' brains, sections of muscle – into figures, graphs, diagrams, reports. These latter represent the 'writerly' end-products of the scientist's work. A significant feature of these inscribed end-products is that once they become available, 'all the intermediary steps which made their production possible are forgotten' (p. 51). In other words, inscription is viewed not as a means of constructing the product but rather as a device for communicating the product's existence: 'Inscriptions are regarded as having a direct relationship to the 'original substance'. The intervening material activity and all aspects of what is often a prolonged and costly process are bracketed off in discussions about what the figure means. The process of writing articles about the substance thus takes the end diagram as the starting point' (p. 51). The essential point here is that these scientific products don't just depend for their realization on material instrumentation – instead, they are completely constituted by the material setting of the laboratory. It is therefore not correct to say that the material and conceptual components of the work of the laboratory are distinctly different, as is often suggested.

Scientific statements begin laboratory life as tentative and uncertain inscriptions. Eventually, the 'successful' inscriptions move beyond their materialist, graphic status and end up as 'ideas', 'theories' and 'reasons'.

In this process, as Latour and Woolgar constantly remind us, the 'craft' basis of scientific production is forgotten or repressed: 'Our argument is not just that facts are socially constructed. We also wish to show that the process of construction involves the use of certain devices whereby all traces of production are made extremely difficult to detect' (p. 176). Two steps are apparently responsible for this mental sleight-of-hand: (1) the splitting of the statement, and (2) its inversion.

In the first step, 'the statement becomes a split entity'. 'On the one hand, it is a set of words which represents a statement about an object. On the other hand, it corresponds to an object in itself which takes on a life of its own. It is as if the original statement had projected a virtual image of itself which exists outside the statement. Previously, scientists were dealing with statements. At the point of stabilization, however, there appears to be both objects and statements about these objects. Before long, more and more reality is attributed to the object and less and less to the statement about the object. Consequently, an inversion takes place: the object becomes the reason why the statement was formulated in the first place. At the outset of stabilization, the object was the virtual image of the statement; subsequently, the statement becomes the mirror image of the reality 'out there' ' (pp. 176-7). In addition, the past also becomes inverted, for the object has been there all the time, just waiting for the scientist to come along and notice it.

Our argument here is that organization is *immanent* to the process of 'writing'; organization is not something which exists 'out there', independently of us. In Latour and Woolgar's research this idea is illustrated in the fact that laboratory scientists rely massively on inscription (i.e writing) devices for producing order out of the chaos and uncertainty that pervades their work. Thus, order is not 'already there', it does not somehow pre-exist the process of enquiry; in fact, the ordered information produced by the scientist is only 'revealed' through the act of writing. The idea that order is constructed in this way out of disorder is hard for us to grasp since we view the world as somehow intrinsically ordered: order is the norm and disorder is an aberration that should be eliminated wherever possible. Latour and Woolgar's work suggests an inversion of the traditional view, so that disorder becomes the rule and order, the exception. Organization is limited to local islands awash in a sea of disorder. The formally organized products of the laboratory are not just exceptions – as we noted, they are *a posteriori* rationalizations of the real process. Scientific research is beset on all sides by chaos and uncertainty. For example, sociologists have documented the importance of informal communication in scientific work but in Latour and Woolgar's work this finding takes on a new meaning: for 'new information is necessarily obtained by way of unexpected meetings, through old boy networks and social proximity', i.e., new ideas come from outside the formal organization. Another necessary implication of the dominance of disorder in scientific work is the extensive waste of research energy. Citation analysts have shown that 'most published papers are never read, the few that are read are worth little, and the remaining 1 or 2 per cent are transformed and misrepresented by those who use them' (p. 252). But this waste is understandable and no longer paradoxical if we recognize that order is the exception and disorder, the rule. Finally, 'each scientist strives to get by amid a wealth of chaotic events. Every time he sets up an inscription device, he is aware of a massive background of noise . . . every time he reads *Science* or *Nature*, he is confronted by a volume of contradictory concepts, trivia, and errors; every time he participates in some controversy, he finds himself immersed in a storm of political passions. This background is ever present, and it is only rarely that a pocket of stability emerges from it' (p. 252).

Organization as a kind of writing

Douglas (1986) has gone some way towards viewing organizations and institutions in terms similar to those of Latour and Woolgar. She discusses organizations as 'entropy-minimizing devices', thus placing the emphasis on the control mode while recognizing the importance of the nomadic mode. 'Writing' devices occur in Douglas's analysis in terms of analogy, metaphor, identity and classification (i.e., time-space tables). In particular, she discusses the role of 'stabilization' as a condition of entropy-reduction in much the same way that Latour and Woolgar analyse how the materiality of the inscription process becomes 'stabilized' in the 'splitting' and 'inversion' processes. Analogy, for example, serves as a foundation or stabilizer in the construction of social organization: 'In modern industrial society the analogical relation of head to hand was frequently used to justify the class structure, the inequalities of the educational system, and the division of labour between manual and intellectual work. The shared analogy is a device for legitimizing a set of fragile institutions' (Douglas, 1986: 49). Most analogies are based in nature and 'being naturalized, they are part of the order of the universe' (p. 52) but as soon as they are recognized as 'inventions' grounded in nature, they become suspect. This is why, like Latour and Woolgar's forgetting of the material base of scientific findings, 'founding analogies have to be hidden and why the hold of the thought style upon the thought world has to be secret' (Douglas, 1986: 53). What is maintained here is the purity and transparency of writing's 'representations' – or, as Weick (1979) has it, organizational enactment is essentially the maintenance of 'perceptions'.

Another organizational example of this control process is contained in Robert Pirsig's autobiographical 'case study' *Zen and the Art of*

Motorcycle Maintenance (1974). The central character of the 'study' – Pirsig himself – muses on the relationship between knowledge and institutions, concluding that 'organized knowledge' exercises a control 'trap' over individuals: 'He felt that institutions such as school, churches, governments and political organizations of every sort all tended to direct thought for ends other than truth, for the perpetuation of their own functions, and for the control of individuals in the service of these functions' (Pirsig, 1974: 121). In contrast to the controlled knowledge of institutions, Pirsig posits a lateral knowledge – equivalent to the nomadic mode of organization – 'that's from a wholly unexpected direction, from a direction that's not even understood as a direction until the knowledge forces itself upon one' (p. 122). Lateral knowledge is oblique, with a feel of the 'uncanny' about it – it comes from the 'beyond' of institutionalized thought.

Pirsig recalls his days as a graduate student at the University of Chicago, dubbed the 'Church of Reason' because of its massive suppression of everything – including lateral knowledge – that threatened the basis of its power in classical reason (i.e., the control mode of organization) with its emphasis on clear-cut logical analysis and firmly categorical thinking. In the end, Pirsig leaves the university (and suffers a breakdown) because he cannot communicate his own discovery of lateral knowledge within the control norms of institutionalized knowledge. In short, the University not only 'enacts' its 'representations' but mounts a special guard to protect their purity and transparency. Like Latour and Woolgar's research scientists, the university believes that writing and texts point directly to some external reality in an act of pure representation. Pirsig knows that this is an illusion based on the unconscious repression of the nomadic or lateral facet of writing. He knows that writing and texts are nothing other than themselves. The effect is rather like Cezanne's discovery, at the dawn of modern art, that he wasn't really painting houses or mountains but rectangles and triangles of different colours.

The production of serious business: exemplifying the control/nomadic schism in scientific writing

Another way of expressing the control/nomadic opposition is through the sense/nonsense relationship. Making sense is the serious business of scientific communities as well as others engaged more generally in organized working activity, and sense-making is the function of the control mode. Paradoxically, sense derives both its meaning and energy from non-sense, its obverse, so that non-sense as 'nonsense' (joking, punning, absurdity, etc.) is as common as 'sense' in human affairs. Non-sense, therefore, provides a basis for understanding more clearly the censoring function of the control mode.

Douglas (1975), in a rare article on jokes (despite the ubiquity of joking and humour, relatively little has been written on the subject), suggests that: ' . . . the essence of the joke is that something formal is attacked by something informal, something organised and controlled by something vital, energetic . . . the joke is seen as an attack on control.' (Douglas, 1975: 95)

Here, we can see that the control mode, through joking, is actively beset by the nomadic mode; the former's orderings and hierarchies are momentarily upset. Non-sense shadows sense at every turn, emerging as a principle of doubt both in the serious business of everyday living and of thoughtful enquiry (Zijderveld, 1983). Scientific activity oscillates between doubting everything and yet at the same time seeks to build argued versions of 'the Truth'; on balance, however, the serious goal of conventional science is description, explanation, prediction and control. Thus the closer the scientist gets to the realization of a thesis the more rigorously s/he represses the disruptive possibility of alternative meanings. Non-sense at this point is out of the question for the scientist who is no longer interested in alternate possibilities but only in assertion and control. Scientific writings may now be seen as organized textual productions which systematically control and repress the nomadic in favour of one-best-way of 'understanding'. By its nature, the nomadic process of non-sense does not permit any 'natural' condition of organization. Instead, it points freely in all directions. Given this insight, it is not surprising that so little attention has been paid to the humorous aspects of scientific culture, despite the surprise expressed by Mulkay and Gilbert (1982a; 585) in a discussion of the 'funny side' of science in which they suggest that 'the study of scientific humour can help to reveal interesting aspects of the serious side of science'; and in the same way that mother-in-law jokes may tell us things of interest about recurrent patterns of social interaction within certain kinds of family groupings, 'so scientists' articles in satirical journals may reveal something about the processes of literary inscription in science which cannot be so easily obtained from study of their more serious work.' (Mulkay and Gilbert, 1982a: 585)

On the basis of several case studies, Mulkay and Gilbert (e.g., 1981, 1982b; Gilbert and Mulkay, 1980, 1982) propose two different kinds of discourse about science which scientists use depending upon their audience. They term these the 'empiricist' and 'contingent' repertoires and for our purposes they map on to the distinction we have made between the control mode and nomadic mode, respectively. The 'empiricist' repertoire is how scientists talk or write about science on formal occasions in public, with politicians, potential funding bodies and so on. In this discourse all traces of the nomadic are expunged:

. . . genuine scientific knowledge is presented as being determined

253

by the controlled, experimental revelation of 'the facts' about the natural world. The production of experimental facts is taken to follow from scientists' application of impersonal procedural rules, and theoretical interpretation to derive unproblematically from the facts, as long as no personal, or social factors are allowed to influence scientists' judgements. (Mulkay and Gilbert, 1982a: 589)

However, in informal contexts, although this 'empiricist' conception of scientific action and belief is still used and in many ways is still primary, the alternative 'contingent' repertoire is also adopted. This discourse is 'contingent' because:

it treats action in science as much less uniform and scientific belief as much more open-ended. Emphasis is placed on the importance of personal commitment, intuition and practical skills. The production of data is taken to be a highly individual accomplishment. Theoretical interpretation is regarded as problematic and only partially constrained by experimental findings. It is accepted that social factors influence the actions of all scientists. In its strongest formulations, this repertoire enables the speaker to treat scientific knowledge simply as those beliefs which specific collections of specialists happen to have adopted for whatever reasons. (Mulkay and Gilbert, 1982a: 589–90)

Recalling our earlier discussion of the joke where we saw that joking works by the juxtaposition of a control and controlled element in such a way that the latter triumphs (albeit momentarily), Mulkay and Gilbert demonstrate how in scientific humour the contingent, controlled element triumphs over the controlling, empiricist discourse. For example, in one of their visits to a laboratory they came across a notice, in fact a piece of laboratory graffiti, pinned to the lab notice-board, which they later came to see as a 'scientific proto-joke':

What he wrote	*What he meant*
a. It has long been known that. . .	I haven't bothered to look up the reference.
b. While it has not been possible to provide definite answers to these questions	The experiment didn't work out, but I figured I could at least get a publication out of it.
c. The W-PO system was chosen as especially suitable. . .	The fellow in the next lab had some already prepared.
d. Three of the sample were chosen for detailed study. . .	The results on the others didn't make sense and were ignored.

e.	Accidentally strained during mounting. . .	Dropped on the floor.
f.	Handled with extreme care throughout the experiment. . .	Not dropped on the floor.
g.	Typical results are shown. . .	The best results are shown i.e., those that fit the dogma.
h.	Agreement with the predicted curve is: Excellent Good Satisfactory Fair	Fair Poor Doubtful Imaginary
i.	Correct within an order of magnitude. . .	Wrong
j.	Of great theoretical and practical importance. . .	Interesting to me.
k.	It is suggested that . . . it is believed that . . . it appears that. . .	I think
l.	It is generally believed that. . .	A couple of other guys think so too.
m.	The most reliable results are those obtained by Jones. . .	He was my graduate student.
n.	Fascinating work. . .	Work by a member of our group.
o.	Of doubtful significance	Work by someone else.

(from Mulkay and Gilbert, 1982a: p. 593).

This juxtaposition nicely demonstrates how in formal empiricist discourse scientists' back-stage understandings are repressed through a variety of rhetorical persuasive devices which masquerade as objectivity. The notice is funny precisely because of the seriousness applied to that task of repression.

The significance of the joke, however, is not just that even scientists are dimly aware that objectivity is a subtly sustained myth, but that, in fact, we cannot make sense in principle without reliance upon the nomadic mode as in joking, irony, satire and so on. Garfinkel (1967), for instance, notes that when researchers read a journal account of a specific study in order to replicate it exactly, they frequently encounter a gap of insufficient information between the reported procedures and the derived results:

The gap occurs when the reader asks how the investigator decided the correspondence between what was actually observed and the intended event for which the actual observation is treated as evidence. The reader's problem consists of having to decide that the reported observation is a literal instance of the intended occurrence i.e., that the actual observation and the occurrence are identical *in sense*. (Garfinkel, 1967: 96)

Garfinkel goes on to explain that since the relationship between the two is a 'sign relationship', the reader must consult 'some set of grammatical rules', that is, must engage in 'interpretive work and trade upon assumptions "underlying" matters "just known in common" '. Ultimately, 'correct correspondence is the product of the work of investigator and reader as members of a community of cobelievers' (Garfinkel, 1967). This is the position Mulkay and Gilbert alluded to earlier when discussing the 'contingent' repertoire in which scientific knowledge is simply those beliefs which certain specific collections of specialists happen to have adopted.

Garfinkel is not suggesting that this undermines the veracity of scientific findings, nor is he suggesting that if only scientists would 'tell it as it is' in terms of the contingent repertoire then all would be fine. He is pointing to a deeper problem which he has elsewhere (Garfinkel, 1967: 73; also Sacks, 1963) called the *'et cetera'* clause. This is the paradoxical process in which any attempt at literal description simply multiplies the task in an infinite regress. Any attempt at a literal description of reality necessarily involves calling a halt or limit to our description otherwise we are forced to go on indefinitely to describe the 'whole' (an impossibility, in effect). Consequently the question arises as to precisely where we agree to call the limit (and thereby imply *'et cetera'*) in communicating with each other. Garfinkel's point is a recognition of the nomadic principle, which jokes also reveal, concerning the arbitrariness of the limit. The practical upshot is that where there is a cobelief about where to draw the limit then a community of specialists can at least dispute on the same terms. But nonetheless their belief, which produces the controlling effect over their intended observation and therefore data, is fundamentally arbitrary and can only be sustained by recourse to rhetorical or persuasive devices such as those listed on the left-hand side of the laboratory graffiti reported by Mulkay and Gilbert (1982a) Thus in Latour and Woolgar's (1979) work we find great importance attached to agreeing the 'grammatical' ground rules socially constructed into the observation, measurement and inscription devices through which scientists perceive the material world.

The writings of these various authors demonstrate a higher than normal awareness of the subtle dependency of the controlling empiricist discourse (the control mode of organization) upon the controlled but always dangerously shadowing contingent discourse (the nomadic mode of organization).

Implications for organizational analysis

Pirsig's (1974) analysis of organized knowledge discussed above suggests that the control mode rests on a *logic of representation* in which a primary reference — a 'model' or 'original' – organizes (orders and hierarchizes) the less faithful copies that can be struck from it. All the organizational theorists surveyed by Whitley (1977) operated according to this mode, as we noted, and not surprisingly since it is the dominant mode of social scientific writing. Latour and Woolgar's (1979) analysis reveals that the supposed 'original' model to be represented is really a construction of the writing process and therefore comes after the latter and not before as the logic of representation would have us believe. In Pirsig's lateral knowledge, a form of the nomadic mode, the primary reference disappears and things are cast adrift, more or less like one another without any one of them being able to claim the privileged status of 'model'. Instead of control by hierarchy, there is a series of exclusively lateral relations 'that have neither beginning nor end' and 'that can be followed in one direction as easily as in another' (Foucault, 1983: 44). In this mode, constructions are temporary accommodations to the flux and flow of the nomadic and thus have no intrinsic stability of their own.

The logic of representation as a mode of analysis in organizational writing has been critiqued by Degot (1982). Degot singles out the concept of 'representation' as a key factor in the study of organizations but places it in question in much the same way as Latour and Woolgar (1979) do. He argues that while it is generally assumed that orthodox organization theorists study organizations that are actually 'out there' in the real world, it can be shown that this often is not the case. The 'reality' of this literature is that the organization is a cultural object which is the product of a prior model. In effect, what the theorist sees is not the model as a representation of the organization but the organization as a representation of the model. Degot instances the systems model of Katz and Kahn (1966) to illustrate this point: ' . . . the results produced present a relatively tautological structure: the organization is a system ruled by the system's laws: the variables identified in this system are created by laws whose form is such precisely because the organization is a system' (Degot, 1982: 637). Similarly, the work of the Aston Group (e.g., Pugh *et al.*, 1969; Child, 1972) reflects not so much the real world of organizations but rather the methods which come to represent those organizations. Psychological approaches to the study of the individual in the organization – whether based on behaviouristic learning theories or hierarchies of needs – are also

257

afflicted with this paradox of representation. All these approaches are contaminated by a 'metaphysics' of representation which gives priority to an unexamined, taken-for-granted model or method which actually serves to 'represent' the organizational reality; they, therefore, do not stop to analyse their own 'construction' practices: 'The construction of the object results from the application of a theory to the real world; the constructed object exists (has sense) only in relation to this theory . . .' (Degot, 1982: 630).

A related issue (though not directly raised by Degot) concerns the nature of organizational analysis as an academic product of the university organization. Bourdieu and Passeron (1977) have argued (like Pirsig) that the role of the university is to reproduce the control structures of society and thus its claim of academic freedom is therefore largely illusory. As a reproducer of control, the university cultivates a representational mode of research and teaching which, by definition, cannot be radically critical since it rests on 'control' norms of purity and rectitude. The key issue here is the status of writing (including representing) and how it is dealt with in the academic system. The function of the academic division of labour and its representational discourse is to police the effects of writing – paradoxes, contradictions – by maintaining the distinctions between disciplines and the order within them. It is this moral economy of good behaviour that is taught and reproduced in research rather than the quest for enlightenment and truth with which the university is traditionally associated. Organizational analysis in the representational mode is therefore fated to reproduce in its discourse the very structures that give academic organization its communicative power and this is why Degot can describe systems theory as tautologous and criticize empirical studies of organizations for merely 'mimicking' their subject matter. As Latour and Woolgar's (1979) work suggests, a 'deconstruction' of the representational approach shows 'copy' and 'original' to be implicated in each other and therefore to be intrinsically inseparable.

Another version of this argument has been presented by Frug (1984) who has criticized organization theory for justifying and legitimating the control mode basic to the bureaucratic structures of business corporations and the administrative state. Frug shows that the central problem of bureaucracy (as studied by organization theorists and scholars of corporate and administrative law) is that of reconciling the relationship between subjectivity and objectivity. The nomadic mode means essentially that no division can ever realistically be made between these concepts since they are intrinsically inseparable from each other. But the control mode that orders the social world means that (somehow) they must be kept apart – otherwise they could not be 'represented' in a clear and explicit way. 'All the stories of bureaucratic legitimation . . . share a common structure: they attempt to define, distinguish, and render mutually compatible the subjective and objective aspects of life. All the defences of bureaucracy have sought to avoid merging objectivity and subjectivity – uniting the demands of commonness and community with those of individuality and personal separateness – because to do so would be self-contradictory. Moreover, it has never been enough just to separate subjectivity and objectivity; each must be guaranteed a place within the bureaucratic structure' (Frug, 1984: 1287). In this case, the process of making bureaucratic structures clear and explicit is self-deceiving for while the 'objective' qualities of the professional manager are seen 'as something outside the individual to which he must adapt, they are qualities that the professional himself helps to define' (p. 1331).

This interweaving or 'nomadism' of objectivity and subjectivity necessarily undermines the 'transparent' or 'obvious' features of bureaucratic logic – the intrinsic inseparability of the two making it difficult to see either. The theorists' answer to the problem is the creation of a self-deceiving 'fiction' of objectivity which serves to suppress the troublesome and insistent demands of subjectivity. Frug's answer to this problem argues for the recognition of formal organizations as essentially 'nomadic' processes in which human relationships are 'variable, intersubjective (and) interdependent' (Frug, 1984: 1296). By placing the emphasis on the nomadic mode, Frug reveals organization to be a 'participatory' process which becomes 'transparently open to transformation (no form of organization is necessary) and always in need of transformation (all forms of organization create forms of domination that need to be combatted)' (p. 1296). Like Latour and Woolgar (1979), Frug stresses the processes of construction rather than the construction as completed object. This radical shift in focus from the control mode to the nomadic mode becomes a way of 'reinvigorating the notion of democracy' in the field of formal organization as 'the ideal under which the possibilities of joint transformation of social life are collected' (Frug, 1984: 1296).

Frug's critical insights are reproduced in a different analytical context by Westwood (1987) in a study of a 'worker-participation' scheme in the English manufacturing division of a multinational pharmaceutical corporation. Westwood uses a framework which is logically similar to the control–nomadic interaction and, like Frug, shows how 'participation' as a subjective process is naturally grounded in the nomadic mode. The 'problem' with 'participatory democracy' is its spontaneous tendency to subvert formal control, hierarchy and management prerogative by generating an 'overflow' of meanings. As Westwood indicates, this excess is partly the result of the 'need to say more' which is inherent in any discourse (Garfinkel's *et cetera* clause) but it is also the result of the natural nomadic tendency of all language to proliferate meaning and so disrupt coherence. Instead of a democratic sharing of information and decision-making, the participation scheme studied by Westwood becomes a discursive field in which the actors move and countermove according to the incompatible forces of the control and nomadic modes. Management views the scheme as a 'project', 'trial' and 'exercise' forced on them by external forces in the wider society; nevertheless, they define it as 'our scheme', 'how can we involve our employees' (Westwood, 1987: 189), and they give to 'participation' a 'preferred and limited range of meanings' (p. 202). Management assumes the 'right to speak adequately and sensibly about participation whilst at the same time denying the veracity of any other talk which might so presume' (p. 187). The 'official' discourse is somehow 'naturally' dictated by management: 'company' discourse, like 'business' discourse more generally (including, of course, the 'serious business' of Mulkay and Gilbert's research scientists discussed earlier), aspires to a neutral status – 'a right and objective way of speaking about and ordering things within the context of the company' (p. 186) and in which, of course, participation must take its place. The process of participation, 'so contingent, unplanned and off-the-cuff, is transposed and corsetted into a structure . . . The organizational values of order, clarity, coherence and planning are demonstrated to apply in the case of participation' (p. 196).

At this point, we return to Frug's argument that the writings of organizational theorists are themselves subject to a covert organizing process – the control mode – which prevents them seeing organization as a process of construction rather than an already accomplished structure. Westwood ends his analysis with the similar claim that discourse (i.e. 'writing in' in the sense that we have used it here) is the field where the control–nomadic struggle occurs in institutions and where the most vital human problems of organization and management begin and end.

References

Bohm, D. (1980) Wholeness and the implicate order, London: Routledge and Kegan Paul.

Bourdieu, P. and Passeron, J. (1977) *Reproduction in Education, Society and Culture*, London: Sage.

Child, J. (1972) 'Organisational structure and strategies of control: a replication of the Aston study, *Administrative Science Quarterly* 17: 163–72.

Degot, V. (1982) 'Le Modèle de l'Agent et le Problème de la Construction de l'Object dans les Théories de l'Enterprise', *Social Science Information* 21: 627–64.

Douglas, M. (1975) *Implicit Meanings: Essays in Anthropology* London: Routledge and Kegan Paul.

Douglas, M. (1986) *How Institutions Think*, London: Routledge.

Foucault, M. (1983) *This Is Not a Pipe*, Berkeley, CA: University of California Press.

Frug, G.E. (1984) 'The ideology of bureaucracy in American law', *Harvard Law Review* 97: 1276–388.

Garfinkel, H. (1967) *Studies in Ethnomethodology*, Englewood Cliffs, NJ: Prentice Hall.

Giddens, A. (1985) *The Nation-State and Violence*, Cambridge: Polity Press.

Gilbert, G.N. and Mulkay, M. (1980) 'Contexts of scientific discourses: social accounting in experimental papers', in K. D. Knorr *et al.* (eds) *The Social Process of Scientific Investigation*, Dordrecht: Reidel, pp. 269–84.

Gilbert, G.N. and Mulkay, M. (1982) 'Warranting scientific belief', *Social Studies of Science* 12: 363–408.

Katz, D. and Kahn, R.L. (1966) *The Social Psychology of Organisations*, New York: Wiley.

Latour, B. and Woolgar, S. (1979) *Laboratory Life: the Social Construction of Scientific Facts*, Beverley Hills, CA: Sage.

Morgan, G. (1986) *Images of Organisation*, Beverley Hills, CA: Sage.

Mulkay, M. and Gilbert, G.N. (1981) 'Putting philosophy to work: Karl Popper's influence on scientific practice', *Philosophy of the Social Sciences* 11: 389–407.

Mulkay, M. and Gilbert, G.N. (1982a) 'Joking apart: some recommendations concerning the analysis of scientific cultures', *Social Studies of Science* 12:: 585–613.

Mulkay, M. and Gilbert, G.N. (1982b) 'Accounting for error: how scientists construct their social world when they account for correct and incorrect belief', *Sociology*, 16: 165–83.

Pirsig, R. (1974) *Zen and the Art of Motorcycle Maintenance*, London: Bodley Head.

Pugh, D.S., Hickson, D., Hining, R., and Turner, C. (1969) 'The context of organisational structure', *Administrative Science Quarterly* 14: 91–114.

Sacks, H. (1963) 'Sociological description', *Berkeley Journal of Sociology* 8: 1–16.

Westwood, R. (1987)' Social criticism: a social critical practice applied to a discourse on participation', in I.L. Mangham (ed.) *Organisation Analysis and Development: a Social Construction of Organisational Behaviour*, Chichester: Wiley, Chapter 8.

Whitley, R. (1977) 'Organisational control and the problem of order', *Social Science Information* 16: 169–89.

Weick, K. (1979) 'Cognitive processes in organizations', in B. Staw (ed.) *Research in Organizational Behaviour*, vol. 1, Greenwich, CT: JAI Press: 41–74.

Zijderveld, A.C. (1983) 'Trend report: the sociology of humour and laughter', *Current Sociology* 31: 1–59.

Chapter seventeen

Corporate birth, crisis and rebirth: the emergence of four small UK service firms

Martyn Pitt

Introduction

In Britain as elsewhere wealth and job creation benefit from a thriving small-firm sector, notably in services. This chapter reports on four small, founder-managed UK firms offering various industrial and commercial services. Here 'emergence' simply means coming from obscurity, achieving legitimacy via stability in trading patterns, however fragile. The firms are controlled and, except in one case, largely owned by their chief executive (CEO) founders. They are typical small firms, having limited resources but a wide range of practical skills.

Reasons will be offered why these firms have grown, albeit with periodic difficulties, and are still viable. Given the low priority emerging firms accord to documenting their progress for posterity, fieldwork was imperative in constructing an objective account (Burgess, 1984; Glaser and Strauss, 1967; Yin, 1984). Data were collected mainly via taped in-depth interviews with major actors and personal observation. A noteworthy feature of their development has been the periodic incidence of (perceived) crisis. CEOs have been instrumental in diagnosing and responding to these situations. It is pertinent to characterize such change as 'rebirth': firms do not seek crises, but crises can produce constructive outcomes, equipping firms better for the future.

The firms

The firms add value to physical products in a variety of ways, but are not really manufacturers. They are service-oriented, though defining a service activity is problematic (Lovelock, 1983; Shostack, 1977, 1982; Svegintzov, 1984). Here, it means a value-adding activity located on the base plane of Killeya and Armistead's (1984) 'operations tetrahedron', i.e. in supply–transport–service space. The marketing and distribution roles pose special challenges (Berry, 1980), being integral parts of the 'delivery system' (Johnston, 1987) and major *sources* of added value.

For example, a machine tool manufacturer's selling agency performs various user contact and support activities that largely constitute its operations and locus of employment. Levitt (1972) and Shostack (1977) argued that all organizations must provide a substantial element of service to compete effectively: what differs between types of firms is the *mix* of product and service elements in their offerings.

Table 17.1 Strategic development of the firms

Firm	1	2	3	4
Major Activity	Customized abrasives distributor	Machine tool agent	Fire protection distributor	Market analyst
Age (years) and staff	7 18	15 12	14 60	10 12
Post-formation product/market choices	Range and sector extensions	Acquisition and divestment; new agency	UK sales agency; new services	New types of data base and client
Major resource commitments	Inventories; salaries of operations/ sales staff	As 1, plus equipment and freehold premises	As 2	Staff salaries; microcomputers; data licences
Competitive advantages	Customization; Fast response; Low overheads;	Performance of products; applications knowhow	As 2 plus R&D skills	Unique problem-solving skills
Synergies among existing activities	Related offering categories to common customer set	Machinery and supplies to same base of customers	Core business served by new activities	Databases serve variety of customers and solve many problem types

The firms will now be described briefly (see also Tables 17.1 and 17.2 and Pitt, 1988). Firm 1 converts sheet abrasives into pads/belts to customers' requirements; it holds custom stocks for regular clients and responds quickly to their needs. In a mature and competitive market, prospecting for new orders remains a priority. Growth has been cautious, financed without debt. Premises are rented, operations labour-intensive. It continues to grow profitably by developing in new geographic market areas and related applications. There is an ethos of consensual decision-making.

Firm 2 is UK agent for an overseas machine tool maker. Its income derives equally from installing new machines and supplying consumables. Growth has been steady, most sales coming from mechanical and electronic engineering firms. Five years ago it acquired a small manufacturer which soon required heavy investment; its success prompted competition from larger firms. Later it was judged unlikely to make adequate future profits, so it was sold, the proceeds reinvested in extended agency activities. The CEO takes the major decisions after consulting colleagues.

Table 17.2 Operating characteristics of the firms

Firm	1	2	3	4
Capital intensity	F. Low	Moderate	Moderate	F. Low
Mix of tangibles and intangibles in the offering	Balance to tangibles (product)	As 1	As 1	Balance to intangibles (analysis)
Market Focus	Business users within 50 miles	Engineering firms in UK/ Europe	Architects and construction projects (UK)	UK retailers/ manufacturers
Main sort of sales promotion	Direct sales contact by principals	Regular sales force/ advertising	As 2	As 1 plus telephone prospecting
Pricing	Market-led	Contract negotiation (cost-plus)	Premium/ value basis	As 3
Major operating skills	Tech. sales; inventory management; customizing	Negotiating; applications knowhow	Marketing/ selling; R&D; graphic design	As 2; market analysis; software innovation
Customizing potential	High; product supplied to customers' specs.	Low	Low	High: output tailored to clients' problems
Perishability (Time dependence)	High: need for fast delivery	Moderate: synchronized with clients' capex. plans	As 2	High: timing depends on clients' problems
Extent of client contact	High when troubleshooting	High in the specification stage	As 2	High, depends on client
Scope to manage customer expectations	Low	Moderate	Moderate/ high	High

Firm 3 began as a contractor to independent residential businesses. Later it became import agent for a novel fire protection product. Sales accelerated and the original activity ceased. It has grown substantially, extending its offerings via new suppliers and recently, its own R & D function. It is a major force in its product area, specifying, but subcontracting production of its offerings. It has also diversified into new activities, some related, some not; initially they serviced the core activity and later extended outside. Able managers run the core business while the CEO concentrates on new entrepreneurial ventures.

Firm 4 established a retail/market database from which consumer goods manufacturers with large sales forces were offered custom reports/analyses. 'Founding clients' funded the database development over several years; it is now regularly updated. Until he became full-time four years ago, the CEO delegated day-to-day management to his partners. Subsequently, he has extended the range of innovative databased services for manufacturers and retailers. The main activities are now technical marketing consultancy and software development. The firm also innovates by using flexible, powerful microcomputers; its (few) competitors generally use mainframes.

Strategic development and change

The firms, between seven and fifteen years old, with twelve to sixty staff, have secured market footholds. In growing steadily in assets, sales, profits and headcount during a period of major UK economic recession in the early 1980s, they can surely be regarded as successful. How have they done so?

Strategic development is the continual interplay of actors' 'strategic choices' (Child, 1972) with 'environmental determinism' (Hannan and Freeman, 1977). Conventional wisdom suggests matching the firm's actual/potential skills and resources to the opportunities its managers perceive in a competitive context and translating these into achievable goals. Long-run viability implies occupying a niche in a chosen, but possibly quite hostile operating environment. Success then depends on how well the firm implements these important (strategic) choices in context.

Much has been written about managing strategic change, but little relates directly to small firms. One would expect them to be *ideas*-not resources-rich; their early lives entrepreneurial, teasing out and actualizing opportunities. Only later will they focus on the engineering and administrative tasks (Miles and Snow, 1978). Binks and Coyne (1983) examined the birth and early development of small firms; Ward and Jenkins (1984) the impact of context, especially local community; Schermerhorn (1980) interfirm co-operation as a means of overcoming disadvantages of smallness; Rothwell and Zegweld (1982) the role of innovation; Robinson *et al.* (1984) the contribution of strategic planning to firms' performance. Perry (1986) noted 'disturbance events' and 'comfort stages' in firms' development, arguing that the former are the key in triggering change.

In these firms, development has conformed to the well-known pattern of relative continuity punctuated by significant change episodes, often associated with high risk and uncertainty (Hedberg and Jonsson, 1977; Miller and Friesen, 1980; Mintzberg, 1978). Table 17.1 summarizes aspects of the firms' strategic development using a four-way characterization of strategy (Hofer and Schendel, 1978: 25).

In small firms significant changes can be tracked with relative ease. Whilst a stimulus–response model doubtless oversimplifies a complex reality, the analytic construct of the 'change-inducing-action-episode' is considered useful. A relatively stable antecedent organization–environment state may contain the cue for a turbulent sequence of actions that, if triggered, ultimately results in a new continuity or quasi-stable state (Lewin, 1952: 228; Mintzberg and Waters, 1982). Thus:

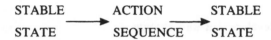

STABLE	ACTION	STABLE
STATE	SEQUENCE	STATE

Action sequences or episodes cumulate and can be mapped as the firm ages. The action cue is hypothesized to be or contain information which actors interpret as requiring a definite response. So, whilst the cue may be external, the galvanizing event is the *managerial response* to it.

Major developmental changes in each firm were analysed as episodes (averaging 7–8 major action elements) on a *post hoc*, 'realized' basis (Mintzberg, 1978). Some fifteen such episodes were identified, excluding start-ups. A typical example is illustrated in Figure 17.1. In retrospect, none of these episodes has had fully intended (deliberate) outcomes. So one must question the degree to which strategic development has been premeditated or planned, at least formally. Excluding start-ups, significant change episodes have occurred about once every three firm-years; in between, developmental changes have been largely incremental, building constructively on antecedents.

In some episodes firms experienced crises, often a significant initiator of change (Starbuck, 1982). In six of the fifteen, CEOs explicitly construed the antecedent state as a crisis, triggering and shaping subsequent events, as in Figure 17.1. The CEO's response to customer perceptions of declining product quality prompted a series of actions that addressed the problem, but in ways that transformed the firm by establishing a product development capability. There is little evidence that this outcome was seriously envisaged until prompted by crisis.

To aid discussion, three categories of firm-change are now posited:

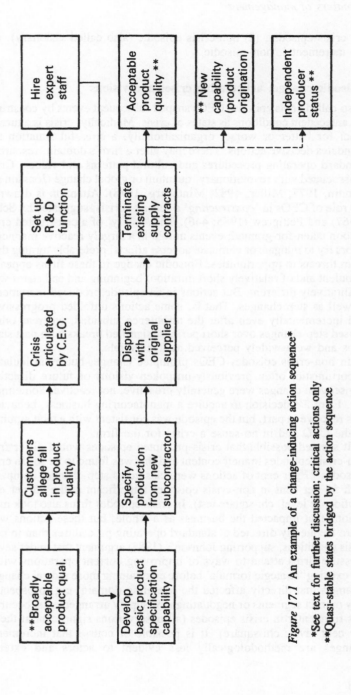

Figure 17.1 An example of a change-inducing action sequence*

*See text for further discussion; critical actions only
**Quasi-stable states bridged by the action sequence

(1) crisis-episodic, (2) non-crisis episodic (also called visionary), and (3) incremental, non-episodic.

Episodic change: articulating crises and visions

In so-called crisis episodes CEOs shaped subsequent events by construing the antecedent conditions as states of crisis. Medically, crisis is a turning point for better or worse; organizationally, a stressful situation that mandates decisive actions. These may alter a firm's domain, resources, standard operating procedures and cultural patterns and values. Crisis is associated with revolutionary, quantum or global change (Jonsson and Lundin, 1977; Miller, 1982; Mintzberg, 1978). Attention is drawn to the role of CEOs in '*constructing*' a sense of crisis, suggested by Schon (1967) and Pettigrew (1985: 446). The 'reality' of a constructed crisis is soon taken-for-granted; events unfold in a largely reactive manner as actors try to mitigate or eliminate adverse affects, preferably turning them from threats to opportunities. Episodic change in these firms appeared turbulent and of relatively short duration: beginning and end states were qualitatively different. But actions in an episode produced incremental as well as step changes. That is, some actions unfolded progressively and incrementally even after the turbulence subsided, whereas others caused step-changes over short periods, signified breaks with past status quos and were widely perceived as irreversible.

In non-crisis episodes CEOs prompted change, but by articulating opportunistic, often previously-unspoken visions of future direction. Consequent changes were generally proactive, not reactive. Sometimes, e.g. Firm 2's decision to acquire a manufacturing business, behaviour was reactive in part, but the episode was consistent with a tacit ambition of the CEO and in no sense a crisis for the firm.

It seemed possible that crisis-prompted episodes would differ from non-crisis episodes in their content and this was found to be so. In crisis episodes 77 per cent of actions were classed as step-changes compared with 56 per cent in non-crisis episodes (significant at the 95 per cent confidence level, chi-square test). In crisis episodes firms also took more actions that impacted the business as a whole, but these actions were more frequently directed at standard operating procedures than in non-crisis conditions, supporting Johnson's (1985) argument that under severe pressure firms attend to ways of improving current operations within the existing 'strategic formula' before entertaining more radical changes. Changes that directly affected the operating domain, e.g. prospecting new market segments or negotiating new supply arrangements, occurred less frequently in crisis episodes (all observations significant at the 95 per cent level, chi-square). It is possible of course that incremental changes are methodologically less evident to actors and external observers, so could have been underemphasized. Though hard to refute, supporting evidence for this view has not yet emerged.

That crisis-change episodes differ from others is consistent with other findings (e.g. Tjosvold, 1984). That they are more likely to involve step-changes or discontinuities seems consistent with arguments about 'myth revision' (Hedberg and Jonsson, 1977), and 'action rationality' (Brunsson, 1982). In retrospect, perhaps the particular significance of episodic change is its role as *a turning point*, not too fancifully character-ized as 'rebirth'. For Firm 1, the hire of a new, although experienced, marketing director produced rapid business growth, but profitability declined. The CEO articulated this situation explicitly as a crisis, committing his firm to painful, but effective metamorphosis to a more tightly controlled, professional business. For Firm 2, a vision took it into manufacturing; later, a profit crisis rejected manufacturing and reaffirmed its agency mission. Firm 3 experienced a visionary trans-formation from contractor to distributor. A crisis later created its research and development capability. For Firm 4, a latent vision allied to crisis-articulation in the context of pressing resource constraints redirected at-tention to a new domain and the exploitation of hitherto undefined market opportunities.

Thus the articulation and enactment of crises by CEOs clearly signalled to fellow actors that slow, marginal adjustments to the status quo were inappropriate. Whilst the enactment of crisis was essentially situation-reactive, firms soon regained a quasi-stable state where they were better equipped to handle hitherto unseen potentialities. At other times CEOs articulated exciting, positive visions of future direction to which they and their colleagues responded. So these firms have shown similar, fairly predictable episodic behaviour in which patterns of change are vigorous but differ between crises and non-crises. It also seems probable that correctly *timing* the articulation of explicit statements was the key to how subsequent events unfolded.

Incremental change and development

Notwithstanding the importance of episodic change, these firms have also developed via minor, continuing incremental adjustments not obviously characterized as episodic. Aspects of such incremental change will now be discussed.

Capitalizing on environmental beneficence

Given radical changes on average only once every three firm-years, much progress has been steady and within an existing domain of activity. Still, progress cannot be isolated from the *quality* of firms' operating

269

environments: one would expect firms' choice and level of resource commitments (and therefore, rate of growth) to be affected by environmental characteristics and contingencies, directly and via interpretation in the light of actors' ambitions and attitudes to risk. Direct environmental constraints included the problem of obtaining finance for working capital and expansion, particularly in the early stages of a firm's life, the continuing high cost of borrowed capital, difficult trading conditions during the early 1980s and in many cases, hostile competition.

Because the firms do not share a common industry sector, assessing environmental impact requires cross-sectoral comparison. One can characterize environments in various ways (Duncan, 1972; Mintzberg, 1979), namely: (1) complexity: the range and sophistication of skills (technologies) needed to compete effectively, (2) rate of change (dynamism) over the medium-to-long-term, (3) diversity of market needs, (4) competitive rivalry, and (5) short-run turbulence and unpredictability. Each firm's core business environment was rated on a five-point scale, then combined to yield a simple, numerical comparison of the relative hostility of each (Table 17.3). The analysis, though crude, suggests moderate if differing degrees of hostility. Linked to age and achievements, the broad conclusion is that a relatively hostile environment probably inhibits a firm's rate of growth, but does not always threaten viability or totally frustrate growth. Firm 3, for example, has enjoyed a persistently high rate of sales growth, consistent with a favourable environment, while Firm 2, of a similar age, operates in a less beneficent environment and has not matched Firm 3's growth rate.

Table 17.3 Environmental characteristics of the four firms

Firm	1	2	3	4
Environmental characteristic[a]				
Complexity: range of factors to be managed (c1)	2	4	3	4
Dynamism: rate of change over medium/long term (c2)	3	5	2	4
Diversity of served market needs (c3)	3	4	2	3
Competitive rivalry/hostility (c4)	5	3	3	3
Turbulence: short-run unpredictability (c5)	3	2	1	3
Composite assessment[b]	3.1	3.4	2.0	3.4

[a.] Rated on a scale from 1 to 5; 1 = most favourable; 5 = most hostile
[b.] Combined geometrically ie fifth root of (c1xc2xc3xc4xc5)

A spin-off for Firm 3 is that strong, internally generated growth enables the CEO to devote increasing time to new ventures which, where successful, have accelerated growth of the core business via synergistic effects and hence of the firm as a whole. So in part long-run viability is linked to environmental beneficence, specifically to a firm's ability to capitalize progressively on the opportunities and lack of obstacles a relatively favourable environment provides.

Understanding customers' needs and priorities: being service-oriented

If survival is achieving an enduring 'fit' with the external environment (Venkatraman and Camillus, 1984), operating activities (Table 17.2) play an important part in creating and reinforcing a defensible position or niche. Here 'fit' is construed as understanding and meeting customers' real needs and priorities over time. CEOs in particular empathasize well with customers, make sense of customers' real-world problems in their own terms and then conceive effective solutions to these problems. 'Close to the customer' (Peters and Waterman, 1982) is not simply physical proximity, but projecting themselves, intellectually and emotionally, into a customer's situation, perceiving it as the other and then interpreting this insight as a business opportunity. In this way, they have become credible suppliers to firms of a comparable size and much larger.

Operationally, there is sometimes a strong, direct sales pitch, other times it is more subtle. For example, in the supply of new fire-proofing materials in preference to asbestos cladding, Firm 3 emphasized the cosmetic benefits to architects, as well as the physical benefits to contractors. By reconceptualizing the nature of the offering, the firm accessed a real and hitherto poorly-served market need.

The phenomenon is usefully examined in service management terms. Services, are said to be characterized by:

1. Relatively intangible offerings,
2. Potential for customization,
3. Considerable interaction of provider and receiver,
4. Limited lifespan or 'perishability' of the offering,
5. Contemporaneous production and consumption, at least where stock-holding is impossible,
6. Quality dependence on idiosyncratic resources,
7. Need to manage customer expectations.

The activities of these firms involve products, but characteristically they have an operational *service-orientation* (Table 17.2). Enduring niche occupation combines utility – the supply of a tangible product – with an intangible service element having consulting or advisory attributes. Firm 1 advises clients which abrasives are likely to be most suitable for a given application, what results to expect and how to overcome

271

problems; Firm 2 demonstrates good machine-operating practice; Firm 3 advises on product applications and realistic performance expectations in particular situations; Firm 4 offers software coupled with expertise and advice which amount to bespoke problem-solving. The less-tangible components of the offering create the distinctiveness *cementing firms to their niches*.

Continuing the service analogy, staff often have the scope and need to exercise initiative in customizing the offering or the manner of delivery. Durable customer relationships derive from small scale; competitive advantage from a customized, personalized and flexible service that large customers value and bigger competitors struggle to emulate. Customer interactions often cut across functional boundaries, since small firms rarely enjoy the luxury of specialist resources to handle each problem. Gronroos (1982) refers to the front-office/back-office division: this is misleading here; a majority of staff think in front-office terms because they deal frequently with customers and affect the perceived quality of the offering. This applies equally to a technical sales representative guiding a customer on specifications and a warehouse operative negotiating cost-effective delivery solutions with the customer and the freight contractor. Staff selection and training ought therefore to be important. Selection is particularly problematic, since a new recruit is a major proportionate increase in total headcount; personal recommendation and prior knowledge are valued indicators of competence and likely 'fit'. Essentially, staff are selected for initiative, enthusiasm, learning capacity, tolerance for hard work and a strong customer orientation. But formal training has played little part in development. Mistakes are not actively encouraged, but are tolerated if they can enhance future performance.

Competence-creating experimentalism

Firms devote much attention to managing their resources and enhancing operating procedures. This dynamic process allows operating competences to develop organically, appropriate metaphors being 'action-experimentation' and 'learning by doing better', not 'planning'. Advantage-conferring competences often result from minor refinements to operational routines and procedures. People experiment judiciously with either the specification of the offering or the manner of its generation or delivery. Successful outcomes create new skills and distinctive competences.

In one sense behaviour is childlike; sometimes things are done that more 'professional' competitors would regard as unrealistic or impossible – as in the case of Firm 4, creating a database with national coverage. As in learning to ride a bicycle, no amount of thinking removes the need for trial and error; modest success prompts further trials. Achieving a threshold level of competence depends on and then sustains momentum and is the basis for future developments. Experience-creation, particularly in crisis-reactive episodes, fosters innovation: CEOs are sensitized to emerging possibilities and options. If a new initiative meets no real obstacle it continues, otherwise direction alters or it is aborted. 'Strategy' is refined in action, but realistically, only *later* when firms have made resource commitments is the strategic shift confirmed.

Being flexible to contain risk

Firms are consciously flexible in their external relations and in operational terms; flexibility is normally achieved by hard work, labour-intensive methods and commitment of staff, not by efficient capital-intensive methods. Firms have few indirect staff, so low indirect overheads means they can operate suboptimally and yet be acceptably profitable.

Being flexible means acquiring fixed assets judiciously: investment is regarded as risky in respect of its asset-specificity and expected duration (conversely, ease of disposal). Therefore, highly specific commitments over long periods, involving plant and equipment, inventories or specialist human resources, look particularly risky. Firms even find ways to contain the risk exposure from major resource commitments, e.g. one regularly acquires larger premises ahead of need, leasing unused space on short, profitable contracts and enjoying capital gains on appreciating freeholds.

These entrepreneurs are not unduly risk-averse, but they use flexibility to offset uncertainty, as a kind of distinctive competence. Flexibility – in the sense of keeping options open – is a valuable holding state in moderately hostile, unpredictable conditions. But too parsimonious an attitude to investment could also mean they trade long-run competitive advantage for short-run flexibility. In practice, if environments become extremely hostile CEOs trade flexibility for assets which they think will improve competitive standing. Put differently, when they perceive operating environments as either benevolent or hostile, they have the confidence to overcome natural caution in making investments. Otherwise they often favour a 'wait-and-see' approach, making their actions hard for competitors to 'read'.

CEOs co-ordinating roles

CEOs play a major part in co-ordinating activities. It is probably their most time-consuming role after purely functional and boundary-spanning activities. They are not intimately involved in every activity, but their wishes, explicit or interpreted, are powerful *guides* for staff as to appropriate action. Conflicting priorities in marketing and operations, for example, are commonplace but staff recognize mutual interests to a degree rarely found in most large firms, enhancing organizational cohesion. Cohesion could break down in crises, but then CEOs encourage constructiveness and enthusiasm for necessary initiatives, getting staff working towards a common goal.

In these firms CEOs are pivotal, involved and charismatic figures. Their disappearance would create major problems. Nonetheless, they are not supermen: administrative operations management requires different skills from entrepreneurial domain selection. Long-term viability almost certainly depends on both and it is problematic when a leader cannot combine both with equal facility or enthusiasm. Each copes differently with this issue. In Firm 1 the CEO insists on consensus decision-making on major issues, delegating much administrative control to trusted colleagues. In Firm 2 the CEO relies on clear functional accountability, fulfilling the key marketing role himself. Strategic decisions are discussed, with the CEO listening to advice but having the final say. In Firm 3 the CEO has largely withdrawn from day-to-day management by delegating to a cohort of mature managers. He concentrates on future developments, particularly moves aimed at diversification. In Firm 4, the management ethos is 'collegiate', as in Mintzberg's (1979) 'adhocracy', consistent with the profesionally qualified staff.

Summary and conclusions

These firms manifest the well-known continuity-and-change syndrome. Major long-run strategic developments result from periodic change-inducing episodes (spurred by crises and visions of the future) and incremental change supported by an implicit philosophy of environmental responsiveness, flexibility, experimentalism and service orientation.

CEOs sometimes 'construct' crises that initially change resource commitments and improve operating procedures, but later result in greater competence in the current domain and the search for an extended domain. In non-crisis conditions changes to environmental domain are typically prompted by CEOs enthusiastic, *ad hoc* visions of new opportunities. Episodic change contains the seeds of metamorphosis; as a change mechanism it has proved successful, but inherently risky and relatively infrequent. By no means all domain-expanding moves have been successful, sometimes they have ended in withdrawal. Here, enhanced business planning would seem particularly beneficial.

Experimental development, 'learning-by-doing-better', often begins with simplistic perceptions of appropriate behaviour in context; largely incremental, producing only small changes in the short term, but creating new distinctive competences which then facilitate new offerings and procedures to secure significant longer-term shifts. Distinctive competences arise from the nature of the service offered and the manner of its production or delivery; from prudent if cautious deployment of scarce resources and from enthusiastic, flexible, adaptive management which keeps firms sensitive to changing circumstances and mitigates uncertainty.

CEOs combine functional and co-ordination roles with innovation. This is an integration task for which they may not always be well-suited by instinct or experience. But failure in these terms would mean losing the organizational *momentum* that is their firms' principal source of dynamic, but always fragile viability.

Growth beyond a certain point may be counter-productive for most small firms. They contribute much by virtue of their modest size and generally do not harm larger firms with whom they nominally compete because they define and occupy niches efficiently. Larger firms have different problems, including diverse areas of activity and bureaucratized structures which make it hard for them to be as responsive. But as markets mature and large organizations increasingly compete via cosmetically, rather than physically differentiated tangible offerings, those who adopt responsive customer-oriented approaches will surely gain. If they keep organizational units lean, compact and staffed by people of the appropriate outlook who can share visions of the future and who are well-rewarded for excellent performance, they may sustain the close involvement of the service provider with the recipient of the service. This motivates staff and adds value for customers by combining the intangible and tangible elements of the offering more effectively (Heskett, 1987).

But in many areas small firms will probably retain a competitive edge in their response to changing situations. With hindsight their actions will not always be optimal, but by evolving and learning and by invoking visions and crises to stimulate change and cohesion, their CEOs can mobilize limited resources towards new opportunities or defend existing ones with an effectiveness that belies the modest size of their firms.

References

Berry, L.L. (1980) 'Services marketing is different', *Business*, Georgia State University, May/June, 24–8.

Binks, M. and Coyne, J. (1983) 'The birth of enterprise: an analytical and empirical study of the growth of small firms', London: Institute of Economic Affairs, Hobart Paper, 98.

Brunsson, N. (1982) 'The irrationality of action and action rationality: decision ideologies and organization actions', *Journal of Management Studies* 19: 29–44.

Burgess, R.G. (1984) *In the Field*, London: George Allen & Unwin.

Child, J. (1972) 'Organizational structure, environment and performance: the role of strategic choice', *Sociology* 6: 1–22.

Duncan, R.B. (1972) 'Characteristics of organizational environments and perceived environmental uncertainty', *Administrative Science Quarterly* 17: 313–27.

Glaser, B.G. and Strauss, A.L. (1967) *The Discovery of Grounded Theory*, New York: Aldine.

Gronroos, C. (1982) 'An applied service marketing theory', *European Journal of Marketing*, 16: 30–41.

Hannan, M.T. and Freeman, J. (1977) 'The population ecology of organizations', *American Journal of Sociology* 82: 929–64.

Hedberg, B. and Jonsson, S. (1977) 'Strategy making as a discontinuous process', *International Studies of Management and Organization* VII: 89–109.

Heskett, J.L. (1987) 'Lessons in the service sector', *Harvard Business Review*, March/April.

Hofer, C.W. and Schendel, D.E. (1978) *Strategy Formulation: Analytical Concepts*, St Paul: West.

Johnson, G.N. (1985) 'Strategic management in action', in V. Hammond (ed.) *Current Research in Management*, London: Pinter.

Johnston, R. (1987) 'Developing competitive strategies in service industries', Paper presented at The EIASM International Workshop on Strategies in Service Industries, Brussels.

Jonsson, S.A. and Lundin, R.A. (1977) 'Myths and wishful thinking as management tools', in P.C. Nystrom and W.H. Starbuck (eds) *Prescriptive Models of Organization*, Amsterdam: North Holland.

Killeya, J.C. and Armistead, C.G. (1984) 'The transfer of concepts and techniques between manufacturing and service systems', in C. Voss (ed.) *Research in Productions/Operations Management*, Aldershot: Gower, 491–505.

Levitt, T. (1972) 'Production line approach to service', *Harvard Business Review*, Sept/Oct: 41–52.

Lewin, K. (1952) *Field Theory in Social Science*, London: Tavistock.

Lovelock, C.H. (1983) 'Classifying services to gain strategic marketing insights', *Journal of Marketing*, 47: 9–20.

Miles, R. and Snow, C.C. (1978) *Organization strategy, structure and process*, New York: McGraw-Hill.

Miller, D. (1982) 'Evolution and revolution: A quantum view of structural change in organizations', *Journal of Management Studies* 19: 131–51.

Miller, D. and Friesen, P. (1980) 'Momentum and revolution in organizational adaptation', *Academy of Management Journal* 23: 591–614.

Mintzberg, H. (1978) 'Patterns in strategy formation', *Management Science* May: 934–48.

Mintzberg, H. (1979) *The Structuring of Organizations*, Englewood Cliffs: Prentice Hall.

Mintzberg, H. and Waters, J.A. (1982) 'Tracking strategy in an entrepreneurial firm', *Academy of Management Journal* 25: 465–99.

Perry, C. (1986) 'Growth strategies for small firms: principles and case studies', *International Small Business Journal* 5: 17–25.

Peters, T. and Waterman, R. (1982) *In Search of Excellence*, New York: Harper & Row

Pettigrew, A. (1985) *The Awakening Giant*, Oxford: Basil Blackwell.

Pitt, M.R. (1988) 'The management of emerging service organizations: an empirical study of strategic and operations management in five small firms', in R. Johnston (ed.) *Proceedings of the Third Annual Conference of the Operations Management Association (U.K.)*, Bedford: I.F.S. Publishing.

Robinson, R.B., Pearce, J.A., Vozikis, G.S. and Mescon, T.S. (1984) 'The relationship between stage of development and small firm planning and performance', *Journal of Small Business Management* 22: 45–52.

Rothwell, R. and Zegweld, W. (1982) *Innovation in the Small and Medium Sized Firm*, London: Pinter.

Schermerhorn, J.R. (1980) 'Inter firm cooperation as a resource for small business development', *Journal of Small Business Management* 18: 48–54.

Schon, D.A. (1967) *Technology and Change: The New Heraclitus*, Oxford: Pergamon.

Shostack, G.L. (1977) 'Breaking free from product marketing', *Journal of Marketing* 41: 73–80.

Shostack, G.L. (1982) 'How to design a service', *European Journal of Marketing* 16: 49–63.

Starbuck, W.H. (1982) 'Congealing oil: inventing ideologies to justify acting ideologies out', *Journal of Management Studies* 19: 3–27.

Svegintsov, S. (1984) 'Services: towards a unified view" in C. Voss (ed.) *Research in Productions/Operations Management*, Aldershot: Gower, 511–17.

Tjosvold, D. (1984) 'Effects of crisis orientation on managers' approach to controversy in decision making', *Academy of Management Journal* 27: 130–8.

Venkatraman, N. and Camillus, J.C. (1984) 'Exploring the concept of "Fit" in strategic management', *Academy of Management Review* 9, 513–25.

Ward, R. and Jenkins, R. (eds) (1984) *Communities in Business*, Cambridge: Cambridge University Press.

Yin, R.K. (1984) *Case Study Research: Design and Methods*, Beverly Hills: Sage.

Index

Index

For Product Safety Concerns and Information please contact our EU representative GPSR@taylorandfrancis.com Taylor & Francis Verlag GmbH, Kaufingerstraße 24, 80331 München, Germany

T - #0036 - 270225 - C0 - 216/138/16 [18] - CB - 9780415720984 - Gloss Lamination